AF707595

The Human Rights-Based Approach to Higher Education

The Human Rights-Based Approach to Higher Education

Why Human Rights Norms Should Guide Higher Education Law and Policy

Jane Kotzmann

OXFORD
UNIVERSITY PRESS

The Human Rights-Based Approach to Higher Education. Jane Kotzmann.
© Oxford University Press 2018. Published 2018 by Oxford University Press.

OXFORD
UNIVERSITY PRESS

Oxford University Press is a department of the University of Oxford. It furthers the University's objective of excellence in research, scholarship, and education by publishing worldwide. Oxford is a registered trademark of Oxford University Press in the UK and certain other countries.

Published in the United States of America by Oxford University Press
198 Madison Avenue, New York, NY 10016, United States of America.

© Oxford University Press 2018

All rights reserved. No part of this publication may be reproduced, stored in a retrieval system, or transmitted, in any form or by any means, without the prior permission in writing of Oxford University Press, or as expressly permitted by law, by license, or under terms agreed with the appropriate reproduction rights organization. Inquiries concerning reproduction outside the scope of the above should be sent to the Rights Department, Oxford University Press, at the address above.

You must not circulate this work in any other form
and you must impose this same condition on any acquirer.

Library of Congress Cataloging-in-Publication Data

Names: Kotzmann, Jane, author.
Title: The human rights-based approach to higher education : why human rights norms should guide higher education law and policy / Jane Kotzmann.
Description: New York : Oxford University Press, 2018. | Includes bibliographical references and index.
Identifiers: LCCN 2017044264 | ISBN 9780190863494 (hardback)
Subjects: LCSH: Education, Higher—Law and legislation. | Human rights.
Classification: LCC K3755 .K68 2018 | DDC 344/ .074—dc23
LC record available at https:// lccn.loc.gov/2017044264

Note to Readers

This publication is designed to provide accurate and authoritative information in regard to the subject matter covered. It is based upon sources believed to be accurate and reliable and is intended to be current as of the time it was written. It is sold with the understanding that the publisher is not engaged in rendering legal, accounting, or other professional services. If legal advice or other expert assistance is required, the services of a competent professional person should be sought. Also, to confirm that the information has not been affected or changed by recent developments, traditional legal research techniques should be used, including checking primary sources where appropriate.

(Based on the Declaration of Principles jointly adopted by a Committee of the American Bar Association and a Committee of Publishers and Associations.)

You may order this or any other Oxford University Press publication by visiting the Oxford University Press website at www.oup.com.

To my husband Ben, who is my rock. And to our daughter, Georgia, and our son, Jonathan, who I hope will be able to enjoy all their human rights.

CONTENTS

LIST OF FIGURES

LIST OF TABLES

LIST OF ABBREVIATIONS

ARUFA	*Arbeitssituation von Universitäts- und FachhochschulabsolventInnen*
ARWU	Academic Ranking of World Universities
AUSSE	Australasian Survey of Student Engagement
CADE	*Convention against Discrimination in Education*
CBI	Confederation of British Industry
CESCR	Committee on Economic, Social and Cultural Rights
CROC	*Convention on the Rights of the Child*
DAC	Development Assistance Committee
ECHR	*European Convention on Human Rights*
ECtHR	European Court of Human Rights
EEA	European Economic Area
EU	European Union
GDP	gross domestic product
ICESCR	*International Covenant on Economic, Social and Cultural Rights*
NSS	National Student Survey
NSSE	National Survey of Student Engagement
OECD	Organisation for Economic Cooperation and Development
SCIE	Science Citation Index-Expanded
SSCI	Social Science Citation Index
TAFE	Technical and Further Education
TEQSA	Tertiary Education Quality and Standards Agency
UDHR	Universal Declaration of Human Rights
UK	United Kingdom
UNESCO	United Nations Educational, Scientific and Cultural Organization
UNICEF	United Nations Children's Fund
US	United States

PREFACE

Although this book was the product of many years of research, its origins may be traced back many more years. Fundamentally, this research has been driven by a passionate and deep-seated interest and belief in justice. It was my passion for the concept of justice that motivated me to study law as an undergraduate student, and in particular to study human rights-related subjects in the Netherlands as part of that degree. Over the years, I have learned that law is not synonymous with, or even necessarily related to, justice. In realising this, however, I have also developed an understanding of the ways in which law can be used in the pursuit of justice. This understanding underpins the ambition for this book: to determine whether and how human rights law can be used to help create a fairer higher education system.[1]

The second major impetus behind this book was my experience as a secondary school teacher. Following the completion of my law degree, I went into practice as a commercial lawyer. The stark contrast between my idealistic notions of law as justice and the reality of commercial legal practice, however, prompted me to engage in much soul-searching. I felt that I needed a change of career, and the idea of teaching appealed to me. A couple of friends mentioned Teach First, and through some internet searching I realised that Teach for Australia was to launch in Victoria in the coming year. It seemed somewhat like fate, and I applied for, and was fortunate to be accepted into, the Teach for Australia program.

1. Note the principles of equity in higher education provided by McCowan: '(1) There must be sufficient places so that all members of society who so desire, and who have a minimum level of preparation, can participate in higher education. (2) Individuals must have a fair opportunity of obtaining a place in the institution of their choice'. Tristan McCowan, 'Expansion without Equity: An Analysis of Current Policy on Access to Higher Education in Brazil' (2007) 53 *Higher Education* 579, 582.

My experience working with Teach for Australia gave me insight into the meaning of disadvantage, and particularly educational disadvantage. Many of the students I taught were bright and hardworking, yet because of their socio-economic situation they were less likely to enjoy the opportunities often enjoyed by students from better circumstances. Following the two years that I worked with Teach for Australia, I taught for a year at a high-performing public school located in eastern metropolitan Melbourne. This experience highlighted for me the educational disadvantage that exists in Australia. I taught students with similar ambitions at each school, who I felt had similar levels of intelligence and work ethic, and yet who ended up with vastly different Australian Tertiary Admission Ranks as a result of their different circumstances.

Educational disadvantage exists at all levels of education. Although this issue is significant at primary, secondary, higher and adult education levels, I decided to focus my research on addressing educational disadvantage at the higher education level. Higher education is unique in that there is no general consensus that all individuals are entitled to higher education. Further, over the past few decades, higher education has been in a state of change. Many states are moving away from a welfare state approach to higher education, perhaps as a response to the massification and thus increasing cost of higher education provision. Instead, many states are embracing a user-pays model of higher education delivery. Yet this model has been criticised, particularly because it generally reinforces social inequality. Despite this state of affairs, attaining higher education has become more important than ever before. Higher education is a prerequisite for many jobs, and those who have attained higher education enjoy improved life circumstances.

This book is interdisciplinary in nature, spanning law, education and discrimination studies. Nevertheless, it is best approached from the disciplinary perspective of law, as the overarching question relates to the most effective legal framework to apply to the higher education sector.

ACKNOWLEDGEMENTS

Although I am the author of this book, I could not have completed it without the assistance and support of others.

I owe greatest thanks to my husband, best friend and soulmate, Ben. I am so grateful for his encouragement and interest in this book, as well as his patience with the time sacrifices and head space that it has required of me. I cannot thank him enough. I also thank my daughter, Georgia, who arrived in this world midway through completion of the book and who sat with me through many hours of writing and reviewing. I am grateful too, to our dogs Teddy and Dasha, who (against their will) have forgone walks and park visits to allow me to continue work and look after Georgia. I must also thank my family, particularly Nana, Auntie Erin and Oma, and our friend Jules, who enabled me to complete this book and care for Georgia at the same time. Credit must also go to family and friends for their interest, support and ideas.

I am fortunate to have received extensive and constructive feedback in relation to this book. Thanks in this respect must go to Professor Mirko Bagaric, Professor Kay Souter, Dr Claire Macken, Dr Neera Bhatia, Professor Doug Hodgson, Professor Kathleen Lynch, and Dr Tristan McCowan, as well as a number of anonymous reviewers. Thanks also to Professor John Tobin and Professor Mirko Bagaric for the initial inspiration behind this book. Of course, any remaining errors are my own.

A version of Chapter 1 of this book was first published by LexisNexis in the *Australian Journal of Human Rights*. (This journal is now published by Taylor & Francis.) The relevant citation is Jane Kotzmann, 'Lifting the Cloak of Conceptual Confusion: Exploring the Meaning of the Human Right to Higher Education' (2015) 21(1) *AJHR* 71. Many thanks to the publisher for providing permission to include this chapter in the book.

Table 3.9 was adapted from Terence Karran, Klaus Beiter and Kwadwo Appiagyei-Atua, 'Measuring Academic Freedom in Europe: A Criterion

Referenced Approach' (2017) 1(2) *Policy Reviews in Higher Education* 209, 213, published by Taylor & Francis Ltd (see www.tandfonline.com). Many thanks to the publisher for providing permission to include this table in the book.

I am also grateful to the following who provided assistance: Elite Editing; Jarkko Päivärinta and User Services, Finnish Social Science Data Archive; Anette Gröjer, Swedish Higher Education Authority; Silvia Gantner, Central Registry of the Swiss Federal Supreme Court; Marko Niemi, Universities Finland UNIFI; and Helen Wood, Angela Kirk and Michelle Bendall, Deakin University Library. Thanks to Teach for Australia, for giving me the opportunity to work with them. A big thanks also to my editor, Blake Ratcliff, and to Oxford University Press, for agreeing to publish the book, for their encouragement and for being so delightful to work with.

Finally, there are, of course, many others to whom I owe thanks. The authors of existing research in this area, acquaintances with whom I have discussed the book and many others who have participated in some form in the dialogue that underlies this book have all contributed to the research that follows. Many thanks to them all.

Introduction

A. EDUCATION AND EDUCATIONAL DISADVANTAGE

Higher education is important. This has been highlighted in recent years by mass student protests and political responses in a variety of world contexts.[1] Student demonstrations in Chile prompted its president, Michelle Bachelet, to commit to the introduction of free higher education.[2] In South Africa, the #FeesMustFall movement beginning in 2015 saw students across the country violently protest an increase in tuition fees; it was subsequently joined by unity protests in London

1. See Lorenzo Cini and César Guzmán-Concha, 'Student Movements in the Age of Austerity. The Cases of Chile and England' (2017) *Social Movement Studies* 1, 1.

2. Maria Elena Hurtado, *Transforming HE from Consumer Good into Social Right* (25 April 2014) University World News <http://www.universityworldnews.com/article.php?story=20140425093353226&query=michelle+bachelet>; Maria Elena Hurtado, *Start of Free Tuition Opens A Pandora's Box* (29 May 2015) University World News <http://www.universityworldnews.com/article.php?story=20150529123109404&query=michelle+bachelet>; Max Radwin, *Students in Chile Are Demanding Free Tuition, and Protests Are Turning Violent* (3 June 2016) Vice News <https://news.vice.com/article/students-in-chile-are-demanding-free-tuition-and-protests-are-turning-violent>; *Thousands of Chilean Students Take to Streets Demanding Education Reform* (11 April 2017) teleSUR <http://www.telesurtv.net/english/news/Thousands-of-Chilean-Students-Take-to-Streets-Demanding-Education-Reform-20170411-0022.html>.

The Human Rights-Based Approach to Higher Education. Jane Kotzmann.
© Oxford University Press 2018. Published 2018 by Oxford University Press.

and New York.[3] United States presidential hopeful Bernie Sanders promised to introduce free college education, and according to polling data has since become one of America's most popular politicians.[4]

This political context should draw attention to the reality that education is of critical importance to all. Education holds intrinsic importance, in that it allows people to learn about themselves and the world they live in.[5] Education also holds significant instrumental importance. People who have attained secondary education are more likely to obtain employment and command higher incomes than those who have not. Similarly, people with higher education are more likely to be employed and enjoy higher incomes than people with only secondary education.[6] Education also has an impact on other aspects of individuals' lives. It is related to improved levels of health, interpersonal trust, participation in volunteering activities and the belief that one can have an impact on the political process.[7] The importance of education in these respects is well expressed by Katarina Tomaševski, who asserts that '[e]ducation operates as multiplier, enhancing the enjoyment of all individual rights and freedoms'.[8]

Education is also essential to social progress and cohesion.[9] Through education and skills, societies are able to increase their available human capital, thus

3. Rosa Lyster, *The Student Protests Roiling South Africa* (21 October 2016) The New Yorker <http://www.newyorker.com/news/news-desk/the-student-protests-roiling-south-africa>; Nuran Davids and Yusef Waghid, *#FeesMustFall: History of South African Student Protests Reflects Inequality's Grip* (10 October 2016) Mail & Guardian <https://mg.co.za/article/2016-10-10-feesmustfall-history-of-south-african-student-protests-reflects-inequalitys-grip>.

4. Bernie Sanders, *Make College Free for All* (22 October 2015) The Washington Post <https://www.washingtonpost.com/opinions/bernie-sanders-america-needs-free-college-now/2015/10/22/a3d05512-7685-11e5-bc80-9091021aeb69_story.html?utm_term=.c127e64d780e>; Joanna Walters, *Bernie Sanders: Free Public College Tuition Is the 'Right Thing To Do'* (23 October 2015) The Guardian <https://www.theguardian.com/us-news/2015/oct/22/bernie-sanders-free-public-college-tuition-higher-education>; Jonathan Easley, *Poll: Bernie Sanders Country's Most Popular Active Politician* (18 April 2017) The Hill <http://thehill.com/homenews/campaign/329404-poll-bernie-sanders-countrys-most-popular-active-politician>; Michael Sainato, *Poll Confirms Bernie Sanders Is the Most Popular Politician in the Country* (11 July 2017) Observer <http://observer.com/2017/07/bernie-sanders-most-popular-politician/>.

5. See Tristan McCowan, *Education as a Human Right: Principles for a Universal Entitlement to Learning* (Bloomsbury Academic, 2013) 121–2.

6. See Organisation for Economic Cooperation and Development ('OECD'), 'Education at a Glance 2014: OECD Indicators' (OECD, September 2014) 13–14.

7. Ibid 14.

8. Katarina Tomaševski, 'Removing Obstacles in the Way of the Right to Education' (Right to Education Primers No 1, 2001) 9.

9. OECD, 'Education at a Glance 2014' above n 6, 13.

enabling improved economic growth.[10] Further, because educated individuals are more likely to gain employment and command higher incomes, education has a significant impact on the level of inequality and inclusion in society. Where levels of inequality are significant, the benefits of education are distributed unequally. Whereas some highly educated individuals will enjoy strong employment opportunities and other life circumstances, poorly educated individuals are likely to experience poverty and social exclusion. Such a state of affairs constitutes a significant threat to social cohesion, and thus to society in general.[11]

In recent times, there has been a trend towards increasing educational disadvantage, or inequality in access to education. The impact of education and skills on life chances has increased, which in turn has increased inequality and disadvantage in many societies.[12] More particularly, data from the Organisation for Economic Cooperation and Development (OECD) indicates that the income gap between people with high levels of education and those with average or poor levels of education has significantly increased,[13] suggesting that the relatively wealthy are increasing their wealth at the cost of the socio-economically disadvantaged and middle classes.

B. HISTORICAL PERSPECTIVES IN RELATION TO HIGHER EDUCATION DELIVERY

The delivery of higher education must be understood in a historical context. Historically, higher education was provided to 'an elite few'.[14] The 1970s, however, saw the commencement of a trend towards a massification of higher education, in which more and more people continued their studies.[15] This trend was related to the increasing prominence of welfare state ideology and concepts of

10. Theodore W Schultz, 'Investment in Human Capital' (1961) 51(1) *American Economic Review* 1, 1. See also Michael Peters, 'Re-thinking Education as a Welfare Right' (2002) 13(5) *School Field* 79, 87.

11. OECD, 'Education at a Glance 2014' above n 6, 14.

12. Ibid 13.

13. Ibid 14.

14. Ibid 13. See also Rebecca Schendel and Tristan McCowan, 'Higher Education and Development: Critical Issues and Debates' in Tristan McCowan and Elaine Unterhalter (eds), *Education and International Development: An Introduction* (2015) 275, 281.

15. See Tristan McCowan, 'Expansion without Equity: An Analysis of Current Policy on Access to Higher Education in Brazil' (2007) 53 *Higher Education* 579, 579.

social mobility.[16] In this context, higher education was frequently subsidised by the state. More recently, concepts of the knowledge economy have led to a view of higher education as being integral to economic growth and competitiveness.[17] Further, the increasing influence of neo-liberal ideology together with a need to finance the massification of higher education has instigated a trend towards the marketisation of higher education. Rather than higher education being subsidised by the state, many countries have implemented reforms designed to shift its cost to the student consumer.[18] Such reforms have been criticised for their negative impact on access to education.

Today, although most countries share a general consensus that primary and secondary education should be provided by the state,[19] debate continues in relation to how to best deliver higher education. Central to this debate is the purposes for which higher education is provided and thus who should be responsible for financing its delivery. Where higher education is considered to be primarily a public good, arguments may be made that the state should subsidise its provision. The issue then becomes how this is to be achieved in the context of massification. However, where higher education is considered to be primarily a private good, it is reasonable to expect individuals to pay for their own education. In this respect, however, policymakers need to consider the impact on access to higher education, inequality and disadvantage, and ultimately the influence of these factors on society.

Discussion around how best to deliver higher education in today's society must take into account the changed historical context. Yet although it is critical to consider the problem in light of contemporary conditions, many arguments made in decades past in relation to higher education delivery may equally apply to today's context. To this extent, consideration of the question of how best to deliver higher education must take all relevant arguments and considerations into account.

16. Jens Jungblut, 'Partisan Politics in Higher Education Policy: How Does the Left-Right Divide of Political Parties Matter in Higher Education Policy in Western Europe?' in Gaële Goastellec and France Picard (eds), *Higher Education in Societies: A Multi-Scale Perspective* (Springer, 2014) 86, 90.

17. Ibid.

18. For example, see Chapter 4 for a description of higher education reforms in England. See generally, Leo Goedegebuure, Frans Kaiser, Peter Maassen and Egbert de Weert, 'Higher Education Policy in International Perspective: An Overview' in Leo Goedegebuure, Frans Kaiser, Peter Maassen, Lyn Meek, Frans van Vught and Egbert de Weert (eds), *Higher Education Policy: An International Comparative Perspective* (Pergamon Press, 1993) 1, 1.

19. For a summary of reasons for this consensus, see Tomaševski, 'Removing Obstacles', above n 8, 14.

C. IMPORTANCE OF POLICY AND LAW FOR HIGHER EDUCATION

Policy frameworks, and the legal means by which they are implemented by states (policy), have a significant impact on access to higher education and educational disadvantage. Some policies are more effective at enabling access to education than others. As Angel Gurria notes, '[d]ifferent policies produce different outcomes, and this is also true with regard to education and skills'.[20] In this respect, consideration of other states' higher education frameworks will be beneficial for policymakers.

The policies that states implement to frame the delivery of higher education teaching and learning are critically important. This is for a number of reasons. One of the key reasons is that higher education policy frameworks have an impact on access to higher education, and access to higher education is linked to improved life chances. Conversely, educational disadvantage has a negative impact on the life chances of the particular individuals who face obstacles to access. It also increases the levels of inequality in society and as a result undermines the cohesiveness of society. A higher education system that excludes or impedes access on the basis of gender, race, nationality and so on, will create a society in which those excluded groups are further marginalised, and will likely create tension between society's haves and have-nots as a result.

Higher education policy also has an impact beyond questions of access. A significant issue, related to that of access, is the charging of fees for higher education. Free provision of higher education is likely to generate a view that higher education is a public good: one which is subsidised with public funds and from which there will be a contribution back to the public. Nevertheless, where regulation requires that higher education is freely provided, there may be insufficient incentive for students to work hard and the public tax burden will be significant. In contrast, requirements for higher education institutions to impose fees may contribute to a perception that higher education is an investment that will primarily benefit the individual and for which the individual should therefore pay. Further, imposition of fees for higher education may lead students to view themselves as consumers who are able to purchase education or certification rather than engage in an ongoing process of learning.

Higher education also makes an important contribution to societal values. In this context, higher education is an important influence on the development of individual personality, values and behaviour. What and how people learn as a result of their experience in education influences the way they see the world and how they act within it. For example, the exclusion of humanities subjects

20. OECD, 'Education at a Glance 2014' above n 6, 15.

from higher education curricula may suggest that only commercially valuable knowledge is worth pursuing. This may have flow-on effects in terms of the value attached to certain types of knowledge, work—and therefore people—in society.

Higher education should thus be viewed as a microcosm of society. The policies that are implemented in relation to a higher education system will impact that system, and that impact will flow on to the broader society. Understanding the effectiveness and consequences of different policy frameworks will enable policymakers to implement policies that improve access to higher education and, more broadly, contribute to a harmonious society, one that is viewed as ideal by the general populace.

D. PURPOSE OF THIS BOOK

This book attempts to identify whether a policy framework for higher education, based on the human right to higher education, might have more to offer in terms of meeting the purposes of higher education teaching and learning than an approach based on market principles. To answer this question, the approach taken is to evaluate first each theoretical model (Chapter 2) and then selected state higher education policies (Chapter 4) in terms of their substance and some of their effects. In pursuing this question, this book seeks to encourage policymakers to ground frameworks in research. Rather than making decisions on the basis of ideological beliefs about the proper role of the state and the rights (or lack of rights) of individuals, this book contends that ensuring policy is research based will result in the development of more considered, sophisticated and ultimately successful higher education systems.[21]

The primary contention of this book is that an approach to higher education that is based on the human right to higher education (a 'human rights-based approach') is more likely to enable the state to meet the purposes of higher education than one based on market principles. Although the relevant international legal provisions are only binding on states parties to the relevant

21. See Linda Hantrais, *International Comparative Research: Theory, Methods and Practice* (Palgrave Macmillan, 2009) 11; Anthony Welch, 'Evidence-Based Policy: Epistemologically Specious, Ideologically Unsound' in Helen Proctor, Patrick Brownlee and Peter Freebody (eds), *Controversies in Education: Orthodoxy and Heresy in Policy and Practice* (Springer, 2015) 63, 69. In relation to current policy development practices in Australia, see Tom Clark, 'Under No Circumstances Resolve the Main Problem: Higher Education Policy Overview in Australia' (2004) 46(2) *Australian Universities Review* 12, 13. It is noted that in pursuing this research question, this book is adopting a consequentialist position on human rights: that the adoption of human rights can be justified by the positive consequences they bring about. In taking this position, it is not suggested that a human rights-based approach to higher education cannot also be justified from a deontological point of view. Nevertheless, such justification is outside the scope of this analysis.

conventions (except to the extent they might constitute customary law),[22] this book posits that the likely consequences of a human rights-based approach to higher education are sufficient to justify the adoption of such an approach regardless of legal obligation. Further, although there is likely to be merit in a human rights-based approach to higher education beyond its probable consequences for teaching and learning, it is contended that these consequences alone are sufficient to justify the adoption of such an approach. Accordingly, this book argues that states that have not yet adopted a human rights-based approach to higher education should consider undertaking policy reform to move in this direction.

This topic carries importance beyond national borders. As Tomaševski identifies, it is easier to realise economic, social and cultural rights, such as the right to education, in wealthy countries. Yet by determining what policies are effective in these contexts, poor countries will also be assisted in addressing similar problems within their own cultural contexts.[23] This book does not suggest that the policies of wealthy countries can be directly transferred to significantly different legal, political and cultural contexts; however, it does suggest that analysis of such policies can provide valuable information for all states to determine the best approach to take within state-specific circumstances.

E. LIMITATIONS

It is a broad question whether a policy framework for higher education, based on the human right to higher education, might have more to offer in terms of meeting the goals of higher education compared with a market-based approach. To attempt to answer it requires some assumptions to be made as well as a degree of subjectivity. For example:

- Although the approach taken here is to compare countries that clearly align with a particular theoretical model, reality is more complex than the theoretical models might suggest. Further, many state higher education systems do not clearly align with a particular model, but rather include elements of more than one.

22. See Stephen Hall, *Principles of International Law* (LexisNexis Butterworths, 4th ed, 2014) 46, 90.

23. See Katarina Tomaševski, 'Unasked Questions about Economic, Social, and Cultural Rights from the Experience of the Special Rapporteur on the Right to Education (1998–2004): A Response to Kenneth Roth, Leonard S. Rubenstein, and Mary Robinson' (2005) 27 *Human Rights Quarterly* 713, 713–4.

- Although efforts have been made to develop a sound research design, it is acknowledged that it has been necessary to make trade-offs and compromise at certain points, which is reflective of the reality that 'it is never possible to find a design that can be operationalized and implemented in all respects in all the units of comparison'.[24]
- To the extent that the conclusions drawn here relate to the effect of higher education policies, they do involve some assumptions being made about the causal nature of higher education policy and the likelihood of achieving higher education purposes. It is likely, however, that the ability of policy to meet the purposes of higher education teaching is also impacted by factors other than the policy framework. For example, the employability of graduates will be impacted by higher education policy, but will also be influenced by the strength of the economy. Further, it is also possible that causality may run both ways; in other words, that achieving higher education purposes might lead a system to take a particular policy approach.[25]

Although these issues do provide limitations, it would not be possible to attempt a meaningful answer to the question without making some assumptions. In terms of the big picture, it is contended that the analysis here indicates trends which suggest that a human rights-based approach is *likely* to offer more than a market-based approach in meeting the purposes of higher education.

In considering the question of whether a human rights-based approach to higher education is more likely to assist a state to achieve the purposes of higher education teaching and learning, the following related issues lie beyond the scope of this book:

- Substantial literature exists in relation to whether human rights exist at all.[26] Even where rights are considered to exist, they have been thought about in different ways.[27] For the purposes of this book, human

24. See Hantrais, above n 21, 69.

25. Ibid 133.

26. Jeremy Bentham, 'Anarchical Fallacies: Being an Examination of the Declaration of Rights Issued during the French Revolution' (1824) in John Bowring (ed), *The Works of Jeremy Bentham* (Russell and Russell, 1962 ed) vol 2, 489, 523–4; H L A Hart, 'Are There Any Natural Rights?' (1955) 64(2) *The Philosophical Review* 175.

27. See Jim Ife, *Human Rights from Below: Achieving Rights through Community Development* (Cambridge University Press, 2010) 73; Kate Halvorsen, 'Notes on the Realization of the Human Right to Education' (1990) 12 *Human Rights Quarterly* 341, 345.

rights are assumed to constitute an intellectually coherent and sound construct. In terms of which human rights exist and their content, this book adopts human rights as they exist in contemporary international legal documentation. Thus, it assumes that there is a right to education (in the same way that there is a right to life, fair trial and property ownership) and examines the extent to which this right should be operationalised and conferred.[28]

- The human right to education includes a number of aspects. This book focuses on those aspects of the right to education that apply to higher education. The right to education in relation to primary, secondary and fundamental education is beyond the scope of this book, as is the right to human rights education and liberty rights in education.[29]
- This book focuses on the likely impact of theoretical frameworks on teaching and learning in higher education. Although it is acknowledged that research and community engagement are also relevant from a human rights perspective, it is not possible to cover all functions of higher education within the word limit of this book. The decision was made to focus on teaching and learning because this is arguably the higher education function to which the right to higher education is most directly relevant.
- This book asserts that any evaluation of higher education systems must be undertaken in relation to the purposes of higher education.[30] Nevertheless, a historical analysis of the purposes of higher education systems lies beyond the scope of this book. Instead, the purposes of higher education are considered in terms of their contemporary relevance.
- Although higher education systems comprise both public and private higher education providers, this book is primarily concerned with the public provision of higher education. By their nature, private higher education institutions may define their own purposes, and thus their

28. See Chapter 1 for an outline of the sources of the right to higher education.

29. In relation to these aspects, see Committee on Economic, Social and Cultural Rights (CESCR), *General Comment No 13: The Right to Education (Article 13 of the Covenant)*, 21st sess, UN Doc E/C.12/1999/10 (8 December 1999) [39–40]; Klaus Dieter Beiter, *The Protection of the Right to Education by International Law: Including a Systematic Analysis of Article 13 of the International Covenant on Economic, Social, and Cultural Rights* (Martinus Nijhoff Publishers, 2006) 483; Fons Coomans, 'Content and Scope of the Right to Education as a Human Right and Obstacles to Its Realization' in Yvonne Donders and Vladimir Volodin (eds), *Human Rights in Education, Science and Culture: Legal Developments and Challenges* (UNESCO Publishing, 2007) 183, 186–7.

30. See Chapter 3 in relation to this argument.

effectiveness might potentially be assessed in a different manner to that of public higher education institutions.[31]

- In undertaking a comparative analysis of state higher education policies, it was not possible to consider the higher education policies of all countries. Those countries that are considered were thought to align well with the theoretical frameworks identified. It is acknowledged that consideration of other higher education policies may shed further light on the potential of the theoretical models to enable the attainment of the purposes of higher education teaching and learning. Further, analysis of the conditions in low and middle-income countries, as compared to OECD countries, may provide different insights.
- The analysis undertaken in this book, and particularly in Chapter 4, is based on the data available at the time of writing. Although the most current data is used where it is available, where it is not available recent data may be drawn upon. Again, more recent data may further elucidate the potential of different models of higher education provision.
- Different areas of government policy may have an impact on participation in higher education. The extent to which they limit participation in higher education—for example through immigration restrictions—lies beyond the scope of this book.

F. WHERE TO FROM HERE?

This book is divided into two parts. Part One is concerned with the theoretical aspects of determining the best approach to providing higher education. In order to determine what an approach to higher education based on the human right to higher education would look like, Chapter 1 of Part One explores the meaning of that human right. The chapter outlines the scope and content of the right to higher education and identifies the various sources of that right in international law. It considers the scope of the right as set out in Article 13 of the *International Covenant on Economic, Social and Cultural Rights,* including an analysis of whether the right includes a right to certification, what constitutes acceptable limitations on access to higher education, and the requirement to progressively introduce free higher education. This discussion underpins the human rights-based approach described in Chapter 2.

31. But see Ronald Barnett and Carolina Guzman, 'The Human Rights University: A Feasible Utopia' in Claudia Brunner and Josefine Scherling (eds), *Bildung, Menschenrechte, Universitat. Menschenrechts-Bildung and Hochschulen im Wandel als gesellschaftliche Herausforderung* (Drava Verlag, 2012) 269.

Chapter 2 explores two general theoretical models that are used to frame higher education policy. The market-based model involves provision of higher education through the free market. In contrast, a human rights-based approach seeks to translate the human right to higher education and operationalise it. The chapter provides an evaluation of these models.

Part Two of this book is concerned with assessing the practical application of different higher education policies. Chapter 3 establishes a framework for evaluating higher education policies in relation to teaching and learning. It identifies the purposes of higher education: individual transformation, improvement of society and social efficiency. It then identifies signs that suggest that the purposes of higher education are being, or may be, met, and outlines a methodology for measuring these signs within a given system.

Chapter 4 builds upon the analysis and framework in Chapter 3 by exploring the real-life operation of six state higher education policies that align with the two theoretical models identified in Chapter 2. The chapter describes each policy in terms of how it aligns with a particular model before evaluating the system in relation to the signs of successful higher education systems identified in Chapter 3. Chapter 4 provides conclusions as to the likelihood that each theoretical model may enable the fulfilment of the purposes of higher education teaching and learning.

REFERENCE LIST

A. Articles/Books/Reports

Barnett, Ronald and Carolina Guzman, 'The Human Rights University: A Feasible Utopia' in Claudia Brunner and Josefine Scherling (eds), *Bildung, Menschenrechte, Universitat. Menschenrechts-Bildung and Hochschulen im Wandel als gesellschaftliche Herausforderung* (Drava Verlag, 2012) 269

Beiter, Klaus Dieter, *The Protection of the Right to Education by International Law: Including a Systematic Analysis of Article 13 of the International Covenant on Economic, Social, and Cultural Rights* (Martinus Nijhoff Publishers, 2006)

Bentham, Jeremy, 'Anarchical Fallacies: Being an Examination of the Declaration of Rights Issued during the French Revolution' (1824) in John Bowring (ed), *The Works of Jeremy Bentham* (Russell and Russell, 1962) vol 2, 489

Cini, Lorenzo and César Guzmán-Concha, 'Student Movements in the Age of Austerity. The Cases of Chile and England' (2017) 16 (5) *Social Movement Studies* 1

Clark, Tom, 'Under No Circumstances Resolve the Main Problem: Higher Education Policy Overview in Australia' (2004) 46(2) *Australian Universities Review* 12

Coomans, Fons, 'Content and Scope of the Right to Education as a Human Right and Obstacles to Its Realization' in Yvonne Donders and Vladimir Volodin (eds), *Human Rights in Education, Science and Culture: Legal Developments and Challenges* (UNESCO Publishing, 2007) 183

Goedegebuure, Leo, Frans Kaiser, Peter Maassen and Egbert de Weert, 'Higher Education Policy in International Perspective: An Overview' in Leo Goedegebuure, Frans Kaiser, Peter Maassen, Lyn Meek, Frans van Vught and Egbert de Weert (eds), *Higher Education Policy: An International Comparative Perspective* (Pergamon Press, 1993) 1

Hall, Stephen, *Principles of International Law* (LexisNexis Butterworths, 4th ed, 2014)

Halvorsen, Kate, 'Notes on the Realization of the Human Right to Education' (1990) 12 *Human Rights Quarterly* 341

Hantrais, Linda, *International Comparative Research: Theory, Methods and Practice* (Palgrave Macmillan, 2009)

Hart, H L A, 'Are There Any Natural Rights?' (1955) 64(2) *The Philosophical Review* 175

Ife, Jim, *Human Rights from Below: Achieving Rights through Community Development* (Cambridge University Press, 2010)

Jungblut, Jens, 'Partisan Politics in Higher Education Policy: How Does the Left-Right Divide of Political Parties Matter in Higher Education Policy in Western Europe?' in Gaële Goastellec and France Picard (eds), *Higher Education in Societies: A Multi-Scale Perspective* (Springer, 2014) 86

McCowan, Tristan, 'Expansion without Equity: An Analysis of Current Policy on Access to Higher Education in Brazil' (2007) 53 *Higher Education* 579

McCowan, Tristan, *Education as a Human Right: Principles for a Universal Entitlement to Learning* (Bloomsbury Academic, 2013)

Peters, Michael, 'Re-thinking Education as a Welfare Right' (2002) 13(5) *School Field* 79

Schendel, Rebecca, and Tristan McCowan, 'Higher Education and Development: Critical Issues and Debates' in Tristan McCowan and Elaine Unterhalter (eds), *Education and International Development: An Introduction* (Bloomsbury Academic, 2015) 275

Schultz, Theodore W, 'Investment in Human Capital' (1961) 51(1) *American Economic Review* 1

Tomaševski, Katarina, 'Unasked Questions about Economic, Social, and Cultural Rights from the Experience of the Special Rapporteur on the Right to Education (1998–2004): A Response to Kenneth Roth, Leonard S. Rubenstein, and Mary Robinson' (2005) 27 *Human Rights Quarterly* 713

Welch, Anthony, 'Evidence-Based Policy: Epistemologically Specious, Ideologically Unsound' in Helen Proctor, Patrick Brownlee and Peter Freebody (eds), *Controversies in Education: Orthodoxy and Heresy in Policy and Practice* (Springer, 2015) 63

B. Official international documents

Committee on Economic, Social and Cultural Rights, *General Comment No 13: The Right to Education (Article 13 of the Covenant)*, 21st sess, UN Doc E/C.12/1999/10 (8 December 1999)

C. Other

Davids, Nuran and Yusef Waghid, *#FeesMustFall: History of South African Student Protests Reflects Inequality's Grip* (10 October 2016) Mail & Guardian <https://mg.co.za/article/2016-10-10-feesmustfall-history-of-south-african-student-protests-reflects-inequalitys-grip>

Easley, Jonathan, *Poll: Bernie Sanders Country's Most Popular Active Politician* (18 April 2017) The Hill <http://thehill.com/homenews/campaign/329404-poll-bernie-sanders-countrys-most-popular-active-politician>

Hurtado, Maria Elena, *Transforming HE from Consumer Good into Social Right* (25 April 2014) University World News <http://www.universityworldnews.com/article.php?story=20140425093353226&query=michelle+bachelet>

Hurtado, Maria Elena, *Start of Free Tuition Opens a Pandora's Box* (29 May 2015) University World News <http://www.universityworldnews.com/article.php?story=20150529123109404&query=michelle+bachelet>

Lyster, Rosa, *The Student Protests Roiling South Africa* (21 October 2016) The New Yorker <http://www.newyorker.com/news/news-desk/the-student-protests-roiling-south-africa>

Organisation for Economic Cooperation and Development, 'Education at a Glance 2014: OECD Indicators' (OECD, September 2014)

Radwin, Max, *Students in Chile Are Demanding Free Tuition, and Protests Are Turning Violent* (3 June 2016) Vice News <https://news.vice.com/article/students-in-chile-are-demanding-free-tuition-and-protests-are-turning-violent>

Sainato, Michael, *Poll Confirms Bernie Sanders Is the Most Popular Politician in the Country* (11 July 2017) Observer <http://observer.com/2017/07/bernie-sanders-most-popular-politician/>

Sanders, Bernie, *Make College Free for All* (22 October 2015) The Washington Post <https://www.washingtonpost.com/opinions/bernie-sanders-america-needs-free-college-now/2015/10/22/a3d05512-7685-11e5-bc80-9091021aeb69_story.html?utm_term=.c127e64d780e>

Thousands of Chilean Students Take to Streets Demanding Education Reform (11 April 2017) teleSUR <http://www.telesurtv.net/english/news/Thousands-of-Chilean-Students-Take-to-Streets-Demanding-Education-Reform-20170411-0022.html>

Tomaševski, Katarina, 'Removing Obstacles in the Way of the Right to Education' (Right to Education Primers No 1, 2001)

Walters, Joanna, *Bernie Sanders: Free Public College Tuition Is the 'Right Thing To Do'* (23 October 2015) The Guardian <https://www.theguardian.com/us-news/2015/oct/22/bernie-sanders-free-public-college-tuition-higher-education>

PART ONE

The Human Rights-Based Approach and the Market-Based Approach

1

The Human Right to Higher Education

A. INTRODUCTION

Despite the right to education existing in international human rights documentation for decades, it remains somewhat veiled by a 'conceptual confusion'.[1] There are many reasons for this confusion. One reason is the lack of 'professional and academic literature which clearly explains what the right to education is and what constitutes a violation'.[2] A second reason is the inability, until the entry into force of the *Optional Protocol to the International Covenant on Economic, Social and Cultural Rights* in 2013,[3] of individuals to make complaints in relation to breach of the *International Covenant on Economic, Social and Cultural Rights* (ICESCR)

1. Katarina Tomaševski, 'Removing Obstacles in the Way of the Right to Education' (Right to Education Primers No 1, 2001) 5.

2. Katarina Tomaševski, 'Has the Right to Education a Future within the United Nations? A Behind-the-Scene Account by the Special Rapporteur on the Right to Education 1998–2004' (2005) 5 *Human Rights Law Review* 205, 210–11.

3. United Nations, *Optional Protocol to the International Covenant on Economic, Social and Cultural Rights* (26 November 2016) United Nations Treaty Collection <https://treaties.un.org/Pages/ViewDetails.aspx?src=IND&mtdsg_no=IV-3-a&chapter=4&clang=_en>.

The Human Rights-Based Approach to Higher Education. Jane Kotzmann.
© Oxford University Press 2018. Published 2018 by Oxford University Press.

rights. Moreover, where the right to education in general is opaque, the right to specifically higher education is even less clear. Any attention given to the right to education tends to focus on primary or basic education, particularly in the context of developing countries. For example, the Education for All goals and Millennium Development Goals are considered by the United Nations to be 'the two most important frameworks in the field of education' and are almost exclusively concerned with primary and basic education.[4] Although there may often be good reasons for prioritisation, unfortunately it also operates to 'implicitly negat[e] the right to . . . [higher] education'.[5]

Higher education is in a state of change.[6] Past decades have seen a significant increase in access, dubbed the 'massification' of higher education.[7] At the same time, it has been primarily the middle and higher classes that have benefited from these changes, and higher education remains a source of social stratification.[8] Increasing access has led to financial pressures on governments (compounded by 'the worst economic crisis of our lifetimes'),[9] which in some countries such as Chile has led to increasing privatisation of the sector.[10] Some general trends in response to these pressures can be identified: the Nordic countries charge low tuition fees and provide generous support systems financed through taxation. Countries including Australia and the United States (US) charge high tuition fees and provide well-developed student support systems, whereas countries including Chile charge high tuition fees but

4. United Nations, *Education*, United Nations <http://www.un.org/en/sections/issues-depth/education/index.html>.

5. Katarina Tomaševski, *Report Submitted by the Special Rapporteur*, UN Doc E/CN.4/2004/45 (15 January 2004) 13. But note that Tomaševski has also criticized the allocation of funding to higher education in preference to primary education, see Katarina Tomaševski, *Preliminary Report of the Special Rapporteur on the Right to Education*, UN Doc E/CN.4/1999/49 (13 January 1999) 34–8.

6. See Saad Rizvi, Katelyn Donnelly and Michael Barber, 'An Avalanche Is Coming: Higher Education and the Revolution Ahead' (Essay, Institute for Public Policy Research, March 2013).

7. Larry Robert Smith, 'Preface' in Larry Robert Smith (ed), *Higher Education: Recent Trends, Emerging Issues and Future Outlook* (Nova Science Publishers, 2013) vii, vii.

8. Heinz-Dieter Meyer, Edward P St John, Maia Chankseliani and Lina Uribe (eds), *Fairness in Access to Higher Education in a Global Perspective: Reconciling Excellence, Efficiency, and Justice* (Sense Publishers, 2013) 3; Organisation for Economic Cooperation and Development (OECD), 'Education at a Glance 2014: OECD Indicators' (OECD, September 2014) 13–15.

9. OECD, 'Education at a Glance 2014', above n 8, 13. See also Rizvi, Donnelly and Barber, above n 6, 11.

10. Meyer, St John, Chankseliani and Uribe, above n 8, 8.

have less-developed student support systems. In the meantime countries such as Austria and France charge low tuition fees and have less-developed support systems.[11] Compounding the need to respond to increased access and financial pressures, however, have been technological changes which impact the way in which higher education can be and often is delivered,[12] as well as increasing globalisation which adds to the changed demographic of higher education students and widens the higher education marketplace.[13] The changing context of higher education demands a response. Before adopting radical changes in the higher education arena, however, it is suggested that we should pause and consider the human rights obligations that have been voluntarily adopted by nations around the world.

Given the lack of detailed analysis of the right to higher education,[14] it is not surprising that recognition and promotion of the right has been patchy and devoid of a concrete overarching framework. This chapter attempts to raise awareness of the complexities associated with the right and the need for rigorous assessment of its meaning and content, in order that some progress can be made towards systematic implementation of the right.[15] This is particularly timely, given the current changes in higher education.

This chapter outlines the scope and content of the right to higher education. It advances Katarina Tomaševski's lead in rejecting a 'chewing-gum approach' to human rights (whereby the concern of human rights is stretched such that 'there is a human rights answer to every question'), and contends that the right needs to be defined with a degree of particularity in order to ensure that it is instrumental in delivering concrete benefits.[16] The understanding of the human right to higher education that is outlined here underpins the human rights-based approach to higher education discussed in Chapter 2 of this book.

11. OECD, 'Education at a Glance 2014', above n 8, 265–6.

12. Smith, above n 7, vii–viii.

13. Ibid viii–x; Meyer, St John, Chankseliani and Uribe, above n 8, 3; Rizvi, Donnelly and Barber, above n 6, 1.

14. Tomaševski, 'Has the Right to Education a Future within the United Nations?' above n 2, 210–11.

15. See John Tobin, 'Understanding a Human Rights Based Approach to Matters Involving Children: Conceptual Foundations and Strategic Considerations' in Antonella Invernizzi and Jane Williams (eds), *The Human Rights of Children: From Visions to Implementation* (Ashgate Publishing, 2011) 61, 77.

16. Tomaševski, 'Has the Right to Education a Future within the United Nations?' above n 2, 225.

B. SOURCES OF THE RIGHT TO HIGHER EDUCATION

The right to higher education has achieved widespread recognition in international law, despite its low profile and the divergent ways that states have approached its implementation.[17] Recognition of the right is reflected in a number of global international legal instruments including declarations and treaties, as well as in some regional international and domestic legal instruments.[18] Legal obligations relating to the right to higher education are only binding on states parties to the relevant conventions, except to the extent that requirements have become customary law.[19]

The most important provisions in relation to the right to higher education are found in the ICESCR and the *Convention on the Rights of the Child* (CROC).[20] Article 13(2)(c) of the ICESCR establishes the right to higher education as a legally binding norm, obligating parties to make higher education 'equally accessible to all, on the basis of capacity'.[21] Similarly, Article 28(1)(c) of the CROC provides that states parties to the *Convention* will '[m]ake higher education accessible to all on the basis of capacity by every appropriate means'. This is a lesser obligation than that set out in the ICESCR, as it fails to oblige states to ensure 'the progressive introduction of free education'.[22] Article 41 of the CROC, however, operates to reinforce the requirements of Article 13(2)(c) of the ICESCR for states that are party to both treaties.[23] Although the CROC applies only to

17. In relation to the varying interpretations of rights, see Ken Brown, *The Right to Learn: Alternatives for a Learning Society* (Routledge Falmer, 2002) 4.

18. Douglas Hodgson, *The Human Right to Education* (Ashgate, 1998) 39; Connie de la Vega, 'The Right to Equal Education: Merely a Guiding Principle or Customary International Legal Right?' (1994) 11 *Harvard Black Letter Journal* 37, 44. Regional international legal instruments are discussed below. Domestic sources of law include, for example, the *Constitution of the Bolivarian Republic of Venezuela* (1999) art 102-103, the *Constitution of India* (2002) art 21A and the *Constitution of Turkey* (1982, amended 2011) art 42.

19. See Stephen Hall, *Principles of International Law* (LexisNexis Butterworths, 4th ed, 2014) 46, 90.

20. Tristan McCowan, *Education as a Human Right: Principles for a Universal Entitlement to Learning* (Bloomsbury Academic, 2013) 26.

21. *International Covenant on Economic, Social and Cultural Rights,* opened for signature 19 December 1966, 993 UNTS 3 (entered into force 3 January 1976) art 13(2)(c).

22. See McCowan, *Education as a Human Right,* above n 20, 30; Douglas Hodgson, 'The International Human Right to Education and Education concerning Human Rights' (1996) 4 *International Journal of Children's Rights* 237, 245.

23. *Convention on the Rights of the Child,* opened for signature 20 November 1989, 1577 UNTS 3 (entered into force 2 September 1990) art 41; Mieke Verheyde, *Article 28: The Right to Education* (Martinus Nijhoff Publishers, 2006) 10.

children, it is the most ratified international treaty in existence, with all but one United Nations member having signed and ratified the document, indicating widespread international support for the right to higher education.[24]

Numerous other international instruments provide for the right to higher education. In particular, the United Nations Educational, Scientific and Cultural Organization's (UNESCO) *Convention against Discrimination in Education* (CADE)[25] operates to require states parties to combat discrimination and provide equality of opportunity and treatment in higher education.[26] The right to higher education is also provided in many treaties applicable to specific groups. For example, Article 10 of the *Convention on the Elimination of All Forms of Discrimination Against Women* requires states parties to ensure women enjoy equality with men at all levels of education,[27] Article 14(2) of the United Nations' *Declaration on the Rights of Indigenous Peoples* provides that indigenous people 'have the right to all levels and forms of education . . . without discrimination',[28] and Article 24(1) of the *Convention on the Rights of Persons with Disabilities* requires states parties to 'ensure an inclusive education system at all levels'.[29]

The right to higher education is also protected in many regional legal documents. In Europe, Article 2 of Protocol No 1 to the *European Convention on Human Rights* (ECHR) provides that '[n]o person shall be denied the right to education'.[30] The right to education in this Article includes a right of access to

24. The United Nations member that has not ratified the *Convention* is the United States. See United Nations Children's Fund (UNICEF), *Convention on the Rights of the Child* (30 November 2005) UNICEF <http://www.unicef.org/crc/index_30229.html>; United Nations, *Convention on the Rights of the Child* (27 November 2016) United Nations Treaty Collection <https://treaties.un.org/Pages/ViewDetails.aspx?src=TREATY&mtdsg_no=IV-11&chapter=4&clang=_en>.

25. *Convention against Discrimination in Education*, opened for signature 14 December 1960, 429 UNTS 93 (entered into force 22 May 1962).

26. McCowan, *Education as a Human Right*, above n 20, 31; Fons Coomans, 'Content and Scope of the Right to Education as a Human Right and Obstacles to Its Realization' in Yvonne Donders and Vladimir Volodin (eds), *Human Rights in Education, Science and Culture: Legal Developments and Challenges* (UNESCO Publishing, 2007) 183, 190; Hodgson, *The Human Right to Education*, above n 18, 47.

27. *Convention on the Elimination of All Forms of Discrimination against Women*, opened for signature 1 March 1980, 1249 UNTS 13 (entered into force 3 September 1981) art 10.

28. *United Nations Declaration on the Rights of Indigenous Peoples*, GA Res 61/295, UN GAOR, 61st sess, 107th plen mtg, Supp No 49, UN Doc A/RES/61/295 (13 September 2007) [art 14(2)].

29. *Convention on the Rights of Persons with Disabilities*, opened for signature 30 March 2007, 2515 UNTS 3 (entered into force 3 May 2008), art 24(1).

30. *European Convention for the Protection of Human Rights and Fundamental Freedoms, as amended by Protocols Nos. 11 and 14*, opened for signature 4 November 1950, ETS 5 (3 September 1953).

educational institutions existing at a given time, including higher education institutions.[31] Further, in the Americas, the right to education is recognised in Article XII of the *American Declaration on the Rights and Duties of Man.*[32] The *Additional Protocol to the American Convention on Human Rights* (San Salvador Protocol) also protects the right to education, in similar terms to Article 13(2)(c) of the ICESCR.[33] In Africa, the *African Charter on Human and Peoples' Rights* provides for a right to education in Article 17,[34] and the *African Charter on the Rights and Welfare of the Child* requires states parties to make higher education 'accessible to all on the basis of capacity and ability by every appropriate means'.[35]

C. SCOPE OF THE RIGHT TO HIGHER EDUCATION: ARTICLE 13 ICESCR

1. Introduction

In analysing the scope of the right to higher education, this chapter focuses on Article 13 of the ICESCR, as the provisions of the ICESCR are the most 'authoritative expression' of the right to higher education.[36] This is for a number of reasons. First, the ICESCR is the main and most wide-reaching treaty covering the

31. *Tarantino v Italy* (2013) 25851/09 Eur Court HR 43; *Leyla Şahin v Turkey* [2005] 44774/98 Eur Court HR 134-42; *Mürsel Eren v Turkey* [2006] 60856/00 Eur Court HR 41. In terms of further European instruments providing for equitable access to higher education see Council of Europe, *Framework Convention for the Protection of National Minorities,* opened for signature 1 February 1995 ETS 157 (1 February 1998) art 12; Council of Europe, *European Charter for Regional or Minority Languages,* opened for signature 5 November 1992 ETS 148 (1 March 1998) art 8e.

32. *American Declaration on the Rights and Duties of Man,* Bogota, Colombia, 2 May 1948, art 12.

33. *Additional Protocol to the American Convention on Human Rights in the Area of Economic, Social and Cultural Rights (Protocol of San Salvador),* opened for signature 17 November 1988, A-52 (entered into force 16 November 1999) art 13.

34. *African Charter on Human and Peoples' Rights (Banjul Charter),* opened for signature 27 June 1981, CAB/LEG/67/3 rev 5, 21 ILM 58 (entered into force 21 October 1986).

35. *African Charter on the Rights and Welfare of the Child,* opened for signature 11 July 1990), OAU Doc CAB/LEG/24.9/49 (entered into force 29 November 1999) art 11(3)(c).

36. McCowan, *Education as a Human Right,* above n 20, 28. Note this approach is also taken in Sital Kalantry, Jocelyn E Getgen and Steven Arrigg Koh, 'Enhancing Enforcement of Economic, Social, and Cultural Rights Using Indicators: A Focus on the Right to Education in the ICESCR' (2010) 32 *Human Rights Quarterly* 253, 261. See also Sezen Kama, 'Another Dimension of the Right to Education: Is "Equally Accessible Higher Education" a Dream?' (2014) 1(1) *Queen Mary Human Rights Review* 149, 153.

right to education.[37] Unlike the provisions in the *Universal Declaration of Human Rights* (UDHR), Article 13 is incontestably legally binding on states parties.[38] Further, the right to education set out in the ICESCR is the most comprehensive of all the rights to education as set forth in international instruments;[39] in particular, it goes further than the UDHR by requiring states to progressively introduce free higher education.[40] Finally, the ICESCR is widely ratified, with 165 states parties,[41] indicating strong support for the right to higher education as set out in Article 13.[42] Nevertheless, as the Optional Protocol to the ICESCR has only recently come into operation,[43] to date there is no jurisprudence from the Committee on Economic, Social and Cultural Rights (CESCR) in relation to Article 13(2)(c).[44] Thus, to the extent that regional or national jurisprudence may shed further light on the content of the right to higher education set out in Article 13(2)(c), it will be incorporated into the following discussion.[45]

The right to education is predominantly an economic, or welfare, right.[46] It requires state governments to direct resources such that the right can be enjoyed.

37. Coomans, 'Content and Scope', above n 26, 184; Fons Coomans, 'Exploring the Normative Content of the Right to Education as a Human Right: Recent Approaches' (2004) 50 *Persona y Derecho* 60, 63.

38. McCowan, *Education as a Human Right*, above n 20, 28; Hodgson, *The Human Right to Education*, above n 18, 41.

39. CESCR, *General Comment No 13: The Right to Education (Article 13 of the Covenant)*, 21st sess, UN Doc E/C.12/1999/10 (8 December 1999).

40. Hodgson, *The Human Right to Education*, above n 18, 43.

41. As of 8 July 2017, see United Nations, *International Covenant on Economic, Social and Cultural Rights* (8 July 2017) United Nations Treaty Collection <https://treaties.un.org/Pages/ViewDetails.aspx?src=TREATY&mtdsg_no=IV-3&chapter=4&clang=_en>.

42. McCowan, *Education as a Human Right*, above n 20, 28. Note that none of the states that have ratified ICESCR have lodged a reservation limiting the application of Article 13(2)(c): see ibid.

43. United Nations, *Optional Protocol to the International Covenant on Economic, Social and Cultural Rights* (26 November 2016) United Nations Treaty Collection <https://treaties.un.org/Pages/ViewDetails.aspx?src=IND&mtdsg_no=IV-3-a&chapter=4&clang=_en>.

44. Office of the High Commissioner for Human Rights, *Jurisprudence*, Office of the High Commissioner for Human Rights <http://juris.ohchr.org/en/search/results?Bodies=9&sortOrder=Date>.

45. As Saul et al. assert: 'In interpreting Article 13, guidance is therefore to be obtained not only from General Comment No 13 and Concluding Observations of the Committee, but also from the jurisprudence, and in particular, decisions of the European Court of Human Rights'. See Ben Saul, David Kinley and Jacqueline Mowbray, *The International Covenant on Economic, Social and Cultural Rights: Commentary, Cases, and Materials* (Oxford University Press, 2014) 1160–1.

46. Hodgson, *The Human Right to Education*, above n 18, 4.

Historically, the right to education is based on socialist philosophy according to which 'rights can only be completely guaranteed by positive State action'.[47] The modern day version of the right to education has evolved, however, requiring both positive steps in the form of resource allocation by the state and negative duties in the form of non-intervention in the right to choose education other than that provided by the state.[48] Although Article 13 encompasses both positive and negative obligations, this analysis is limited to the positive obligations of states parties.[49]

The CESCR is responsible for monitoring implementation of Article 13 of the ICESCR.[50] The CESCR's overall approach to assessing implementation of the right to education was developed together with the former Special Rapporteur on the right to education, Katarina Tomaševski.[51] The approach, referred to as the 4A Scheme, is to ensure that education is available, accessible, acceptable and adaptable. In this respect, availability essentially refers to the availability of educational infrastructure. Accessibility is concerned with non-discrimination, as well as physical and economic accessibility. Education must also be acceptable in that it must be relevant, culturally appropriate and of good quality. Adaptability requires that education be flexible to meet the needs of changing societies and individual students.[52] The CESCR has also indicated that states parties have obligations to 'respect, protect and fulfil' each of these features of the right to education.[53]

Article 13 of the ICESCR provides as follows:

> 1. The States Parties to the present Covenant recognize the right of everyone to education. They agree that education shall be directed to the full development of the human personality and the sense of

47. Ibid 73.

48. Coomans, 'Exploring the Normative Content of the Right to Education as a Human Right' above n 37, 64.

49. The positive obligations associated with the right to higher education are the most contentious and most difficult to satisfy.

50. *Committee on Economic, Social and Cultural Rights*, Office of the High Commissioner for Human Rights <http://ohchr.org/en/hrbodies/cescr/pages/cescrindex.aspx>.

51. See CESCR, *General Comment No 13: The Right to Education (Article 13 of the Covenant)*, 21st sess, UN Doc E/C.12/1999/10 (8 December 1999); Katarina Tomaševski, *Human Rights Obligations in Education: The 4-A Scheme* (Wolf Legal Publishers, 2006); Saul, Kinley and Mowbray, above n 45, 1096.

52. CESCR, *General Comment No 13: The Right to Education (Article 13 of the Covenant)*, 21st sess, UN Doc E/C.12/1999/10 (8 December 1999); Saul, Kinley and Mowbray, above n 45, 1096–101.

53. CESCR, *General Comment No 13: The Right to Education (Article 13 of the Covenant)*, 21st sess, UN Doc E/C.12/1999/10 (8 December 1999) [50].

its dignity, and shall strengthen the respect for human rights and fundamental freedoms. They further agree that education shall enable all persons to participate effectively in a free society, promote understanding, tolerance and friendship among all nations and all racial, ethnic or religious groups, and further the activities of the United Nations for the maintenance of peace.

2. The States Parties to the present Covenant recognize that, with a view to achieving the full realization of this right:

...

(c) Higher education shall be made equally accessible to all, on the basis of capacity, by every appropriate means, and in particular by the progressive introduction of free education.

...

(e) The development of a system of schools at all levels shall be actively pursued, an adequate fellowship system shall be established, and the material conditions of teaching staff shall be continuously improved.[54]

2. The Duty Bearer

Rights can only exist where there are corresponding duties on others to ensure that the right can be enjoyed.[55] Article 13 imposes obligations which rest primarily on the state.[56] In this sense, '[t]he state is responsible for fulfilling or making it possible to fulfill this right for everyone'.[57] Although the state bears primary responsibility for ensuring the right to higher education is enjoyed, other decision makers, such as higher education institutions, must also be accountable.[58]

54. *International Covenant on Economic, Social and Cultural Rights*, opened for signature 19 December 1966, 993 UNTS 3 (entered into force 3 January 1976) art 13(2).

55. Katarina Tomaševski, *Education Denied: Costs and Remedies* (Zed Books, 2006) 51. See also Douglas Hodgson, *Individual Duty within a Human Rights Discourse* (Ashgate, 2003) 2.

56. Pierrick Devidal, 'Trading Away Human Rights? The GATS and the Right to Education: A Legal Perspective' in Dave Hill and Ravi Kumar (eds), *Global Neoliberalism and Education and Its Consequences* (Routledge, 2009) 73, 80; McCowan, *Education as a Human Right*, above n 20, 36; Kate Halvorsen, 'Notes on the Realization of the Human Right to Education' (1990) 12 *Human Rights Quarterly* 341, 342; Hodgson, 'The International Human Right to Education and Education Concerning Human Rights', above n 22, 238.

57. Halvorsen, above n 56, 341.

58. United Nations Educational, Scientific and Cultural Organization (UNESCO), *2009 World Conference on Higher Education: The New Dynamics of Higher Education and Research for Societal*

Relevant institutions must ensure that their policies and practices adhere to the requirements of the right to higher education.[59] Rights holders are able to claim their rights from the 'people or institutions that . . . should help, assist, or collaborate in ensuring access to freedom'.[60]

3. The Rights Holder

The right to education (as with all human rights) is a right to which all human beings are equally entitled 'from childhood until the end of life'.[61] In essence, it means that all people should have an equal opportunity to access education, regardless of their race, sex, nationality or any other differentiating characteristic—in other words 'without discrimination under any grounds'.[62] The non-discriminatory nature of this right is inherent within international documentation, for example Article 26 of the UDHR, '[e]veryone has the right to education' and Article 13(1) of the ICESCR, '[t]he States Parties to the present *Covenant* recognize the right of everyone to education'.

Although the right to education is usually discussed in reference to the rights of the child, it is a right of all people at all stages of life.[63] This is important in that higher education is generally provided to adults. It is also important in terms of the coherence of the human rights doctrine, as Tristan McCowan points out, 'if we uphold a general right to education it is arbitrary to create cut-off points . . . the

Change and Development: Communique (8 July 2009) 1; Paul Gready and Jonathan Ensor 'Introduction' in Paul Gready and Jonathan Ensor (eds), *Reinventing Development? Translating Rights-Based Approaches from Theory into Practice* (Zed Books, 2005) 1, 6; C Raj Kumar, 'International Human Rights Perspectives on the Fundamental Right to Education—Integration of Human Rights and Human Development in the Indian Constitution' (2004) 12 *Tulane Journal of International and Comparative Law* 237, 260; Hodgson, *Individual Duty within a Human Rights Discourse*, above n 55, 85.

59. Tomaševski, 'Removing Obstacles', above n 1, 12.

60. Kumar, above n 58, 282.

61. A Reis Monteiro, 'The Right of the Child to Education: What Right to What Education?' (2010) 9 *Procedia Social and Behavioral Sciences* 1989, 1989. See also *Velyo Velev v Bulgaria* (2014) 16032/07 Eur Court HR; European Court of Human Rights, 'Guide on Article 2 of Protocol No 1 to the *European Convention on Human Rights*: Right to Education' (Guide, European Court of Human Rights, December 2015) 6.

62. Monteiro, above n 61, 1989; de la Vega, above n 18, 38.

63. Tristan McCowan, 'Is There a Universal Right to Higher Education?' (2012) 60(2) *British Journal of Educational Studies* 116; Hodgson, 'The International Human Right to Education and Education concerning Human Rights', above n 22, 238.

entitlement must exist in some form throughout life'.[64] Thus, the right to education is a right of all people irrespective of age.

4. The Meaning of 'Higher Education'

(a) Broad Interpretation

Although the term 'education' is not defined in the ICESCR, it is to be interpreted broadly.[65] Education encompasses all forms of learning that individuals undertake throughout their lives and extends far beyond the formal systems of education established in most states.[66] Although education in this sense is an extremely wide-ranging concept, it is suggested that the constraints outlined by R S Peters should be accepted in relation to higher education. According to Peters, education must involve an aspect of 'wittingness', meaning that the student understands that he or she is being educated.[67] Further, there must also be an aspect of 'voluntariness' in that the student must be undertaking the education voluntarily.[68] These constraints are morally desirable in that they exclude the potential for indoctrination. Moreover, they align with the historical development of the right to education in that states parties developed and adopted the right to education in Article 26 of the UDHR and Article 13 of the ICESCR in an endeavour to prevent adoption of the type of education systems implemented in Nazi Germany.[69]

(b) Rights Respecting Education

The right to higher education is also a right to *rights respecting* higher education.[70] In other words, although the entitlement is equal access to higher education, there

64. McCowan, *Education as a Human Right*, above n 20, 128.

65. P Arajarvi 'Article 26' in A Eide (ed), *The Universal Declaration of Human Rights: A Commentary* (Scandinavian University Press, 1992) 408.

66. Committee on the Rights of the Child, *General Comment No 1: Article 29(1): The Aims of Education*, UN Doc CRC/GC/2001/1 (17 April 2001) [2]. See also UNESCO, *Recommendation concerning Education for International Understanding, Co-operation and Peace and Education Relating to Human Rights and Fundamental Freedoms*, 18th sess (19 November 1974) [art 1(a)]. See also Hodgson, *The Human Right to Education*, above n 18, 3.

67. McCowan, *Education as a Human Right*, above n 20, 92–3.

68. Ibid.

69. Antonio Cassese, *International Law* (Oxford University Press, 2nd ed, 2005) 377; Elizabeth Craig, 'Accommodation of Diversity in Education—A Human Rights Agenda?' (2003) 15 *Child & Family Law Quarterly* 279, 279.

70. McCowan, *Education as a Human Right*, above n 20, 172. In relation to the justifications for human rights within education, see Tristan McCowan, 'Human Rights within Education: Assessing the Justifications' (2012) 42(1) *Cambridge Journal of Education* 67.

is also an entitlement to education conducted in a way that recognises and respects all human rights.[71] This requirement is a consequence of the principle of indivisibility of human rights. In particular, it requires higher education institutions and those working within them to respect students' right to work, to treat all students equally and without discrimination and to respect students' right to freedom of thought.[72] It also requires the education provided to be underpinned by values that accord with human rights.[73] For example, education will need to be learner centred, and student participation in all aspects of the education system should be encouraged.[74] All aspects of the education system should be considered in light of human rights. For example, high-stakes testing should be avoided where possible as '[c]hildren and adults . . . suffer extreme stress in systems in which high stakes testing is common',[75] potentially infringing students' right to health.

(c) 'Higher' Education

Article 13(2)(c) refers to 'higher' education. According to UNESCO, higher education, or tertiary education, 'builds on secondary education, providing learning activities in specialised fields of education' which may comprise 'academic education' or 'advanced vocational or professional education'.[76] Further, unlike secondary education, higher education involves 'a high level of complexity and specialisation'.[77]

The focus of Article 13 of the ICESCR is on the institutional provision of education.[78] As noted by McCowan, this is clear from the division of Article 13(2) into requirements for primary, secondary and higher education.[79] Thus, Article

71. *Contra* Peodair Leihy and Jose M Salazar, 'The Moral Dimension in Chilean Higher Education's Expansion' (2017) 74 *Higher Education* 147, 156.

72. McCowan, *Education as a Human Right*, above n 20, 172.

73. Committee on the Rights of the Child, *General Comment No 1: Article 29(1): The Aims of Education*, UN Doc CRC/GC/2001/1 (17 April 2001) [3].

74. Ibid [2].

75. McCowan, *Education as a Human Right*, above n 20, 101.

76. UNESCO, *International Standard Classification of Education* (UNESCO, 2011) 84.

77. Ibid 83; see also Klaus Dieter Beiter, *The Protection of the Right to Education by International Law: Including a Systematic Analysis of Article 13 of the International Covenant on Economic, Social, and Cultural Rights* (Martinus Nijhoff Publishers, 2006) 521–2.

78. Hodgson, *The Human Right to Education*, above n 18, 4. See generally Tristan McCowan, 'Reframing the Universal Right to Education' (2010) 46(4) *Comparative Education* 509.

79. McCowan, *Education as a Human Right*, above n 20, 69.

13(2)(c) implies a focus on higher education institutions. This institutional focus is reinforced by the definition of higher education approved by the General Conference of UNESCO, which states that it includes studies 'provided by universities or other educational establishments that are approved as institutions of higher education.'[80]

Higher education institutions have two particular attributes.[81] First, it is a prerequisite that students entering 'higher' education have completed prior study or equivalent experience because they are by definition building on the learning that they have already achieved. Second, 'higher' education 'involves in-depth and sustained study'.[82] This definition of higher education clearly includes university study, but may extend to education provided by other institutions.

(d) Certification

Completion of higher education generally results in the attainment of some form of certification, for example a degree, which presents evidence of achievement of particular skills and knowledge. The attainment of certification usually provides for opportunities in terms of further study and employment.[83] Certification is therefore a method used to distinguish between individuals, with those people more highly qualified enjoying greater access to higher education and higher paid jobs. Thus certificates, such as diplomas and degrees, lead to positional benefits that are not available to all.

The right to education set out in Article 2 of Protocol 1 of the ECHR includes the possibility of profiting from the education received.[84] This means that the right to higher education set out in Article 2 includes a 'right to obtain, in conformity with the rules in force in each State and in one form or another, the

80. UNESCO, *World Conference on Higher Education: World Declaration on Higher Education for the Twenty-First Century: Vision and Action* (9 October 1998) 1. See also Hodgson, 'The International Human Right to Education and Education Concerning Human Rights', above n 22, 237–8; Douglas Hodgson, 'The Educational Rights of Persons with Disabilities: International Human Rights Law and Australian Law Perspectives' (2013) 12(4) *International Journal of Discrimination and the Law* 183, 185.

81. McCowan, *Education as a Human Right*, above n 20, 116.

82. Ibid.

83. Ibid 92.

84. *Case "Relating to Certain Aspects of the Laws on the Use of Languages in Education in Belgium" v Belgium (Belgian Linguistic Case)* (1968) 1474/62 Eur Court HR.

official recognition of studies which have been completed'.[85] Thus, the right to education in Article 2 includes a right to certification.[86]

It is unclear whether certification falls within the right to higher education as set out in Article 13(2)(c) of the ICESCR. It could be argued that the Article should be interpreted as including a right to certification.[87] Although beneficial learning can be achieved through both formal and informal means, informal education rarely leads to the positional benefits that result from formal education.[88] Without access to such positional benefits, individuals are less likely to enjoy the same opportunities as others with similar education for which a certificate has been awarded. This argument for a right to certification is premised on the notion that there is a right to education, and specifically higher education, *because* of the positional benefits attached to that education: in other words, that there are instrumental reasons (as opposed to, or in addition to, intrinsic reasons) for the existence of the right to education.

Yet the argument in favour of a right to certification is problematic for a number of reasons. First, if the right to education were justified by only instrumental reasons, it would not be a right in the first place. Rather, the ends achieved by education (for example, to work or a particular standard of living) would be the right.[89] Further, premising a right to certification on the basis of positional benefits does not make sense because 'not everyone can have positional advantage over everyone else'.[90] Moreover, human rights are premised on fundamental values of equality and fairness. To allow a right to certification on the basis that it will lead to the attainment of benefits that are not available to all seems to undermine these values and thus be inconsistent with the human rights doctrine.

Although these criticisms have some merit, a right to higher education without a right to receive certification for education completed would seriously undermine the basic objectives of Article 13(2)(c).[91] The preferable view is that although there can be no right to certification without demonstrating specified knowledge and skills, upon such demonstration the right to higher education

85. *Belgian Linguistic Case* (1968) 1474/62 Eur Court HR [3]–[5]. See also *Kjeldsen, Busk Madsen and Pedersen v Denmark* (1976) 5095/71 Eur Court HR 52.

86. See also European Court of Human Rights, above n 61, 6.

87. See McCowan, *Education as a Human Right*, above n 20, 120.

88. Ibid 92.

89. See ibid 120.

90. Ibid 121.

91. Thus, to the extent that massive open online courses involve provision of higher education without certification, it is contended that their availability is not sufficient to meet the requirements of a right to higher education.

should be interpreted to require that certification be provided. Further, given the stratified nature of certification, the certification provided must be appropriate to the particular knowledge and skills demonstrated. Absent certification, the capacity of the individual to realise the incidental (career enhancing and community developing) aspects of education is curtailed. In keeping with the objectives of Article 13(2)(c) and in particular the requirements of equal access, the Article should also be interpreted to require 'a right not to be unfairly denied the opportunity to achieve [certification]'.[92]

5. The Purposes of Higher Education

Article 13(1) sets out the purposes of education which apply to all forms of education, including higher education.[93] These aims were included in Article 13 in the historical context of the disastrous impact of the national socialist education system in Germany, which emphasised obedience to the state and racial discrimination.[94] Thus, the aims were included in order to 'strengthen the UN's role in maintaining global peace'.[95]

The aims included in Article 13 are both significant and legally binding. The aims emphasise that the right to higher education must be student-centred and empowering and is related not just to access, but also to the content of education provided.[96] Further, not only must higher education be directed towards the values set out in the Article, but educational processes must also be based on those values.[97] A holistic approach to higher education must be pursued.[98] That the aims are legally binding is indicated by their status as material provisions of the Covenant, the deliberate inclusion of the aims and the practice of the CESCR in relation to them.[99]

To discuss the purposes of higher education, Hodgson's categorisation of purposes into four general groups will be adopted.[100] It should be noted at the outset

92. McCowan, *Education as a Human Right*, above n 20, 92.

93. See Beiter, above n 77, 463.

94. Ibid 463–4.

95. Ibid 464.

96. Ibid 464–5.

97. Ibid 465.

98. Ibid 466–7.

99. Ibid 469–70.

100. See Hodgson, *The Human Right to Education*, above n 18, 74–7.

that the purposes of higher education as set out in Article 13(1) are interpreted in light of subsequent instruments that have elaborated on those aims.[101]

(A) Full Development of the Human Personality and the Sense of Its Dignity

The most important purpose of higher education is 'the full development of [students'] individual human personality' including the sense of 'dignity' that being human entails.[102] In this context, the 'human personality' relates to all aspects of personality. This will include aspects such as the 'physical, intellectual, psychological and social', with the aim being that these differing aspects will be developed as much as possible.[103] This indicates that rather than the provision of a uniform education for all, education must be provided in such a way as to recognise and develop the unique characteristics of each individual. This also entails an understanding that the contents and methods of delivering education should be centred on the individual involved, rather than perceived market needs or state objectives.[104] Moreover, when considering the student's unique personality, his or her particular context and potential future must also be taken into account.[105]

Interestingly in the modern context, the Committee on the Rights of the Child has indicated that teaching which is 'focussed . . . on accumulation of knowledge, prompting competition and leading to an excessive burden of work . . . may seriously hamper the harmonious development of the child'.[106] Although this comment is in relation to the rights of the child, there is no reason it should not equally apply to adult learners. In contrast, rather than pushing students to accumulate information and compete with one another, '[e]ducation should be [student]-friendly, inspiring and motivating', allowing students to develop themselves without pressure and at their own pace.[107]

101. CESCR, *General Comment No 13: The Right to Education (Article 13 of the Covenant)*, 21st sess, UN Doc E/C.12/1999/10 (8 December 1999).

102. *International Covenant on Economic, Social and Cultural Rights*, opened for signature 19 December 1966, 993 UNTS 3 (entered into force 3 January 1976), art 13(1); Monteiro, above n 61, 1989; Beiter, above n 77, 470.

103. Arajarvi, above n 65, 409; Hodgson, *The Human Right to Education*, above n 18, 73–4, 83.

104. Monteiro, above n 61, 1990.

105. Committee on the Rights of the Child, *General Comment No 1: Article 29(1): The Aims of Education*, UN Doc CRC/GC/2001/1 (17 April 2001) [4].

106. Ibid [5].

107. Ibid.

(b) Strengthen the Respect for Human Rights and Fundamental Freedoms

Under the right to higher education, education must also be directed towards the reinforcement of human rights and freedoms. Directing education towards this purpose should serve as a means of preventing future human rights abuses.[108] At a minimum, this means that higher education must not be in contradiction with international or domestic human rights instruments.[109] Further, according to the natural meaning of the words, higher education must also positively encourage respect for human rights. In turn, this should lead to increased 'social justice and equality'.[110] Human rights education is the means by which respect for human rights is encouraged and should assist in the development of a human rights-respecting culture.[111]

(c) Participate Effectively in a Free Society

The third overarching purpose of higher education under a rights framework is the enabling of community participation. Here, education should be provided in order to empower students to be able to contribute to society and be actively engaged in the community.[112] In this respect, it is helpful to note that one of UNESCO's guiding principles for education policy is 'readiness on the part of the individual to participate in solving the problems of his community, his country and the world at large'.[113] This indicates that education must have an aspect of practicality and be directed towards interaction with the future community.[114] In order to participate in a free society, individuals need to develop the capacity to engage in work and employment of their choosing, consistent with their interests, passions and capabilities. Education, and in particular credentialism, is a threshold requirement for individuals to work or practice in many vocations and professions.

108. Paula Gerber, *Understanding Human Rights: Educational Challenges for the Future* (Edward Elgar Publishing, 2013) 1.

109. Arajarvi, above n 65, 409.

110. Halvorsen, above n 56, 342.

111. Gerber, above n 108, 1–12.

112. Committee on the Rights of the Child, *General Comment No 1: Article 29(1): The Aims of Education*, UN Doc CRC/GC/2001/1 (17 April 2001) [5].

113. UNESCO, *Recommendation concerning Education for International Understanding, Co-operation and Peace and Education Relating to Human Rights and Fundamental Freedoms*, 18th sess (19 November 1974) [art 4(g)]. See also Hodgson, *The Human Right to Education*, above n 18, 83.

114. See Beiter, above n 77, 471.

(d) Promote Understanding, Tolerance and Friendship among All Nations and All Racial, Ethnic or Religious Groups, and Further the Activities of the United Nations for the Maintenance of Peace

Finally, higher education must promote 'understanding, tolerance and friendship' and further efforts to achieve peace. In other words, students should be exposed to notions of difference and taught to value diversity. Students should 'become aware of the diversity of beliefs people hold and appreciate what it is to be part of a society where these differences exist'.[115] In the higher education context, this could involve, for example, ensuring diversity of student enrolments as well as approaching subject content from various racial, ethnic and religious perspectives.

6. The Requirement of Equal Accessibility

One of the key requirements of Article 13(2)(c) is that prospective students be provided with equal access to higher education.[116] Higher education institutions generally have a limited number of available places. Further, many barriers exist for individuals and groups to higher education, for example, social, economic and geographic ones.[117] Equal access requires that access to higher education programmes is determined without discrimination.[118] In this respect, states must adopt policies that ensure that places are available without discrimination. This aspect of the right to higher education requires parties not only to remove legal and administrative impediments to access,[119] but also to '[adopt] specific policies, often targeted, to reduce social and economic barriers'[120] and thus ensure that higher education is not only available to a privileged elite.[121] This may involve the adoption of particular policies or strategies

115. Hodgson, *The Human Right to Education*, above n 18, 73–84.

116. Saul, Kinley and Mowbray, above n 45, 1104; Kama, above n 36, 160.

117. Neville Harris, *Education, Law and Diversity* (Hart Publishing, 2007) 43.

118. CESCR, *General Comment No 13: The Right to Education (Article 13 of the Covenant)*, 21st sess, UN Doc E/C.12/1999/10 (8 December 1999) [6–7].

119. Beiter, above n 77, 523.

120. Harris, above n 117, 145.

121. Kenneth Lawson, 'The Concept of Higher Education for All Explored', in Gordon Roderick and Michael Stephens (eds), *Higher Education for All?* (Routledge, 2012) 27, 30.

to encourage representation of marginalised groups in higher education.[122] The actual content of education must also be accessible to all students; in other words, it will need to be 'relevant, culturally appropriate and of good quality' for all students.[123] The overarching goal is the promotion of equality of opportunity and treatment in access to higher education.[124] Particular issues that have arisen in relation to equal access to higher education include religion, citizenship or residence status, economic circumstances, language and access while in prison.

(A) Religion

Pursuant to Article 13(2)(c), individuals must have equal access to higher education regardless of their religion. An issue that has arisen in this respect is whether regulations that restrict the wearing of religious dress in educational institutions infringe the affected students' right to education. Such regulations are common in a number of countries, including France, Belgium, the Netherlands, Bulgaria and Russia.[125] That these type of regulations may affect the ability of some students to attend educational institutions has been acknowledged by the Human Rights Committee and the Committee on the Rights of the Child.[126]

The issue was brought to the European Court of Human Rights (ECtHR) in *Leyla Şahin v Turkey.*[127] In that case, Istanbul University introduced regulations that prohibited the wearing of Islamic headscarves.[128] The applicant, a Muslim woman who wore a headscarf, was studying medicine at the University, and pursuant to the regulations was denied entry to examinations and lectures.[129] She

122. Beiter, above n 77, 523. See, for example, *Grutter v Bollinger,* 539 US 306 (2003), *Motala v University of Natal* [1995] 3 BCLR 374 D (The Constitutional Court of South Africa), *contra Gratz v Bollinger* 539 US 244 (2003).

123. CESCR, *General Comment No 13: The Right to Education (Article 13 of the Covenant),* 21st sess, UN Doc E/C.12/1999/10 (8 December 1999) [6–7].

124. Beiter, above n 77, 523.

125. See 'Which Countries Have Banned the Burka?' *Radio Australia* (online), 7 December 2016 <http://www.radioaustralia.net.au/international/2016-12-07/which-countries-have-banned-the-burka/1637886>.

126. See Human Rights Committee, *Concluding Observations: France,* UN Doc CCPR/C/FRA/CO/4 (31 July 2008) [28]; Committee on the Rights of the Child, *Concluding Observations: France,* UN Doc CRC/C/15/Add.240 (30 June 2004) [25]–[26].

127. *Leyla Şahin v Turkey* (2007) 44774/98 Eur Court HR.

128. Ibid 16.

129. Ibid 17.

argued before the ECtHR that her right to education (amongst other rights) had, as a result, been violated.[130] The ECtHR asserted that 'analysis of the case by reference to the right to education cannot . . . be divorced from the conclusion reached by the Court with respect to [freedom of religion]'.[131] It held that the regulations were justified by the legitimate aim of preserving the secular nature of the university and were proportionate to that aim, and thus the applicant's right to education had not been breached.[132] Although this decision has been widely criticised,[133] subsequent jurisprudence suggests that the Court will continue to grant states 'a wide margin of appreciation'.[134] Whether the CESCR adopts the same approach remains to be seen.

(B) Citizenship or Residence Status

Non-citizens and those without permanent resident status who are resident in a state party should be provided with equal access to higher education institutions. Pursuant to Article 3(e) of the CADE, states parties must 'give foreign nationals resident within their territory the same access to education as that given to their own nationals'.[135] Thus, in its Concluding Observations in relation to Canada, the CESCR expressed its concern that 'loan programmes for post-secondary education are available only to Canadian citizens and permanent residents' and not recognised refugees or asylum seekers.[136]

130. Ibid 3.

131. Ibid 157.

132. Ibid 158–62.

133. For example, see Judge Tulkens dissenting judgment in ibid. See also Armin Steinbach, 'Burqas and Bans: The Wearing of Religious Symbols under the *European Convention of Human Rights*' (2015) 4 *Cambridge Journal of International and Comparative Law* 29; Niraj Nathwani, 'Islamic Headscarves and Human Rights: A Critical Analysis of the Relevant Case Law of the European Court of Human Rights' (2007) 25 *Netherlands Quarterly of Human Rights* 221; Nicholas Gibson, 'An Unwelcome Trend: Religious Dress and Human Rights following Leyla Şahin vs Turkey' (2007) 25 *Netherlands Quarterly of Human Rights* 599.

134. *SAS v France* (2014) 43835/11 Eur Court HR 155. See also *Lautsi v Italy* (2012) 30814/06 Eur Court HR.

135. *Convention against Discrimination in Education*, opened for signature 14 December 1960, 429 UNTS 93 (entered into force 22 May 1962) art 3(e).

136. CESCR, *Concluding Observations: Canada*, UN Doc E/C.12/1/Add.31 (10 December 1998) [39]. See also CESCR, *Concluding Observations: Norway*, UN Doc E/C.12/1/Add.109 (23 June 2005) [22] and [43]. See also Vernor Muñoz, *The Right to Education of Migrants, Refugees and Asylum-Seekers*, UN Doc A/HRC/14/25 (16 April 2010) [63].

In general, a difference in access to education based solely on nationality is unlikely to be compatible with the right to education.[137] In terms of the ECtHR jurisprudence, however, it is clear that the right to education does not provide individuals with a right to enter or to stay in a foreign country.[138] Further, where deportation results in an individual's inability to continue his or her education, it will not constitute a breach of the right to education.[139] The ECtHR's judgment in *Ponomaryov v Bulgaria*[140] suggests that there may be some flexibility for states in relation to citizenship or resident status. Although the case was concerned with the charging of fees to non-citizens for secondary school, the Court made it clear that 'in the present circumstances' it considered charging higher fees to aliens for higher education 'fully justified'.[141]

(c) Economic Circumstances

One of the most contentious aspects of the right to higher education is that education must be provided without discrimination on the basis of economic circumstances.[142] In other words, those without means to pay for higher education must be provided with equal access, subject to the requirement that states need only take progressive steps towards the provision of free higher education.[143] One means by which equality of access must be achieved is through the establishment of an adequate fellowship system (see discussion of Article 13(2)(e) at 9 below).[144] Where a state introduces or increases tuition fees, or reduces the availability of student loans or other financial support, this may prevent candidates with lesser means from accessing higher education, and may therefore discriminate against them on the basis of their economic circumstances.

137. *Ponomaryov v Bulgaria* (2011) 5335/05, Eur Court HR; European Court of Human Rights, above n 61, 9.

138. *Foreign Students v The United Kingdom* (1977) 7671/76 Eur Court HR 4.

139. European Court of Human Rights, above n 61, 10. See also *Sorabjee v the United Kingdom* (1995) 23938/94 Eur Court HR; *Jaramillo v the United Kingdom* (1995) 24865/94 Eur Court HR; *Dabhi v the United Kingdom* (1997) 28627/95 Eur Court HR.

140. *Ponomaryov v Bulgaria* (2011) 5335/05, Eur Court HR.

141. Ibid 56.

142. CESCR, *General Comment No 13: The Right to Education (Article 13 of the Covenant)*, 21st sess, UN Doc E/C.12/1999/10 (8 December 1999) [6–7]. See generally, Kama, above n 36.

143. *International Covenant on Economic, Social and Cultural Rights*, opened for signature 19 December 1966, 993 UNTS 3 (entered into force 3 January 1976) art 13(2)(c).

144. Ibid art 13(2)(e). See also Beiter, above n 77, 532–3.

The CESCR has often expressed concern in relation to the impact of fees on access to higher education. For example, in relation to the United Kingdom (UK) of Great Britain and Northern Ireland, the CESCR stated that '[w]hile noting that various systems to support access to higher education are in place in the State party, the Committee is concerned that university fees are increasing, which affects equal access to higher education' and recommended that the state party take steps to comply with Article 13.[145] Similarly, in relation to Canada, the CESCR stated its concern at 'increasing tuition fees in post-secondary education, combined with decreasing governmental funding, which disproportionately impacts students and families with low income and indigenous peoples'.[146] In relation to Bulgaria, the CESCR indicated its concern 'that the fees introduced in higher education may represent a serious obstacle for disadvantaged groups of society seeking such an education'.[147]

The impact of increased fees on access to higher education was considered in the recent UK case of *Hurley and Moore v Secretary of State for Business Innovation & Skills* (*Hurley*).[148] In that case, the claimants argued that regulations that operated to significantly increase higher education fees were contrary to the right to education provided for in Article 2 of Protocol 1 to the ECHR.[149] The Court noted that the fee increases were part of a package of measures introduced in order to assist students from lower socio-economic backgrounds.[150] Although the Court was not sufficiently satisfied that the regulations would discriminate against students from low socio-economic backgrounds, it found that even if they were discriminatory, the impact was justified.[151] Accordingly, the Court found no breach of Article 2.

Although *Hurley* appears to suggest that the availability of student loans and financial support can offset the discriminatory effect of fees, whether the right

145. CESCR, *Concluding Observations on the Sixth Periodic Report of the United Kingdom of Great Britain and Northern Ireland*, UN Doc E/C.12/GBR/CO/6 (14 July 2016) [65]–[66].

146. CESCR, *Concluding Observations on the Sixth Periodic Report of Canada*, UN Doc E/C.12/CAN/CO/6 (23 March 2016) [57]–[58]. See also CESCR, *Concluding Observations: Canada*, UN Doc E/C.12/CAN/CO/4-E/C.12/CAN/CO/5 (22 May 2006) [31]; CESCR, *Concluding Observations: Canada*, UN Doc E/C.12/1/Add.31 (10 December 1998) [39].

147. CESCR, *Concluding Observations: Bulgaria*, UN Doc E/C.12/1/Add.37 (8 December 1999) [21].

148. [2012] EWHC 201.

149. Ibid 4.

150. Ibid 22–5.

151. Ibid 26–45.

to education as set out in Article 2 of Protocol 1 to the ECHR requires the state to provide access to loan finance will depend on the particular context. In the case of *(R) Douglas v North Tyneside Metropolitan Borough Council,* the Court of Appeal held that loan arrangements in the English regulations could 'be described as a facilitator of education but . . . [were] one stage removed from the education itself' and thus were not sufficiently linked to 'education' for the purposes of Article 2.[152] In *(R) Kebede v Secretary of State for Business Innovation and Skills,* however, the Court departed from this approach and found that the arrangements for funding access to higher education did fall within the scope of Article 2.[153] Similarly, in *(R) Tigere v Secretary of State for Business, Innovation and Skills,* the Supreme Court found that laws that placed blanket exclusions on accessing student loans on students with limited or discretionary leave to remain in the UK fell within the scope of Article 2 and unjustifiably infringed the right to education.[154] Most recently, the Court in *Hunter v Student Awards Agency Scotland* held that student loans for living expenses fell within the ambit of Article 2.[155] This case law can be distinguished from the obligations imposed by the right to higher education set out in Article 13(2) of the ICESCR, however, in that Article 13(2)(e) expressly requires states to establish an adequate fellowship system (see discussion of Article 13(2)(e) at 9 below).

The requirement to provide equal access to higher education regardless of economic status has also been considered in terms of regulations on access. In proceedings initiated against St Hugh's College, Damien Shannon argued that the University of Oxford's financial guarantee policy discriminated against poorer students by requiring them to establish access to a particular amount of living costs. The proceedings were settled and prompted Oxford to review its financial guarantee policy.[156] Similarly, in the case of *Mohini Jain v Karnataka,*[157] the Supreme Court of India held that charging 'capitation fees' was contrary to the right to education, because they based access to education on income rather than merit.

152. [2004] 1 All ER 709, 56. See also Harris, above n 117, 142.

153. [2014] PTSR 92.

154. [2015] UKSC 57.

155. [2016] CSOH 71.

156. See Elizabeth Gibney, *St Hugh's Settles Shannon Case,* (25 March 2013) Times Higher Education <https://www.timeshighereducation.com/news/st-hughs-settles-shannon-case/2002745.article>.

157. *Mohini Jain v Karnataka* (1992) AIR 1858.

(d) Language

Language can operate as an obstacle to equal access to higher education. Where education is not provided in the language used by individuals, they will not be able to obtain effective access. Accordingly, the right to education provided for in the ECHR includes a right to be educated in the national language or one of the national languages.[158] In the case of *İrfan Temel v Turkey,* the ECtHR held that temporarily expelling students who had requested the introduction of optional classes in the Kurdish language violated their right to education.[159]

(e) Prisoners

Prisoners are entitled to enjoy all of their human rights with the exception of the right to liberty.[160] Thus, the right to education set out in the ECHR provides prisoners with a right to access existing education systems established in prison.[161] It does not, however, provide prisoners with an entitlement to have higher education made available to them where a system is not established.[162]

7. Limiting the Provision of Higher Education to Those with 'Capacity'

Although primary education must be provided to all under Article 13 of the ICESCR, higher education is to be limited to those with 'capacity'.[163] This is a development from the language in Article 26 of the UDHR, which permits higher education to be limited on the basis of 'merit', or the 'ability to absorb the education'.[164] This is an important modification, in that although the notion of 'merit' 'is backward-looking and emphasises the student's past academic achievements, 'capacity' 'is forward-looking and stresses the student's future potential'.[165]

158. *Belgian Linguistic Case* (1968) 1474/62 Eur Court HR 3.

159. (2009) 36458/02 Eur Court HR.

160. European Court of Human Rights, above n 61, 9.

161. *Velyo Velev v Bulgaria* (2014) 16032/07 Eur Court HR.

162. European Court of Human Rights, above n 61, 9. See also *Georgiou v Greece* (2000) 45138/98 Eur Court HR.

163. *International Covenant on Economic, Social and Cultural Rights,* opened for signature 19 December 1966, 993 UNTS 3 (entered into force 3 January 1976) art 13; Beiter, above n 77, 456–8.

164. Arajarvi, above n 65, 409.

165. Beiter, above n 77, 97. See also Kama, above n 36, 154.

The limitation on the basis of capacity constitutes recognition that 'not everyone may have the necessary capacity or ability to benefit from [higher education]'.[166] In other words, the successful undertaking of higher education requires a particular level of intellectual ability as well as the attainment of relevant prior knowledge and skills.[167] This limitation constitutes a recognition that '[k]nowledge is not something that can simply be given to someone'.[168] Rather, when assessing whether individuals should be granted admission, the consideration should be essentially 'whether they will learn'[169] or have 'scholarly potential'.[170] Where the capacity for learning does not exist, state resources would be wasted by offering higher education, and more importantly, the best interests of the student, who would 'be at best wasting their time by pursuing a course that they are not yet able to engage with', would not be served.[171]

The capacity limitation can operate in two ways. First, the requirement that education be made available on the basis of 'capacity' indicates that 'some entrance restrictions on the part of institutions are justified'.[172] The jurisprudence of the ECtHR is helpful in understanding what restrictions might be legitimate, but it is clear that states enjoy a 'margin of appreciation' in university regulation.[173] In *Tarantino v Italy*, the ECtHR indicated that the right of equal access to higher education is not absolute and may be subject to limitations.[174] Valid limitations must be 'foreseeable for those concerned and pursue a legitimate aim'.[175] There must also be 'a reasonable relationship of proportionality between the means employed and the aim sought to be achieved'.[176] In the particular circumstances of the case, the relevant laws limited access to particular faculties of universities

166. Harris, above n 117, 39.

167. McCowan, *Education as a Human Right*, above n 20, 125; Beiter, above n 77, 524–5.

168. Ben Kotzee and Christopher Martin, 'Who Should Go to University? Justice in University Admissions' (2013) 47(4) *Journal of Philosophy of Education* 623, 636.

169. Ibid 637–8.

170. Ibid 629–30.

171. McCowan, *Education as a Human Right*, above n 20, 125.

172. McCowan, 'Is There a Universal Right to Higher Education?', above n 63, 121–2; Saul, Kinley and Mowbray, above n 45, 1104.

173. *Lautsi v Italy* (2011) 30814/06 Eur Court HR; *Tarantino v Italy* (2013) 25851/09 Eur Court HR 44.

174. *Tarantino v Italy* (2013) 25851/09 Eur Court HR [44].

175. Ibid [45].

176. Ibid.

(including medicine and dentistry) by establishing quotas for admission and requiring applicants to pass an entrance examination.[177] The ECtHR found that these laws were foreseeable and pursued a legitimate aim of 'achieving high levels of professionalism, by ensuring a minimum and adequate education level in universities running in appropriate conditions, which is in the general interest'.[178] Further, they were not disproportionate to the aims sought to be achieved, and accordingly it was held that there had been no violation of Article 2 of Protocol 1 to the ECHR.[179] Conversely, in *Altınay v Turkey* the Court found that changes to the admission rules were unforeseeable and without transitional corrective measures were not reasonably proportionate to the aim pursued, and thus constituted a violation of the applicant's right to education.[180]

Second, capacity may be used to restrict which students are able to progress within higher education. For example, where students are unable to demonstrate particular knowledge or skills, they 'may legitimately be denied access to the next stage'.[181] In the case of *X v United Kingdom*, for example, the fact that the applicant failed his first year examination requirements and had a poor attendance record at compulsory classes justified the University's decision to refuse him re-entry.[182] It should also be noted that states are able to set a maximum duration for higher education studies.[183]

In terms of measuring 'capacity', as noted above, measures must be used in order to assess 'the student's future potential'.[184] Such measures should aim to take into account 'all [the student's] . . . relevant expertise and experience'[185] and 'merit, capacity, efforts, perseverance and devotion'.[186] In this context, methods of

177. Ibid [15]–[20].

178. Ibid [48].

179. Ibid [49]–[59]. See also *X v United Kingdom* (1980) 8844/80 Eur Court HR. Although note that annulling a candidate's positive entrance examination result on the basis of previous poor results may constitute a violation of the candidate's right to education: *Mürsel Eren v Turkey* (2006) 60856/00 Eur Court HR.

180. *Altınay v Turkey* (2013) 37222/04 Eur Court HR 56-61.

181. Beiter, above n 77, 456–8.

182. *X v United Kingdom* (1980) 8844/80 Eur Court HR.

183. See *X v Austria* (1973) 5492/72 Eur Comm HR.

184. Beiter, above n 77, 97.

185. CESCR, *General Comment No 13: The Right to Education (Article 13 of the Covenant)*, 21st sess, UN Doc E/C.12/1999/10 (8 December 1999) [19].

186. UNESCO, *World Conference on Higher Education: World Declaration on Higher Education for the Twenty-First Century: Vision and Action* (9 October 1998) [art 3(a)].

measurement could include 'proof of the successful completion of prior education... oral and/or written entrance examinations, occupational experience, an interview, a period of probation, or a combination of the mentioned methods'.[187] Further, in terms of entry to courses leading to professions where particular knowledge or skills are required, measures testing whether the student has the future capacity to exercise those skills or gain that knowledge would be appropriate.[188]

8. The Requirement of 'Progressive Introduction of Free Education'

The most controversial aspect of the right to higher education is the directive in Article 13(2)(c) that states parties take steps towards the introduction of free higher education.[189] In the context of the entirety of Article 13, this means that states must provide free primary education, then with remaining state resources work towards the progressive realisation of free secondary and higher education.[190] As noted by Sonja Grover, this means that 'there is no international obligation to free of charge... higher education.[191] Rather, there is only an obligation for states to work towards that objective within an unlimited time frame. Until states parties achieve free higher education, Article 13(2)(e) imposes an obligation to establish an adequate fellowship system (see discussion of Article 13(2)(e) at 9 below).[192]

The underlying rationale for the requirement of progressive realisation of free higher education is that, ultimately, all higher education fees act as a form of disincentive to the enjoyment of the right to higher education for those who lack the means or have a lower capacity to pay fees.[193] As a result, such fees are a form of subtle discrimination.[194] This perspective is supported by McCowan, who notes

187. Beiter, above n 77, 524–5.

188. Ibid.

189. *International Covenant on Economic, Social and Cultural Rights,* opened for signature 19 December 1966, 993 UNTS 3 (entered into force 3 January 1976) art 13(2). See also McCowan, *Education as a Human Right,* above n 20, 27; Kalantry, Getgen and Koh, above n 36, 270.

190. CESCR, *General Comment No 13: The Right to Education (Article 13 of the Covenant),* 21st sess, UN Doc E/C.12/1999/10 (8 December 1999) [14].

191. McCowan, *Education as a Human Right,* above n 20, 27–8.

192. *International Covenant on Economic, Social and Cultural Rights,* opened for signature 19 December 1966, 993 UNTS 3 (entered into force 3 January 1976) art 13(2)(e).

193. CESCR, *General Comment No 11: Plans of Action for Primary Education,* 20th sess, UN Doc E/C.12/1999/4 (10 May 1999) [7]; Fons Coomans, 'Justiciability of the Right to Education' (2009) 2 *Erasmus Law Review* 427, 437.

194. Coomans, 'Justiciability of the Right to Education', above n 193, 442.

that the 'most obvious' barriers to higher education are financial ones; as a result, if higher education is a right then it should be provided 'either free or at such a low cost that it would not provide an obstacle to any segment of society'.[195] In this respect, Neville Harris notes the 'huge amount of accumulated evidence' that exists 'concerning the deterrent effects of the costs of participation in higher education in the form of fees, maintenance costs and lack of income'.[196]

Although Article 13(2)(e) requires that states parties establish an adequate fellowship system, presumably to reduce the disincentive of higher education fees, forms of higher education subsidisation such as loan schemes are also problematic. McCowan observes that student loans 'do not completely remove' the discriminatory impact of student fees, and 'can still represent a disproportionate disincentive to students from low-income backgrounds on account of fear of debt or lack of confidence in the benefits of HE [higher education] study'.[197] Moreover, charging different levels of fees depending on the particular course chosen can also undermine the requirement for access on the basis of merit or capacity'.[198]

The CESCR's position in relation to the meaning of the requirement to make higher education progressively free is unequivocal. The CESCR has confirmed that states parties are to make higher education progressively free.[199] Although there is no set time frame to achieve this objective, Article 2(2) imposes immediate obligations to provide higher education without discrimination, including financial discrimination. In its country observations, the CESCR has often expressed concern about the imposition of higher education fees. For example, in relation to Mauritius, the CESCR stated that it is 'concerned about the re-introduction of fees at the tertiary level of education, which constitutes a deliberately retrogressive step'.[200] Similarly, the CESCR recommended that Chile, '[a]dopt specific measures to progressively introduce free ... higher education based on the capacity of each individual'.[201]

195. McCowan, *Education as a Human Right*, above n 20, 125.

196. Harris, above n 117, 228.

197. McCowan, *Education as a Human Right*, above n 20, 118. See also *Hurley and Moore v Secretary of State for Business Innovation & Skills* [2012] EWHC 201, 17 and 39.

198. McCowan, *Education as a Human Right*, above n 20, 118.

199. Kalantry, Getgen and Koh, above n 36, 277.

200. CESCR, *Concluding Observations: Mauritius*, UN Doc E/C.12/1994/8 (31 May 1994) [16]. See also CESCR, *Concluding Observations: Germany*, UN Doc E/C.12/1/Add.68 (24 September 2001) [29]; CESCR *Concluding Observations: Germany*, UN Doc E/C.12/1/Add.29 (4 December 1998) [22].

201. CESCR, *Concluding Observations: Chile*, UN Doc E/C.12/CHL/CO/4 (7 July 2015) [30].

This aspect of the right to higher education has come under intense criticism. The thrust of such criticism is essentially that it is very difficult for states parties to provide higher education for free. For example, in the context of the massification of higher education, globalisation and other demands on government resources, it has been argued that this aspect of the right is ultimately 'susceptib[le] . . . to economic and political pressures'[202] and 'cannot be considered an absolute right'.[203]

The obligation to progressively introduce free higher education was considered in *Hurley*.[204] The High Court noted the CESCR's position in relation to the imposition of fees[205] and had regard to Article 13(2)(c).[206] Nevertheless, as the progressive introduction of free education is not an absolute obligation,[207] the Court asserted that 'there must be a serious question whether the UK is in breach of the provision'.[208] Ultimately, the Court did not need to answer this question, as the proceedings were brought under Article 2 of Protocol 1 of the ECHR, which does not include a specific obligation to progressively introduce free higher education.

The Federal Tribunal of Switzerland has directly considered the obligation to progressively introduce free higher education set out in Article 13(2)(c). In that case, a student union brought an action alleging that an increase in registration fees at Zurich University was in breach of Article 13(2)(c).[209] In its decision, the Federal Tribunal stated that the provisions of Article 13(2)(c) were 'addressed only to the legislator' and did not constitute an individual human right to the progressive introduction of free higher education.[210] According to the Tribunal, the words 'in particular' in Article 13(2)(c) indicated only that progressive realisation of free higher education was 'one of the possible means' available to a legislator to achieve the objective of accessibility.[211] It was up to the legislator to 'choose the [appropriate] means'.[212]

202. Harris, above n 117, 45.

203. Ibid 70.

204. [2012] EWHC 201.

205. Ibid 38.

206. Ibid 43–4.

207. Ibid 44.

208. Ibid.

209. Economic and Social Council, *Implementation of the International Covenant on Economic, Social and Cultural Rights*, UN Doc E/1990/5/Add.33 (18 September 1996) [676].

210. Ibid [676–7].

211. Ibid.

212. Ibid.

The decision of the Federal Tribunal is problematic in light of the seemingly plain words of Article 13(2)(c) and their interpretation by the CESCR. The goal of accessibility is to be achieved by 'every' appropriate means, which explicitly includes 'the progressive introduction of free education'. Further, the word 'and' prefaces 'in particular', indicating that it is both the progressive introduction of free education *as well as* other appropriate means which are to be used. As Klaus Deiter Beiter indicates, 'states parties do not have a "choice of policy" as regards the possible introduction or increase of study fees'.[213] The Federal Tribunal's decision is likely useful in terms of domestic politics. Yet it seems contra to the wording of Article 13(2)(c).

The reality, however, is that general state practice has moved towards the introduction and increase of fees, rather than the realisation of free higher education.[214] Even states parties to the ICESCR, 'tend to exhibit a commitment to for-fee rather than free university education'.[215] Only a small number of countries have enacted a legislative obligation to provide higher education free of charge.[216] Nevertheless, those countries that have done so have demonstrated that it is not unrealistic for states to adopt such a policy, as is shown in the human rights-based approach case studies in Chapter 4.

9. Obligation to Develop a System of Schools, Establish a Fellowship System and Continuously Improve the Material Conditions of Teaching Staff

Article 13(2)(e) sets out obligations on states parties to:

- Actively pursue the development of a system of schools at all levels;
- Establish an adequate fellowship system; and
- Continuously improve the material conditions of teaching staff.[217]

213. Beiter, above n 77, 400–1.

214. Tomaševski, *Human Rights Obligations in Education,* above n 51, 51–3; McCowan, *Education as a Human Right,* above n 20, 118. See also Michael Mansfield, *Fees Deny the Basic Human Right to Education* (11 October 2011) The Guardian <https://www.theguardian.com/education/2011/oct/10/education-human-right-not-commodity>.

215. Tomaševski, *Human Rights Obligations in Education,* above n 51, 51–3.

216. McCowan, *Education as a Human Right,* above n 20, 27–8.

217. *International Covenant on Economic, Social and Cultural Rights,* opened for signature 19 December 1966, 993 UNTS 3 (entered into force 3 January 1976) art 13(2)(e); Beiter, above n 77, 530.

In relation to higher education, these obligations are essentially steps that a state party is required to take in order to meet its obligations under Article 13(2)(c).[218]

The obligation to develop a system of schools requires the state to establish and maintain higher education infrastructure, including buildings, teaching materials and equipment. The obligation thus requires that higher education be made available. This obligation is not clear from the language of Article 13(2)(c) and thus Article 13(2)(e) operates to extend this obligation to higher education.[219]

The obligation to establish an adequate fellowship system refers to the requirement that states ensure that financial support is available to higher education students to help cover the costs of education. This assistance is usually provided to those students who may not otherwise be able to afford the costs of higher education. Thus, the obligation assists in ensuring the accessibility, and particularly economic accessibility, of higher education. Although states must make higher education progressively free, until that goal is achieved accessibility must be assisted via 'appropriate means', including the establishment of an adequate fellowship system.[220]

The requirement to continuously improve the material conditions of teaching staff is connected to the objective of ensuring the provision of quality teaching. In this respect, ensuring favourable working conditions will enable higher education institutions to recruit quality teachers, a prerequisite to providing quality teaching. The obligation requires the state to ensure the protection of teachers' labour and trade union rights, provision of an acceptable salary and protection via social security measures.[221]

10. Obligations in Relation to Higher Education

(a) Immediate Obligations

Although the right to higher education is to be progressively implemented, some aspects of the right require immediate implementation by states parties and cannot be deferred indefinitely.[222] This is a result of Article 2 of the ICESCR, which

218. Beiter, above n 77, 530–1.

219. Ibid 532.

220. Ibid 532–3.

221. Ibid 533–6.

222. CESCR, *General Comment No 13: The Right to Education (Article 13 of the Covenant)*, 21st sess, UN Doc E/C.12/1999/10 (8 December 1999) [43–45]; Hodgson, *The Human Right to Education*, above n 18, 43; Manisuli Ssenyonjo, 'Economic, Social and Cultural Rights' in Mashood A Baderin and Manisuli Ssenyonjo (eds), *International Human Rights Law Six Decades after the UDHR and Beyond* (Ashgate Publishing, 2010) 49, 59.

provides that parties will take steps to achieve the progressive realisation of the rights set out in the *Covenant* and that these rights 'will be exercised without discrimination.'[223] In relation to the right to higher education, this results in a number of obligations.

First, a state party has an immediate obligation 'to take steps' towards making higher education equally accessible to all.[224] Both legislative and non-legislative steps should be put into effect.[225] In particular, this requires states parties to adopt and implement a national higher education strategy that outlines how the state proposes to achieve realisation of the right to higher education. [226] The strategy must include methods to monitor the progress towards realisation of the right.[227] Further, where appropriate, programmes should be implemented to protect vulnerable groups within society.[228]

Second, states parties are obliged to ensure that higher education is provided without discrimination.[229] This obligation 'applies fully and immediately to all aspects of education and encompasses all internationally prohibited grounds of discrimination.'[230] It extends to discrimination in law as well as discrimination in fact.[231]

(B) Progressive Obligations

States are obliged to work towards the progressive realisation of the right to higher education.[232] This means that '[s]tates parties have a specific and continuing

223. *International Covenant on Economic, Social and Cultural Rights*, opened for signature 19 December 1966, 993 UNTS 3 (entered into force 3 January 1976) art 2(1) and (2).

224. CESCR, *General Comment No 13: The Right to Education (Article 13 of the Covenant)*, 21st sess, UN Doc E/C.12/1999/10 (8 December 1999) [52]; Ssenyonjo, above n 222, 56.

225. Ssenyonjo, above n 222, 56.

226. Coomans, 'Content and Scope', above n 26, 203.

227. CESCR, *General Comment No 13: The Right to Education (Article 13 of the Covenant)*, 21st sess, UN Doc E/C.12/1999/10 (8 December 1999) [52]; Ssenyonjo, above n 222, 61.

228. Coomans, 'Content and Scope', above n 26, 203.

229. Ssenyonjo, above n 222, 59. See also Kama, above n 36, 166.

230. CESCR, *General Comment No 13: The Right to Education (Article 13 of the Covenant)*, 21st sess, UN Doc E/C.12/1999/10 (8 December 1999) [31]. See also Katarina Tomaševski, *Preliminary Report of the Special Rapporteur on the Right to Education*, UN Doc E/CN.4/1999/49 (13 January 1999) 13–14.

231. Coomans, 'Content and Scope', above n 26, 203.

232. Ssenyonjo, above n 222, 56. See also Hodgson, 'The Educational Rights of Persons with Disabilities', above n 80, 189.

obligation "to move as expeditiously and effectively as possible" towards the full realization of [A]rticle 13'.[233] Progressive realisation may involve many different strategies. It may include, for example, the development of curricula that aligns with the purposes set out in Article 13 or the establishment of a '[higher education] inspection system'.[234] Further, states parties are also required to use 'maximum available resources' to achieve realisation of the right to higher education.[235] In this context, the state should ensure that sufficient resources are directed to support marginalised groups.[236]

Finally, states are required, depending on their circumstances, to seek or provide international assistance and cooperation.[237] This is a result of the wording of Article 2(1), which provides that states parties are to take steps 'individually and through international assistance and co-operation' to achieve the ICESCR rights.[238] While wealthy states have tended to treat any education aid as being voluntary, this provision indicates that there may well be an international law obligation to provide such aid.

(c) No Retrogressive Measures

Retrogressive measures are those steps that move a state further away from, rather than toward, realisation of a *Convention* right, in this case the progressive achievement of equal access to free higher education. It is clear from the terms of Article 13, when read in light of Article 2, that retrogressive measures in relation to higher education are prohibited.[239] Retrogressive measures in the context of higher education are most likely to comprise the introduction or increase in higher education fees, sometimes coupled with the introduction of student

233. CESCR, *General Comment No 13: The Right to Education (Article 13 of the Covenant)*, 21st sess, UN Doc E/C.12/1999/10 (8 December 1999) [44]. See also CESCR, *Question of the Realization in All Countries of the Economic, Social and Cultural Rights Contained in the Universal Declaration of Human Rights in the International Covenant on Economic, Social and Cultural Rights, and Study of Special Problems Which the Developing Countries Face in Their Efforts to Achieve These Human Rights*, 43rd sess, Agenda Item 8 and 18, UN Doc E/CN.4/1987/17 (8 January 1987) 21 (*The Limburg Principles*).

234. Coomans, 'Content and Scope', above n 26, 203.

235. Ssenyonjo, above n 222, 56.

236. Ibid 62.

237. Ibid 56.

238. *International Covenant on Economic, Social and Cultural Rights*, opened for signature 19 December 1966, 993 UNTS 3 (entered into force 3 January 1976) art 2(1).

239. See Ssenyonjo, above n 222, 61.

loans.[240] This has been a common practice in many states parties, for example the United Kingdom, in recent times.[241] The prevalence of retrogressive measures in higher education is reflected in the comments of Tomaševski, the previous Special Rapporteur for the right to education, who noted following her mission to the UK that 'the government openly breached the ICESCR by introducing fees in university education'. She described it as a 'sobering' experience to discover the lack of awareness of the obligations imposed by the ICESCR and the ease with which the government was able to introduce fees.[242]

Retrogressive measures are 'definitely not legitimate' and according to the CESCR constitute 'a deliberate retrogressive step'.[243] Further, following the Limburg Principles on the Implementation of the International Covenant on Economic, Social and Cultural Rights, retrogressive measures, to the extent that they constitute '[a] failure by a State party to comply with an obligation contained in the *Covenant*', are considered 'a violation of the *Covenant*'.[244]

It is, nevertheless, legitimate to introduce retrogressive measures in particular circumstances. In order to legitimately do so, the state needs to show it has carefully considered all alternatives and can justify them 'by reference to the totality of the rights provided for in the *Covenant* and in the context of the full use of the State party's maximum available resources'.[245] Alternatively, under Article 4 of the ICESCR, rights may only be restricted to the extent that such measures are 'compatible with the nature of these rights and solely for the purpose of promoting the general welfare in a democratic society'.[246]

It may be difficult to justify the introduction or increase in higher education fees following the guidelines set down by the Committee. States parties would first need to demonstrate that they had considered all the alternatives, such as budgetary cuts in other areas, reduction of available student places or alternative methods of delivery. States would also need to demonstrate that the introduction or increase of fees was justified in the context of all the rights set out in the ICESCR. According to Beiter, this seemingly permits some form of 'trade-off' between or within rights; '[i]t might thus be open for a state party to lower the

240. See Coomans, 'Content and Scope', above n 26, 203; Beiter, above n 77, 593–4.

241. Beiter, above n 77, 387–8.

242. Tomaševski, 'Has the Right to Education a Future within the United Nations?' above n 2, 229.

243. Beiter, above n 77, 593–4.

244. CESCR, *The Limburg Principles*, UN Doc E/CN.4/1987/17, para 70.

245. CESCR, *General Comment No 13: The Right to Education (Article 13 of the Covenant)*, 21st sess, UN Doc E/C.12/1999/10 (8 December 1999) [43–5].

246. *International Covenant on Economic, Social and Cultural Rights*, opened for signature 19 December 1966, 993 UNTS 3 (entered into force 3 January 1976) art 4.

enjoyment of a right or an aspect thereof, if, at the same time, it substantially raises the enjoyment of another or an aspect of the same right'.[247] So, for example, a state party could potentially argue that the introduction of fees, although impeding access for particular groups, enabled the provision of an increased number of higher education places. A further requirement must be shown, however, in that the justification must also be in the context of the full use of the state party's maximum available resources.

Alternatively, in accordance with Article 4, states would need to demonstrate that restrictions on access to higher education caused by the introduction or increase of fees are compatible with the nature of the right to higher education and solely for the purpose of promoting the general welfare in a democratic society. This may prove difficult, as according to Beiter, 'unhampered and non-discriminatory access to education may be said to form part of the nucleus of the right to education', and as a result such measures would impact the 'essence' of the right to higher education.[248] Nevertheless, if fees were imposed and scholarships or other subsidy was provided to those unable to afford the fees (in accordance with Article 13(2)(e)), arguably access could be improved. The difficulty of drawing a line between those who can and cannot afford a certain level of fee, however, may prove difficult.

Finally, regardless of which defence a state asserts, it will need to show that measures have been implemented to support disadvantaged groups.[249] In particular, potential students from low socio-economic backgrounds must be provided with assistance, for example in the form of fee exemptions, scholarships or low interest loan schemes. Moreover, even where an introduction or increase in fees is justified, the state is not exempt from the requirement of progressive realisation of the right to education, including through the provision of free higher education,[250] meaning that the state is not able to continually increase fees whatever the justifications offered.

11. Accountability and the Right to Higher Education

(A) Violations

Although Article 13(2)(c) requires progressive realisation of the right to higher education, a number of acts are likely to constitute violations of the right. As noted above, retrogressive measures will generally constitute a prima facie breach

247. Beiter, above n 77, 387–8.

248. Ibid 456–8.

249. *International Covenant on Economic, Social and Cultural Rights*, opened for signature 19 December 1966, 993 UNTS 3 (entered into force 3 January 1976) art 13(2)(e); ibid 387–8.

250. Beiter, above n 77, 387–8.

of Article 13(2)(c).[251] Other violations might include intentionally failing to make higher education progressively free or reducing the state budget for higher education.[252] As described above, justifications for such measures may be raised by a state party, although they will still need to show sufficient support is being provided to disadvantaged groups.

(B) Justiciability

Although the justiciability of economic, social and cultural rights has been controversial, it is difficult to deny Tomaševski's argument that '[n]o right can exist without remedies'. [253] This perspective is confirmed in the Limburg Principles which require states to provide 'effective remedies including, where appropriate, judicial remedies'[254] and by the reality that the right to education 'is litigated both domestically and internationally'.[255] Accordingly, some aspects of the right to higher education should be made justiciable. In terms of which aspects, Manisuli Ssenyonjo's argument is compelling: the right to higher education should be justiciable 'whenever [the right] ... cannot be made fully effective without some role for the judiciary'.[256]

In particular, the requirement of non-discrimination in higher education is appropriate for judicial review given that the ICESCR requires its immediate implementation.[257] Further, this aspect of the right appears to also be 'the most effective way of challenging a violation of the right to education before the courts'.[258] Given the immediate nature of the obligation, it may also be appropriate to make the taking of retrogressive measures, such as the introduction or increase of higher education fees, justiciable.[259]

251. See Kama, above n 36, 158.

252. Beiter, above n 77, 651.

253. Katarina Tomaševski, *Report Submitted by the Special Rapporteur*, UN Doc E/CN.4/2004/45 (15 January 2004) [45].

254. CESCR, *The Limburg Principles*, UN Doc E/CN.4/1987/17, 19.

255. Katarina Tomaševski, *Progress Report of the Special Rapporteur on the Right to Education*, UN Doc E/CN.4/2000/6 (1 February 2000) [30]. See also Vernor Muñoz Villalobos, *Report Submitted by the Special Rapporteur on the Right to Education, Mr Vernor Muñoz Villalobos*, UN Doc E/CN.4/2005/50 (17 December 2004) 130.

256. Ssenyonjo, above n 222, 54, quoting CESCR, *General Comment 9: The Domestic Application of the Covenant*, UN Doc E/C.12/1998/24 (3 December 1998) [9].

257. CESCR, *The Limburg Principles*, UN Doc E/CN.4/1987/17, 35.

258. Coomans, 'Justiciability of the Right to Education', above n 193, 443.

259. Beiter, above n 77, 400–1.

D. CONCLUSION

The ICESCR opened to nations around the world for signature over half a century ago. This *Covenant,* together with a raft of other treaties, declarations, regional agreements and domestic legislation provides for a human right to higher education. Yet although the right to higher education clearly exists in international law, its meaning remains cloudy. In this respect, the recent entry into force of the Optional Protocol to the ICESCR is a welcome development, which should assist in further clarifying the obligations the right to higher education imposes on states parties.

The world has changed significantly since the ICESCR was drafted. State legislation and policies have followed a neo-liberal trajectory, shifting the perception of higher education from being a public good to being a commodity able to be bought and sold. Is there any place for a human right to higher education in this context? If so, what would it look like?

This chapter has raised awareness of the conceptual and pragmatic difficulties and complexities associated with the right to higher education. It has indicated how aspects of the right should be understood and applied. As Tomaševski noted in 2005, answering questions such as these is 'urgent' work, compelled by '[t]he risk of global retrogression in economic, social and cultural rights'.[260] In order for the normative virtue that is the right to higher education to play a meaningful role in advancing educational policy, the issues discussed in this chapter must be further refined, resulting in a core common understanding of the concrete content of the right. Absent this, the right to higher education will remain conceptually confusing, and higher education opportunities will continue to be determined by (often) haphazard political decisions and imperatives at the national level.[261]

REFERENCE LIST

A. Articles/Books/Reports

Arajarvi, P, 'Article 26' in A Eide (ed), *The Universal Declaration of Human Rights: A Commentary* (Scandinavian University Press, 1992) 408

Beiter, Klaus Dieter, *The Protection of the Right to Education by International Law: Including a Systematic Analysis of Article 13 of the International Covenant on Economic, Social, and Cultural Rights* (Martinus Nijhoff Publishers, 2006)

260. Tomaševski, 'Has the Right to Education a Future within the United Nations?' above n 2, 237.

261. See Linda Hantrais, *International Comparative Research: Theory, Methods and Practice* (Palgrave Macmillan, 2009) 120–1.

Brown, Ken, *The Right to Learn: Alternatives for a Learning Society* (Routledge Falmer, 2002)

Cassese, Antonio, *International Law* (Oxford University Press, 2nd ed, 2005)

Coomans, Fons, 'Exploring the Normative Content of the Right to Education as a Human Right: Recent Approaches' (2004) 50 *Persona y Derecho* 60

Coomans, Fons, 'Content and Scope of the Right to Education as a Human Right and Obstacles to Its Realization' in Yvonne Donders and Vladimir Volodin (eds), *Human Rights in Education, Science and Culture: Legal Developments and Challenges* (UNESCO Publishing, 2007) 183

Coomans, Fons, 'Justiciability of the Right to Education' (2009) 2 *Erasmus Law Review* 427

Craig, Elizabeth, 'Accommodation of Diversity in Education—A Human Rights Agenda?' (2003) 15 *Child & Family Law Quarterly* 279

De la Vega, Connie, 'The Right to Equal Education: Merely a Guiding Principle or Customary International Legal Right?' (1994) 11 *Harvard Black Letter Journal* 37

Devidal, Pierrick, 'Trading Away Human Rights? The GATS and the Right to Education: A Legal Perspective' in Dave Hill and Ravi Kumar (eds), *Global Neoliberalism and Education and its Consequences* (Routledge, 2009) 73

Gerber, Paula, *Understanding Human Rights: Educational Challenges for the Future* (Edward Elgar Publishing, 2013)

Gibson, Nicholas, 'An Unwelcome Trend: Religious Dress and Human Rights following Leyla Şahin vs Turkey' (2007) 25 *Netherlands Quarterly of Human Rights* 599

Gready, Paul and Jonathan Ensor, 'Introduction' in Paul Gready and Jonathan Ensor (eds), *Reinventing Development? Translating Rights-Based Approaches from Theory into Practice* (Zed Books, 2005) 1

Hall, Stephen, *Principles of International Law* (LexisNexis Butterworths, 4th ed, 2014)

Halvorsen, Kate, 'Notes on the Realization of the Human Right to Education' (1990) 12 *Human Rights Quarterly* 341

Hantrais, Linda, *International Comparative Research: Theory, Methods and Practice* (Palgrave Macmillan, 2009)

Harris, Neville, *Education, Law and Diversity* (Hart Publishing, 2007)

Hodgson, Douglas, 'The International Human Right to Education and Education concerning Human Rights' (1996) 4 *International Journal of Children's Rights* 237

Hodgson, Douglas, *The Human Right to Education* (Ashgate, 1998)

Hodgson, Douglas, *Individual Duty within a Human Rights Discourse* (Ashgate, 2003)

Hodgson, Douglas, 'The Educational Rights of Persons with Disabilities: International Human Rights Law and Australian Law Perspectives' (2013) 12(4) *International Journal of Discrimination and the Law* 183

Kalantry, Sital, Jocelyn E Getgen and Steven Arrigg Koh, 'Enhancing Enforcement of Economic, Social, and Cultural Rights Using Indicators: A Focus on the Right to Education in the ICESCR' (2010) 32 *Human Rights Quarterly* 253, 270

Kama, Sezen, 'Another Dimension of the Right to Education: Is "Equally Accessible Higher Education" a Dream?' (2014) 1(1) *Queen Mary Human Rights Review* 149, 160

Kotzee, Ben and Christopher Martin, 'Who Should Go to University? Justice in University Admissions' (2013) 47(4) *Journal of Philosophy of Education* 623, 636

Kumar, C Raj, 'International Human Rights Perspectives on the Fundamental Right to Education—Integration of Human Rights and Human Development in the Indian Constitution' (2004) 12 *Tulane Journal of International and Comparative Law* 237

Lawson, Kenneth, 'The Concept of Higher Education for All Explored', in Gordon Roderick and Michael Stephens (eds), *Higher Education for All?* (Routledge, 2012) 27

Leihy, Peodair and Jose M Salazar, 'The Moral Dimension in Chilean Higher Education's Expansion' (2017) 74 *Higher Education* 147

McCowan, Tristan, 'Reframing the Universal Right to Education' (2010) 46(4) *Comparative Education* 509

McCowan, Tristan, 'Human Rights within Education: Assessing the Justifications' (2012) 42(1) *Cambridge Journal of Education* 67

McCowan, Tristan, 'Is There a Universal Right to Higher Education?' (2012) 60(2) *British Journal of Educational Studies* 116

McCowan, Tristan, *Education as a Human Right: Principles for a Universal Entitlement to Learning* (Bloomsbury Academic, 2013)

Meyer, Heinz-Dieter, Edward P St John, Maia Chankseliani and Lina Uribe (eds), *Fairness in Access to Higher Education in a Global Perspective: Reconciling Excellence, Efficiency, and Justice* (Sense Publishers, 2013) 3

Monteiro, A Reis, 'The Right of the Child to Education: What Right to What Education?' (2010) 9 *Procedia Social and Behavioral Sciences* 1989

Nathwani, Niraj, 'Islamic Headscarves and Human Rights: A Critical Analysis of the Relevant Case Law of the European Court of Human Rights' (2007) 25 *Netherlands Quarterly of Human Rights* 221

Rizvi, Saad, Katelyn Donnelly and Michael Barber, 'An Avalanche Is Coming: Higher Education and the Revolution Ahead' (Essay, Institute for Public Policy Research, March 2013)

Saul, Ben, David Kinley and Jacqueline Mowbray, *The International Covenant on Economic, Social and Cultural Rights: Commentary, Cases, and Materials* (Oxford University Press, 2014)

Smith, Larry Robert (ed), *Higher Education: Recent Trends, Emerging Issues and Future Outlook* (Nova Science Publishers, 2013)

Ssenyonjo, Manisuli, 'Economic, Social and Cultural Rights' in Mashood A Baderin and Manisuli Ssenyonjo (eds), *International Human Rights Law Six Decades after the UDHR and Beyond* (Ashgate Publishing, 2010) 49

Steinbach, Armin, 'Burqas and Bans: The Wearing of Religious Symbols under the *European Convention of Human Rights*' (2015) 4 *Cambridge Journal of International and Comparative Law* 29

Tobin, John, 'Understanding a Human Rights Based Approach to Matters Involving Children: Conceptual Foundations and Strategic Considerations' in Antonella Invernizzi and Jane Williams (eds), *The Human Rights of Children: From Visions to Implementation* (Ashgate Publishing, 2011) 61

Tomaševski, Katarina, 'Has the Right to Education a Future within the United Nations? A Behind-the-Scene Account by the Special Rapporteur on the Right to Education 1998–2004' (2005) 5 *Human Rights Law Review* 205

Tomaševski, Katarina, *Education Denied: Costs and Remedies* (Zed Books, 2006)

Tomaševski, Katarina, *Human Rights Obligations in Education: The 4-A Scheme* (Wolf Legal Publishers, 2006)
Verheyde, Mieke, *Article 28: The Right to Education* (Martinus Nijhoff Publishers, 2006)

B. Cases/Constitutions/Legislation

Altınay v Turkey (2013) 37222/04 Eur Court HR
Case "Relating to Certain Aspects of the Laws on the Use of Languages in Education in Belgium" v Belgium (Belgian Linguistic Case) (1968) 1474/62 Eur Court HR
Constitution of India (2002)
Constitution of the Bolivarian Republic of Venezuela (1999)
Constitution of Turkey (1982, amended 2011)
Dabhi v the United Kingdom (1997) 28627/95 Eur Court HR
Foreign Students v The United Kingdom (1977) 7671/76 Eur Court HR
Georgiou v Greece (2000) 45138/98 Eur Court HR
Gratz v Bollinger 539 US 244 (2003) (US Supreme Court)
Grutter v Bollinger, 539 US 306 (2003) (US Supreme Court)
Hunter v Student Awards Agency Scotland [2016] CSOH 71
Hurley and Moore v Secretary of State for Business Innovation & Skills [2012] EWHC 201
İrfan Temel v Turkey (2009) 36458/02 Eur Court HR
Jaramillo v the United Kingdom (1995) 24865/94 Eur Court HR
Kjeldsen, Busk Madsen and Pedersen v Denmark (1976) 5095/71 Eur Court HR 52
Lautsi v Italy (2012) 30814/06 Eur Court HR
Leyla Şahin v Turkey (2007) 44774/98 Eur Court HR
Mohini Jain v Karnataka (1992) AIR 1858
Motala v University of Natal [1995] 3 BCLR 374 D (The Constitutional Court of South Africa)
Mürsel Eren v Turkey (2006) 60856/00 Eur Court HR
Ponomaryov v Bulgaria (2011) 5335/05, Eur Court HR
R (Douglas) v North Tyneside Metropolitan Borough Council [2004] 1 All ER 709
R (Kebede) v *Secretary of State for Business Innovation and Skills* [2014] PTSR 92
R (Tigere) v Secretary of State for Business, Innovation and Skills [2015] UKSC 57
SAS v France (2014) 43835/11 Eur Court HR
Sorabjee v the United Kingdom (1995) 23938/94 Eur Court HR
Tarantino v Italy (2013) 25851/09 Eur Court HR
Velyo Velev v Bulgaria (2014) 16032/07 Eur Court HR
X v Austria (1973) 5492/72 Eur Comm HR
X v United Kingdom (1980) 8844/80 Eur Court HR

C. Official international documents

Additional Protocol to the American Convention on Human Rights in the Area of Economic, Social and Cultural Rights (Protocol of San Salvador), opened for signature 17 November 1988, A-52 (entered into force 16 November 1999)
African Charter on Human and Peoples' Rights ("Banjul Charter"), opened for signature 27 June 1981, CAB/LEG/67/3 rev 5, 21 ILM 58 (entered into force 21 October 1986)

African Charter on the Rights and Welfare of the Child, opened for signature 11 July 1990), OAU Doc CAB/LEG/24.9/49 (entered into force 29 November 1999)
American Declaration on the Rights and Duties of Man, Bogota, Colombia, 2 May 1948
CESCR, *Concluding Observations: Bulgaria*, UN Doc E/C.12/1/Add.37 (8 December 1999)
CESCR, *Concluding Observations: Canada*, UN Doc E/C.12/1/Add.31 (10 December 1998)
CESCR, *Concluding Observations: Canada*, UN Doc E/C.12/CAN/CO/4-E/C.12/CAN/CO/5 (22 May 2006)
CESCR, *Concluding Observations: Canada*, UN Doc E/C.12/CAN/CO/6 (23 March 2016)
CESCR, *Concluding Observations: Chile*, UN Doc E/C.12/CHL/CO/4 (7 July 2015)
CESCR, *Concluding Observations: Germany*, UN Doc E/C.12/1/Add.29 (4 December 1998)
CESCR, *Concluding Observations: Germany*, UN Doc E/C.12/1/Add.68 (24 September 2001)
CESCR, *Concluding Observations: Mauritius*, UN Doc E/C.12/1994/8 (31 May 1994)
CESCR, *Concluding Observations: Norway*, UN Doc E/C.12/1/Add.109 (23 June 2005)
CESCR, *Concluding Observations: United Kingdom of Great Britain and Northern Ireland*, UN Doc E/C.12/GBR/CO/6 (14 July 2016)
CESCR, *General Comment No 11: Plans of Action for Primary Education*, 20th sess, UN Doc E/C.12/1999/4 (10 May 1999)
CESCR, *General Comment No 13: The Right to Education (Article 13 of the Covenant)*, 21st sess, UN Doc E/C.12/1999/10 (8 December 1999)
CESCR, *Question of the Realization in All Countries of the Economic, Social and Cultural Rights Contained in the Universal Declaration of Human Rights in the International Covenant on Economic, Social and Cultural Rights, and Study of Special Problems with the Developing Countries Face in Their Efforts to Achieve These Human Rights*, 43rd sess, Agenda Item 8 and 18, UN Doc E/CN.4/1987/17 (8 January 1987) 21 ('*The Limburg Principles*')
Committee on the Rights of the Child, *Concluding Observations: France*, UN Doc CRC/C/15/Add.240 (30 June 2004)
Committee on the Rights of the Child, *General Comment No 1: Article 29(1): The Aims of Education*, UN Doc CRC/GC/2001/1 (17 April 2001)
Convention against Discrimination in Education, opened for signature 14 December 1960, 429 UNTS 93 (entered into force 22 May 1962)
Convention on the Elimination of All Forms of Discrimination against Women, opened for signature 1 March 1980, 1249 UNTS 13 (entered into force 3 September 1981)
Convention on the Rights of Persons with Disabilities, opened for signature 30 March 2007, 2515 UNTS 3 (entered into force 3 May 2008)
Convention on the Rights of the Child, opened for signature 20 November 1989, 1577 UNTS 3 (entered into force 2 September 1990)
Council of Europe, *European Charter for Regional or Minority Languages*, opened for signature 5 November 1992 ETS 148 (1 March 1998)
Council of Europe, *Framework Convention for the Protection of National Minorities*, opened for signature 1 February 1995 ETS 157 (1 February 1998)

Economic and Social Council, *Implementation of the International Covenant on Economic, Social and Cultural Rights*, UN Doc E/1990/5/Add.33 (18 September 1996)

European Convention for the Protection of Human Rights and Fundamental Freedoms, as amended by Protocols Nos 11 and 14, opened for signature 4 November 1950, ETS 5 (3 September 1953)

Human Rights Committee, *Concluding Observations: France*, CCPR/C/FRA/CO/4 (31 July 2008)

International Covenant on Economic, Social and Cultural Rights, opened for signature 19 December 1966, 993 UNTS 3 (entered into force 3 January 1976)

Muñoz Villalobos, Vernor, *Report Submitted by the Special Rapporteur on the Right to Education, Mr Vernor Muñoz Villalobos*, UN Doc E/CN.4/2005/50 (17 December 2004) 130

Muñoz Villalobos, Vernor, *The Right to Education of Migrants, Refugees and Asylum-Seekers*, UN Doc A/HRC/14/25 (16 April 2010)

Tomaševski, Katarina, *Preliminary Report of the Special Rapporteur on the Right to Education*, UN Doc E/CN.4/1999/49 (13 January 1999)

Tomaševski, Katarina, *Progress Report of the Special Rapporteur on the Right to Education*, UN Doc E/CN.4/2000/6 (1 February 2000) [30]

Tomaševski, Katarina, *Report Submitted by the Special Rapporteur*, UN Doc E/CN.4/2004/45 (15 January 2004)

United Nations Declaration on the Rights of Indigenous Peoples, GA Res 61/295, UN GAOR, 61st sess, 107th plen mtg, Supp No 49, UN Doc A/RES/61/295 (13 September 2007)

D. Other

'Which Countries Have Banned the Burka?' *Radio Australia* (online), 7 December 2016 <http://www.radioaustralia.net.au/international/2016-12-07/which-countries-have-banned-the-burka/1637886>

Committee on Economic, Social and Cultural Rights, Office of the High Commissioner for Human Rights <http://ohchr.org/en/hrbodies/cescr/pages/cescrindex.aspx>

European Court of Human Rights, 'Guide on Article 2 of Protocol No 1 to the *European Convention on Human Rights*: Right to Education' (Guide, European Court of Human Rights, December 2015)

Gibney, Elizabeth, *St Hugh's Settles Shannon Case*, (25 March 2013) Times Higher Education <https://www.timeshighereducation.com/news/st-hughs-settles-shannon-case/2002745.article>

Mansfield, Michael, *Fees Deny the Basic Human Right to Education* (11 October 2011) The Guardian <https://www.theguardian.com/education/2011/oct/10/education-human-right-not-commodity>

Office of the High Commissioner for Human Rights, Jurisprudence, Office of the High Commissioner for Human Rights <http://juris.ohchr.org/en/search/results?Bodies=9&sortOrder=Date>

Organisation for Economic Cooperation and Development, 'Education at a Glance 2014: OECD Indicators' (OECD, September 2014)

Tomaševski, Katarina, 'Removing Obstacles in the Way of the Right to Education' (Right to Education Primers No 1, 2001)

UNESCO, *2009 World Conference on Higher Education: The New Dynamics of Higher Education and Research for Societal Change and Development: Communique* (8 July 2009)

UNESCO, *Recommendation concerning Education for International Understanding, Co-operation and Peace and Education Relating to Human Rights and Fundamental Freedoms*, 18th sess (19 November 1974)

UNESCO, *World Conference on Higher Education: World Declaration on Higher Education for the Twenty-First Century: Vision and Action* (9 October 1998)

UNESCO, *International Standard Classification of Education* (UNESCO, 2011)

United Nations Children's Fund ('UNICEF'), *Convention on the Rights of the Child* (30 November 2005) UNICEF <http://www.unicef.org/crc/index_30229.html>

United Nations, *Convention on the Rights of the Child* (27 November 2016) United Nations Treaty Collection <https://treaties.un.org/Pages/ViewDetails.aspx?src=TREATY&mtdsg_no=IV-11&chapter=4&clang=_en>

United Nations, *Education for All (EFA)* <http://www.un.org/en/globalissues/briefingpapers/efa/>

United Nations, *Optional Protocol to the International Covenant on Economic, Social and Cultural Rights* (26 November 2016) United Nations Treaty Collection <https://treaties.un.org/Pages/ViewDetails.aspx?src=IND&mtdsg_no=IV-3-a&chapter=4&clang=_en>

United Nations, *International Covenant on Economic, Social and Cultural Rights* (19 December 2016) United Nations Treaty Collection <https://treaties.un.org/Pages/ViewDetails.aspx?src=TREATY&mtdsg_no=IV-3&chapter=4&clang=_en>

Van Bueren, Geraldine, *If University Education Is a Human Right, High Fees May Be Legally Wrong, argues Geraldine Van Bueren* (25 April 2013) Times Higher Education <https://www.timeshighereducation.com/if-university-education-is-a-human-right-high-fees-may-be-legally-wrong-argues-geraldine-van-bueren/2003391.article>

2

Theoretical Approaches to Higher Education

A. INTRODUCTION

Higher education policy, and the legislation used to enact it, as with other areas of law and policy is underpinned and reflective of an ideology, or a system of beliefs, relating to the role of government within the state. As Simon Marginson explains, '[p]olicy-making is iterative and reproductive on the basis of the dominant ideas which become institutionalised over time'.[1] These ideas remain in place until alternative ideologies take hold of government and filter down to the institution level. Analysis of a particular higher education legal and policy system should make evident the underpinning set of ideas.[2]

The ideas that may inform higher education policy are numerous. For example, they may include the purpose of 'nation-building . . . alleviat[ion] of poverty . . . social justice . . . [or] rights'.[3] It is likely that more than one set of ideas will be reflected in any one system. Similar to Gosta Esping-Andersen's

1. Simon Marginson, 'The Impossibility of Capitalist Markets in Higher Education' (2013) 28(3) *Journal of Education Policy* 353, 353.

2. See also Ronald Barnett, 'Editorial' (1996) 21(1) *Studies in Higher Education* 3, 3.

3. Tristan McCowan, *Education as a Human Right: Principles for a Universal Entitlement to Learning* (Bloomsbury Academic, 2013) 10–11.

The Human Rights-Based Approach to Higher Education. Jane Kotzmann.
© Oxford University Press 2018. Published 2018 by Oxford University Press.

observation in relation to different types of welfare states, it is unlikely that there is any 'single pure case' of a system representing a particular ideology.[4] Yet, as with Esping-Andersen's analysis, 'the world is obviously composed of distinct regime-clusters'.[5] In particular, two approaches to higher education regulation may be contrasted. A market-based approach to higher education is reflective of classic liberal or neo-liberal economic theory that higher education will be most effective when it is left to the market. A human rights-based approach, on the other hand, may be adopted under which higher education is seen as being a right belonging to all people, for which the state has primary responsibility.[6]

The regulatory framework currently in ascendancy in many states in the context of higher education is largely representative of a market-based or neo-liberal approach.[7] This can be seen partly as an aspect of a widespread embrace of neo-liberal ideology as well as a response to the massification of higher education[8] and the need to find a sustainable way to finance far more extensive access to higher education.[9] Neo-liberalism is reflected in domestic higher education systems in the sense that students have been reconceptualised as consumers,[10] as well as in international trade law within which higher education is considered

4. Gosta Esping-Andersen, *The Three Worlds of Welfare Capitalism* (Polity Press, 1990) 28–9. In relation to the lack of a 'pure' market-based system see Leo Goedegebuure, Frans Kaiser, Peter Maassen and Egbert de Weert, 'Higher Education Policy in International Perspective: An Overview' in Leo Goedegebuure, Frans Kaiser, Peter Maassen, Lyn Meek, Frans van Vught and Egbert de Weert (eds), *Higher Education Policy: An International Comparative Perspective* (Pergamon Press, 1993) 1, 5.

5. Esping-Andersen, above n 4, 28–9.

6. Although a capabilities approach to higher education is also possible, it has not influenced higher education systems to the same extent as the two named approaches, and is best seen as a supplement to a human rights-based approach. See Tristan McCowan, 'Human Rights, Capabilities and the Normative Basis of "Education for All"' (2011) 9(3) *Theory and Research in Education* 283. Further, although other approaches to higher education might be implemented (for example, religious, postcolonial or Marxist approaches), in particular outside of liberal societies, it is not possible to canvass all approaches within the parameters of this book.

7. See Marginson, above n 1, 353; Kathleen Lynch, 'New Managerialism, Neoliberalism and Ranking' (2014) 13 *Ethics in Science and Environmental Politics* 141, 142. Such an approach results in the relationship between the state and higher education being 'reconfigured and recast, not severed': Andrew Gunn, 'The Role of Political and Policy Studies in Higher Education Policy Research' 1 *Theory and Method in Higher Education Research* 27, 29.

8. Katarina Tomaševski, 'Globalizing What: Education as a Human Right or as a Traded Service?' (2005) 12(1) *Indiana Journal of Global Legal Studies* 1, 9–10.

9. See Rajani Naidoo, Avi Shankar and Ekant Veer, 'The Consumerist Turn in Higher Education: Policy Aspirations and Outcomes' (2011) 27(11–12) *Journal of Marketing Management* 1142, 1144.

10. Michael Peters, 'Re-Thinking Education as a Welfare Right' (2002) 13(5) *School Field* 79, 80.

an exportable service.[11] The market-based approach is generally characterised by the introduction of or increase in tuition fees, a shift towards privatisation[12] and treatment of higher education as an 'export commodity'.[13]

The market-based approach to higher education has been criticised, in particular for its impact on equity and social justice and its potential to burden students with debts they may never be able to pay. In response to this situation, this chapter explores the particular characteristics of the market-based approach and the human rights-based approach to higher education policy, and undertakes a broad analysis of the potential strengths and weaknesses of each approach. In undertaking this examination, it should be acknowledged that there is a distinction between the characteristics of a theoretical model in principle, and the extent to which it is effectively implemented. Nevertheless, weaknesses in implementation can also be indicative of flaws in the approach itself, and the reverse also applies in terms of the strengths of a particular approach. Thus, the analysis here canvasses strengths and weaknesses both in principle and in practice. The objective is to move closer to an understanding of the ideal regulatory system for higher education, which is 'nuanced . . . sector specific . . . attuned to the character of higher education and knowledge that would establish a dynamic of reflexive continuous improvement across the full range of activity in the sector'.[14] In this chapter, it is contended that a human rights-based approach is likely to be preferable to a market-based approach to higher education policy.

B. THE MARKET-BASED APPROACH

1. Introduction to the Market-Based Approach

The market-based approach to higher education posits that higher education is most effectively provided through the free market.[15] In the free market, goods and services are exchanged purely on the basis of price.[16] Thus, a market for higher education involves higher education institutions as suppliers, selling education

11. Tomaševski, 'Globalizing What', above n 8, 1.

12. Peters, above n 10, 80.

13. Tomaševski, 'Globalizing What', above n 8, 9–10.

14. Marginson, above n 1, 353.

15. See Roger Brown, 'Introduction' in Roger Brown (ed), *Higher Education and the Market* (Routledge, 2011) 1, 1; Goedegebuure, Kaiser, Maassen, Meek, van Vught and de Weert, above n 4, 323.

16. David D Dill, 'Higher Education Markets and Public Policy' (1997) 10(3)–(4) *Higher Education Policy* 167, 168.

as a service to be traded to students conceptualised as 'consumers of higher education'.[17] Such an approach is evident in the highly privatised Chilean higher education system.[18]

The market-based approach to higher education is founded on classical liberal and neo-liberal beliefs. Through minimal state intervention and fostering competition in the marketplace, liberals hold that the market is a 'superior means for the abolition of class, inequality, and privilege'.[19] Thus, in the context of higher education, the market-based approach encourages competition between higher education providers, as well as the incorporation of private-sector management principles, which should result in greater efficiency and effectiveness in institutional operations.[20] Further, because institutions will need to compete against each other for student consumers, the price of higher education should be kept at the level of efficiency where supply meets demand. In terms of financing the cost of higher education, the market-based approach emphasises the private benefits that flow from education and therefore requires that individuals, rather than taxpayers, pay higher education costs.

According to Jeffrey Williams, the market-based approach 'represents a shift in the idea of higher education from a public entitlement to a private service'.[21] As a result, government intervention is minimised; rather than ensuring access to higher education, the state's role is to ensure that the market for higher education is operating efficiently.[22] This in turn is felt to lead to greater experimentation and innovation on the part of higher education institutions.[23] Higher education providers are forced to test different ideas in order to attract students; those ideas that are demanded in the market will flourish, whereas those with low demand will not be offered.[24] The result should be higher education institutions that offer high-quality, sought-after educational products at a price to match demand.

17. Naidoo, Shankar and Veer, above n 9, 1144, 1142.

18. See José Joaquín Brunner, 'Chile: Challenges to Autonomy and Accountability in a Privatized Context' (2013) 3 *Leadership and Governance in Higher Education* 1.

19. Esping-Andersen, above n 4, 9.

20. Naidoo, Shankar and Veer, above n 9, 1144–5.

21. Jeffrey Williams, 'The Pedagogy of Debt' (2006) 33(4) *College Literature* 155, 159 (emphasis altered).

22. Ibid 159–60.

23. Daniel L Bennett, 'Myth Busting: The Laissez-Faire Origins of American Higher Education' (2014) 18(4) *The Independent Review* 503, 504.

24. Ibid.

The market-based approach ascribes value to higher education largely because of its instrumental role in assisting people to participate in the labour force and consequent benefit to the economy.[25] People that engage in education develop knowledge and skills that are economically valuable[26] and improve productivity.[27] As a result, educated people are sought after in the labour market and receive higher wages. [28] In this sense, investment in education is considered an 'investment in human capital'[29] for which the 'economic returns to education' can be calculated.[30] From the individual perspective, education is attractive because it maximises a person's potential standard of living. From the societal perspective, investment in education should be encouraged in order to increase workforce productivity and thus foster economic growth.

It is important, however, to distinguish between the market-based approach and human capital theory. Although human capital theory focuses on the role of education in economic growth, it is not incompatible with other theoretical approaches that may be adopted in the context of higher education. Unlike the market-based approach, it does not necessarily posit that higher education should be delivered by the free market.

2. Principles of a Market-Based Approach

(a) Competition

A key principle of the market-based approach is competition.[31] One aspect of competition is the absence of any barriers to entry to the market.[32] This means that any institution is able to enter the higher education market and compete with existing providers, with minimal costs (eg, setup costs) and without a need to satisfy government regulation. Second, competition involves competitors

25. Melanie Walker, 'A Capital or Capabilities Education Narrative in a World of Staggering Inequalities?' (2012) 32 *International Journal of Educational Development* 384, 385.

26. Theodore W Schultz, 'Investment in Human Capital' (1961) 51(1) *American Economic Review* 1, 1. See also Peters, above n 10, 3.

27. Ingrid Robeyns, 'Three Models of Education: Rights, Capabilities and Human Capital' (2006) 4(1) *Theory and Research in Education* 69, 72.

28. Ibid.

29. Schultz, above n 26, 87.

30. Robeyns, above n 27, 72.

31. Bennett, above n 23, 505.

32. Ibid 505. See also Roger Brown, 'Markets and Non-Markets' in Roger Brown (ed), *Higher Education and the Market* (Routledge, 2011) 6, 7.

being able to openly compete for profits and market share.[33] In the higher education context, this is likely to entail competition in attracting students, as well as increased reliance on tuition fees and private fundraising as forms of revenue.[34] Third, in competitive markets, price is set on the basis of demand and supply.[35] Thus, in the higher education context, fees are unregulated by government and differ between higher education institutions on the basis of student demand. Finally, competition requires that consumers have open access to information and make choices 'consistent with competition, commodity production and profit'.[36] In higher education, this means that prospective students will have access to information about higher education courses (including fees), graduation rates, and job prospects resulting from course completion and rankings, and will enrol in a course on the basis of such information.

(b) Privatisation

The market-based approach is likely to involve privatisation, which has a number of aspects.[37] First, in a privatised system, property rights are 'clearly defined', meaning higher education institutions are able to manage their property free of government regulation.[38] Second, financing of providers is through private bodies rather than government. In the higher education context, a pure form of privatisation would involve private bodies delivering the initial capital for the institution, an absence of government subsidies and an increased focus on tuition fees, private fundraising and research grants.[39] Third, transition towards privatisation may involve 'de-monopolization' or the relaxing of government regulations in relation to higher education. 'De-nationalization' is the shift of higher education institutions from public to private; 'contracting out' means that services provided within higher education institutions are contracted to private providers rather than being provided by the public sector.[40]

33. Marginson, above n 1, 356.

34. Dill, above n 16, 172.

35. Marginson, above n 1, 356. See also Brown, 'Markets and Non-Markets', above n 32, 8.

36. Marginson, above n 1, 356. See also Brown, 'Markets and Non-Markets', above n 32, 8.

37. Bennett, above n 23, 505.

38. Ibid.

39. Ibid.

40. Dill, above n 16, 176.

(c) Absence of Government Intervention

A key aspect of a market-based approach is the absence of government intervention. This is because intervention is thought to be inefficient, increase costs and distort market allocation.[41] Under the market-based approach, government spending on higher education is minimised, in part because individuals are expected to finance the private benefit that they gain from higher education. Government regulation should also, in theory, be minimised, as regulation is likely to increase the costs of service provision and undermine competition between higher education institutions. A reduction in government regulation permits higher education institutions themselves to manage their operations, including staffing, enrolments, teaching and research.[42] Nevertheless, the contemporary trend of adopting market-based approaches to higher education has not resulted in a reduction of government regulation; rather, according to Rajani Naidoo, Avi Shankar and Ekant Veer, '[g]overnments create the conditions for a quasi-market, and at the same time market mechanisms are deployed to achieve governmental goals'.[43]

3. Strengths of the Market-Based Approach

Before discussing the specific strengths of the market-based approach, it should be acknowledged that the literature in favour of it is 'scarce' and relatively general.[44]

(a) Quality, Productivity and Innovation

The market-based approach has the potential to improve the quality and productivity of teaching in higher education institutions as well as stimulate innovation.[45] In a context where institutions are required to compete for students, significant incentives exist to improve teaching standards and output and consequently the reputation of the institution.[46] This may result in institutional requirements for academics to not only meet their teaching obligations, but to focus on improving

41. Bennett, above n 23, 504.

42. Dill, above n 16, 176.

43. Naidoo, Shankar and Veer, above n 9, 1144–5.

44. Roger Brown, 'The Impact of Markets' in Roger Brown (ed), *Higher Education and the Market* (Routledge, 2011) 20, 21.

45. See Francis A Steier, 'The Changing Nexus: Tertiary Education Institutions, the Marketplace and the State' (2003) 57(2) *Higher Education Quarterly* 158, 163; Brown, 'Introduction', above n 15, 1.

46. Dill, above n 16, 169.

teaching quality. Nevertheless, it should be noted that demand for higher education is unlikely to be based only on the quality of education offered. People seek higher education not just for the education itself, but for improved employment prospects and other opportunities.[47] Thus, demand for higher education may also result from other factors such as 'skilful branding and advertising', 'lifestyle images' attached to the brand[48] and the potential for networking.[49]

It is also possible that by charging fees, higher education will become more valued within society and therefore of better quality. Jandhyala Tilak notes a common argument for market-based higher education provision is that 'any good or service provided free or at a heavily subsidized price, is not valued by the consumers'.[50] Following this argument, attaching fees to higher education is likely to encourage people to value higher education and attract better-quality students.[51] Further, students who value their education are more likely to be successful in their studies, which in turn will have a beneficial impact on the reputation of the higher education institution.

(b) Efficiency and Responsiveness

Economic efficiency, one of the underpinning values of a market-based approach, is one of its key strengths.[52] The market-based approach is focused on removing inefficiency. In the context of higher education, government subsidisation is considered inefficient because it removes the incentive for higher education institutions to allocate resources efficiently.[53] The removal of government regulation and the imperative to cover costs in the absence of government subsidisation are likely to improve efficiency of operations and in turn lower the cost of higher education and improve quality.[54] Conversely, the long-term economic prospects of a market-based approach are not clear-cut; it could be argued that a human rights-based

47. Tristan McCowan, 'Higher Education and the Profit Incentive' in Dave Hill and Ravi Kumar (eds), *Global Neoliberalism and Education and Its Consequences* (Routledge, 2009) 54, 62.

48. Ibid 63.

49. Ibid 61.

50. Jandhyala B G Tilak, 'Financing of Higher Education: Traditional versus Modern Approaches' (2012) 2(1) *Yuksekogretim Dergisi Journal of Higher Education* 28, 31.

51. Ibid.

52. Dill, above n 16, 172.

53. Tilak, above n 50, 31.

54. See Mark Sinclair, 'Three Futures for University Provision: The Social Justice Market, Capitalism and Private For-Profit Universities' (2003) 25(2) *Journal of Higher Education Policy and Management* 161, 168, 170; Brown, 'The Impact of Markets', above n 44, 21.

approach will increase the number of tertiary-educated people in society, thus increasing human capital and improving the economy in the long term.[55]

A market-based approach is also said to improve institutional responsiveness. Proponents argue that the market assists higher education institutions to better observe their performance and costs.[56] Accordingly, market competition is better able to incentivise institutions to be more responsive to the needs of students and other stakeholders.[57]

(c) Prioritisation of Government Subsidies

A market-based approach to higher education could be argued to be appropriate in light of government subsidy priorities—government funding is limited and, in terms of education, funds should be directed towards primary and secondary education rather than higher education. This is because the economic and 'social rates of return' are thought to be much higher at the primary and secondary levels than for higher education.[58] Further, without adequate primary and secondary education, people will not develop the capacity necessary for higher education. Nevertheless, distribution of funding is not a 'one-or-the-other' question, and governments will need to consider all budgetary items. The limited nature of government funding is not in itself a sufficient justification for adoption of a market-based approach to higher education.

(d) Equity

The market-based approach to higher education is also argued to be more equitable than approaches that rely on government subsidies.[59] First, as the

55. United Nations Children's Fund and United Nations Educational, Scientific and Cultural Organization (UNICEF and UNESCO), 'A Human Rights-Based Approach to Education for All' (UNICEF/UNESCO, 2007) 12–13.

56. Brown, 'The Impact of Markets', above n 44, 21.

57. Brown, 'Introduction', above n 15, 1.

58. Tilak, above n 50, 30; Tristan McCowan, 'The Growth of Private Higher Education in Brazil: Implications for Equity and Quality' (2004) 19(4) *Journal of Education Policy* 453, 454–5. But see Rebecca Schendel, Tristan McCowan and Moses Oketch, 'The Economic and Non-Economic Benefits of Tertiary Education in Low-Income Contexts' (2014) 77 *International Higher Education* 6; Moses Oketch, Tristan McCowan and Rebecca Schendel, 'The Impact of Tertiary Education on Development: A Rigorous Literature Review' (Literature Review, Department for International Development, April 2014) 5–7; Rebecca Schendel and Tristan McCowan, 'Higher Education and Development: Critical Issues and Debates' in Tristan McCowan and Elaine Unterhalter (eds), *Education and International Development: An Introduction* (2015) 275, 275–6.

59. See generally McCowan, 'The Growth of Private Higher Education in Brazil', above n 58, 459–62.

private benefits that flow from higher education are considered to outweigh the social benefits, it is considered fair that students be asked to pay for those benefits.[60] Further, directing government subsidies towards higher education arguably exacerbates inequality, because the middle and upper classes are more likely to undertake higher education.[61] Accordingly, requiring higher education students to finance their own education can reduce or eliminate the regressive nature of public subsidisation of higher education.[62] To the extent that low socio-economic and disadvantaged groups are not represented in higher education, the market-based approach may be considered more equitable.

4. Weaknesses of the Market-Based Approach

(a) Lack of Service Information

A significant limitation of the market-based approach is the distinct lack of information about the services being offered by different higher education institutions. This is a result of the 'insuperable difficulty of producing valid, reliable and accessible information about product quality'.[63] Consequently, stakeholders rely on proxy information to substitute for quality, which in the case of higher education tends to be institutional prestige.[64] This in turn creates issues; in particular, because high prestige is associated with high fees, higher fees operate as an indicator of higher quality,[65] and thus tuition fees increase rather than decrease.

(b) Undermining Academic Quality and Focus

While proponents of the market-based approach argue that it will improve academic quality, critics contend that it will have the opposite effect. Where higher education institutions operate in a market, they rely on student tuition fees. In this context and without government research grants, research is unlikely to be profitable, and is therefore at risk of being devalued and not undertaken as a core academic activity. This is supported by evidence that for-profit higher education institutions have enjoyed success in part because they do not invest in

60. Tilak, above n 50, 30.

61. Ibid 30–1.

62. Ibid.

63. Brown, 'The Impact of Markets', above n 44, 20–3.

64. Ibid 20–6. See also, Michael Tomlinson, 'The Impact of Market-Driven Higher Education on Student-University Relations: Investing, Consuming and Competing' (2016) 29 *Higher Education Policy* 149, 151–2.

65. Brown, 'The Impact of Markets', above n 44, 47.

research.[66] This is detrimental to academic quality, as it limits the extent of public good emerging from higher education, and students are unable to benefit from exposure to academic research.[67]

The market-based approach is also likely to have a negative impact on teaching quality.[68] First, although it may be argued that teaching quality will improve because institutions will be competing for students, this is premised on the student being the adjudicator of quality. Where students are satisfied with the teaching service provided, teaching is considered to be of good quality.[69] In effect, however, what this means is that rather than focusing teaching efforts on learning, academics will be incentivised to ensure students are happy. As students may have more interest in achieving certification than in learning, there is potential for this focus to undermine teaching quality.

A market-based approach to higher education may have further problems for teaching quality. Students who view themselves as consumers may be less likely to engage in, and thus achieve, learning, because they expect to be able to easily obtain what they have paid for.[70] In relation to higher education institutions themselves, teaching activities are likely to be prioritised on the basis of their commercial potential, rather than their capacity to lead to real learning. This may result in a preference for disciplines and courses that are economically relevant, at the cost of less commercialisable knowledge and skills that may assist with the achievement of societal aims such as political participation or social harmony.[71]

(c) The Notion of Human Capital Devalues Human Beings

Within a market perspective, people are viewed as human capital rather than human beings, which, according to Katarina Tomaševski, 'questions the inherent worth of each human being'.[72] This aspect of the approach is highly criticised. Amartya Sen, for example, asserts that 'being a fine piece of capital is not the

66. McCowan, 'Higher Education and the Profit Incentive', above n 47, 64.

67. Ibid.

68. Brown, 'The Impact of Markets', above n 44, 41–2.

69. Henry A Giroux, 'Neoliberalism, Corporate Culture, and the Promise of Higher Education' (2002) 72(4) *Harvard Educational Review* 425, 446.

70. Although note the results discussed in Tomlinson, above n 64, 157.

71. Katarina Tomaševski, *Progress Report of the Special Rapporteur on the Right to Education*, UN Doc E/CN.4/2000/6 (1 February 2000) [67]. See also Giroux, above n 69, 434, 442.

72. Katarina Tomaševski, *Progress Report of the Special Rapporteur on the Right to Education*, UN Doc E/CN.4/2000/6 (1 February 2000) [67]. See also Katarina Tomaševski, *Report of the Special Rapporteur*, UN Doc E/CN.4/2003/9 (21 January 2003) [34].

most exalted state that can happen to a human being'.[73] By tying the value of a human being to his or her ability to contribute to the market, other aspects of being human are devalued, such as being part of a family, experiencing emotion and being able to empathise with others. Further, those people who are unable to contribute to the market, for reasons of illness or family commitments, for example, are excluded. From this perspective, the role of the individual is to serve the market, whereas it may instead be argued that the economy is a construct in place to serve people.[74]

The market-based approach is also problematic in the education-specific context. Given that people are valued for their ability to contribute to the market, those people deemed unlikely to be able to contribute may be denied education. Tomaševski provides the example of 'children with physical and learning disabilities . . . [who] may be excluded from school because providing wheelchair access might be deemed too expensive or their learning deemed not to yield a sufficient marginal return on investment'.[75] Although such a scenario might be acceptable in a market-based approach, many would find it morally unacceptable.

(d) Impact on Equity and Social Justice

The adoption of a market-based approach to higher education would have harmful effects on equity and social justice.[76] One of the key aspects of the approach is the minimisation of any government subsidies provided to higher education institutions and the reliance on tuition fees for cost recovery. Effectively, this means that people with sufficient financial means will be able to enjoy higher education, while those without such means will be excluded or only have access to lower-quality (cheaper) courses.[77] As Pierrick Devidal identifies, this will

73. Amartya Sen, 'Human Development and Financial Conservatism' (1998) 26(4) *World Development* 733, 734.

74. Katarina Tomaševski, *Progress Report of the Special Rapporteur on the Right to Education,* UN Doc E/CN.4/2000/6 (1 February 2000) [67].

75. Katarina Tomaševski, 'Removing Obstacles in the Way of the Right to Education' (Right to Education Primers No 1, 2001) 9, 37–8. See also Katarina Tomaševski, *Manual on Rights-Based Education: Global Human Rights Requirements Made Simple* (2004) UNESCO <http://unesdoc.unesco.org/images/0013/001351/135168e.pdf> 50.

76. See James Tooley, 'The "Neo-Liberal" Critique of State Intervention in Education: A Reply to Winch' (1998) 32(2) *Journal of Philosophy of Education* 267, 276.

77. See Tilak, above n 50, 32; Giroux, above n 69, 448–9; Gareth Williams, 'The Problems of Financing Higher Education', in Gordon Roderick and Michael Stephens (eds), *Higher Education for All?* (Routledge, 2012) 106–7; Katarina Tomaševski, *Human Rights Obligations in Education: The 4-A Scheme* (Wolf Legal Publishers, 2006) 17; McCowan, 'The Growth of Private Higher Education in Brazil', above n 58, 453; Tristan McCowan, 'Expansion without Equity: An Analysis of Current

'create a dual market, where the best programs will be accessible only to the richest groups of individuals'.[78] Further, given the link between higher education and employment prospects, this regressive[79] impact is likely to pervade society and lead to increasing social stratification.[80]

In order to ameliorate this unfairness, states implementing a market-based approach to higher education may ensure loans are available to assist students paying tuition fees, or provide a 'funding safety-net'[81] for the poor. Yet this is unlikely to fix the problem. As Tilak notes, 'students from lower socioeconomic backgrounds . . . [may] be reluctant to saddle themselves with debt burden', meaning fees will likely still act as a disincentive for them to enrol in higher education.[82] Further, interest charged on loan repayments will penalise people on low incomes as well as women who take time off work to have children, contributing further to social inequality. In terms of a funding safety net, the provision of means-based assistance may stigmatise recipients, resulting in increased social stratification.

(E) Ignores Other Purposes of Education

The market-based approach to higher education is focused on the individual economic benefits of education and ignores other benefits.[83] It is true that the individual gains significant economic benefits by undertaking higher education, for example, economically valued knowledge as well as skills such as critical thinking

Policy on Access to Higher Education in Brazil' (2007) 53 *Higher Education* 579, 579; Kathleen Lynch, 'International League Tables and Rankings in Higher Education: An Appraisal' in Imelda Elliott, Michael Murphy, Alain Payeur, Raymond Duval (eds), *Mutations de L'Enseignement Supérieur et Internationalisation* (De Boeck, 2011) 19, 26; Mark Fincher and Stephen Katsinas, 'Testing the Limits of the Price Elasticity of Potential Students at Colleges and Universities: Has the Increased Direct Cost to the Student Begun to Drive Down Higher Education Enrolment?' (2017) 39(1) *Journal of Higher Education Policy and Management* 31, 31.

78. Pierrick Devidal, 'Trading Away Human Rights? The GATS and the Right to Education: A Legal Perspective' in Dave Hill and Ravi Kumar (eds), *Global Neoliberalism and Education and Its Consequences* (Routledge, 2009) 73, 94.

79. Tilak, above n 50, 33.

80. Neville Harris, *Education, Law and Diversity* (Hart Publishing, 2007) 44–5. See also McCowan, 'Higher Education and the Profit Incentive', above n 47, 68; Olivia Ball 'Conclusion' in Paul Gready and Jonathan Ensor (eds), *Reinventing Development? Translating Rights-Based Approaches from Theory into Practice* (Zed Books, 2005) 278, 286.

81. Tooley, above n 76, 278–9.

82. Tilak, above n 50, 33. See also Giroux, above n 69, 445; Fincher and Katsinas, above n 77.

83. Robeyns, above n 27, 72. See also Williams, above n 21, 160; Tomlinson, above n 64, 150–65.

or teamwork. Yet, as McCowan asserts, focusing on these benefits alone ignores 'more general benefits . . . in terms of critical, intellectual, aesthetic and emotional abilities that are hard to quantify'.[84] Further, the intrinsic importance of education to the individual is also ignored under the market-based approach, which views education only as a means to an end.[85]

Similarly, the market-based approach to higher education overlooks the public benefits that higher education produces.[86] Public benefits cannot be factored into tuition fees, and as a result higher education is likely to be 'undersupplied' under the market-based approach.[87] Overlooking and devaluing these public benefits of education is likely to marginalise and possibly eliminate them, potentially leading people to treat higher education as just another form of financial investment.[88]

5. Conclusion: Market-Based Approach

Although a market-based approach to higher education has the potential to improve institutional efficiency and—where low socio-economic groups are underrepresented—equity, such an approach is significantly undermined by serious weaknesses. At its core, a market-based approach focuses only on the economically relevant aspects of higher education and overlooks the non-economic dimensions. In this respect, higher education can contribute to society via its impact on values and culture, and its positive effect on the economy as well as long-term gains from research and technology development.

C. THE HUMAN RIGHTS-BASED APPROACH

1. Introduction to the Human Rights-Based Approach

Human rights-based approaches seek to translate contemporary human rights norms and operationalise them.[89] Although there is no single human rights-based

84. McCowan, 'Higher Education and the Profit Incentive', above n 47, 70.

85. Robeyns, above n 27, 74.

86. Stephen J Klees, 'A Quarter Century of Neoliberal Thinking in Education: Misleading Analyses and Failed Policies' *Globalisation, Societies and Education* (2008) 6(4) 311, 316. See generally Goedegebuure, Kaiser, Maassen, Meek, van Vught and de Weert, above n 4, 5.

87. Brown, 'Markets and Non-Markets', above n 32, 10.

88. Robeyns, above n 27, 74. See generally, Tomlinson, above n 64, 163.

89. Australian Human Rights Commission, *Human Rights Based Approaches* <https://www.humanrights.gov.au/human-rights-based-approaches>; Kirsten Anderson, 'How Can a Rights-Based

approach, such approaches share common elements, and are informed by the principles of the particular right being operationalised.[90] Thus, a human rights-based approach to higher education is directed towards ensuring the enjoyment of the human right to higher education and the integration of human rights generally into the higher education system.[91] By way of example, the Finnish higher education system is underpinned by the entrenchment of the right to higher education in the Finnish Constitution.[92]

As outlined in Chapter 1 of this book, the human right to higher education (and thus a human rights-based approach to higher education) is concerned with ensuring that there is equal access to higher education. This concern, however, goes beyond financial obstacles to access, and extends to overcoming social and environmental obstacles as well.[93] Beyond access, the human right to higher education is concerned with the quality of education and respect for human rights within education.[94] According to UNICEF and UNESCO, these three aspects of the human rights focus 'are interdependent and interlinked, and a rights-based education necessitates the realization of all three'.[95]

Ensuring respect for human rights within education means that the full range of human rights must be afforded to students within the higher education system in order to respect each student's dignity.[96] Thus, government must ensure

Approach to Development Programming Help to Achieve Quality Education? Evaluating the Education Guarantee Scheme in Madhya Pradesh' (2006) 2 *Asia-Pacific Journal on Human Rights and the Law* 75, 84.

90. John Tobin, 'Understanding a Human Rights Based Approach to Matters Involving Children: Conceptual Foundations and Strategic Considerations' in Antonella Invernizzi and Jane Williams, *The Human Rights of Children: From Visions to Implementation* (Ashgate Publishing, 2011) 61, 64–75.

91. See United Nations Children's Fund and United Nations Educational, Scientific and Cultural Organization (UNICEF and UNESCO), 'A Human Rights-Based Approach to Education for All' (UNICEF/UNESCO, 2007) xii.

92. *Suomen perustuslaki* 11.6.1999/731, 16 [Ministry of Justice (Finland) unofficial trans, *The Constitution of Finland 11 June 1999*, s 16 <http://www.finlex.fi/fi/laki/kaannokset/1999/en19990731.pdf>]; Parliament of Finland, *Constitution of Finland* <http://web.eduskunta.fi/Resource.phx/parliament/relatedinformation/constitution.htx?lng=en>.

93. Marcia H Rioux and Paula C Pinto, 'A Time for the Universal Right to Education: Back to Basics' (2010) 31(5) *British Journal of Sociology of Education* 621, 635.

94. United Nations Children's Fund and United Nations Educational, Scientific and Cultural Organization (UNICEF and UNESCO), 'A Human Rights-Based Approach to Education for All' (UNICEF/UNESCO, 2007) 27.

95. Ibid.

96. Rioux and Pinto, above n 93, 626.

higher education policy and planning are informed by the human rights-based approach, which may require 'reforming the educational system'.[97] Further, higher education institutions will need to review course content and pedagogy as well as institutional processes and policies to ensure that they are rights respecting.[98] As Marcia H Rioux and Paula C Pinto assert, the human rights-based approach to higher education is a 'commitment . . . to social justice' and is likely to require 'radical reform . . . that removes gender inequality, illiteracy, disability discrimination and barriers to schooling'.[99]

2. Principles of a Human Rights-Based Approach

To ensure that the human rights-based approach outlined here is conceptually coherent, the principles described by John Tobin have been incorporated.[100] According to Tobin, the principles of a human rights-based approach include core principles, express principles and implied principles.[101] The core principles are those principles common to all rights-based approaches and include the integration and mainstreaming of human rights norms. The express principles of a human rights-based approach are those overarching principles that are expressly stated in the relevant international legal instruments. Here, they include accountability, non-discrimination and equality, and participation. Implied principles of a human rights-based approach are those principles that 'represent the fundamental values upon which the international human rights systems is said to be based',[102] which are often included in the preambles to international conventions and in human rights resolutions and declarations. These principles include dignity, interdependence and indivisibility, and cultural sensitivity.[103]

97. Olof Sandkull, 'Strengthening Inclusive Education by Applying a Rights-Based Approach to Education Programming' (Paper presented at the Inclusive and Supportive Education Congress Conference, Glasgow, Scotland, August 2005) 1.

98. McCowan, *Education as a Human Right*, above n 3, 179–80.

99. Rioux and Pinto, above n 93, 635.

100. See Tobin, 'Understanding a Human Rights Based Approach', above n 90, 64–75.

101. See ibid 65.

102. Ibid 73.

103. Tobin, 'Understanding a Human Rights Based Approach', above n 90, 64–75. See also, UNESCO, *The Human Rights-Based Approach: Statement of Common Understanding* (2004) UNICEF <http://www.unicef.org/sowc04/files/AnnexB.pdf>; Australian Human Rights Commission, above n 89; Sandkull, above n 97, 3; Ian Macpherson, 'The Rights-Based Approach to Adult Education: Implications for NGO-Government Partnerships in Southern Tanzania' (2009) 39(2) *Compare: A Journal of Comparative and International Education* 263, 264.

(a) Integration and Mainstreaming of Human Rights Norms

The key defining feature of a human rights-based approach is that it is based on human rights norms.[104] Thus, the objective of the human rights-based approach is the integration of human rights norms into policy, procedure and programming within a particular context.[105] In the context of this discussion of higher education policy, the relevant human rights drawn upon are those set out in international human rights treaties, as discussed in Chapter 1. This is because the right to higher education set out in those documents has received broad international acceptance.[106]

Mainstreaming refers to the importance of embedding human rights at all levels, 'assessing the human rights implications of any planned action including legislation, policies or programs, in all areas and at all levels'.[107] In the context of higher education, mainstreaming requires 'integrating human rights throughout [higher] education policy-making and practice at all levels',[108] and consideration of rights implications of higher education legislation and policies, as well as education programs to ensure those involved in higher education are aware of rights and obligations.

(b) Accountability

The human rights-based approach is based on the rule of law, in that human rights law provides the foundation for the approach.[109] Where states ratify international human rights instruments, they agree to be accountable for ensuring the enjoyment of the relevant human rights within their jurisdiction.[110] For example, pursuant to Article 2 states parties to the ICESCR agree 'to take steps . . . to the maximum of [their] available resources, with a view to achieving progressively

104. Tobin, 'Understanding a Human Rights Based Approach', above n 90, 66; Anderson, above n 89, 87.

105. Tobin, 'Understanding a Human Rights Based Approach', above n 90, 66; Sandkull, above n 97, 3.

106. Tobin, 'Understanding a Human Rights Based Approach', above n 90, 67.

107. John Tobin, 'Beyond the Supermarket Shelf: Using a Rights Based Approach to Address Children's Health Needs' (2006) 14 *The International Journal of Children's Rights* 275, 276–7.

108. Katarina Tomaševski, *Manual on Rights-Based Education: Global Human Rights Requirements Made Simple* (2004) UNESCO <http://unesdoc.unesco.org/images/0013/001351/135168e.pdf> 1.

109. Katarina Tomaševski, *Report Submitted by the Special Rapporteur*, UN Doc E/CN.4/2004/45 (15 January 2004) [43].

110. Tobin, 'Beyond the Supermarket Shelf', above n 107, 283–4.

the full realization of the rights recognized in the [ICESCR]'.[111] The state holds the ultimate responsibility to protect and secure rights, and to ensure accountability in this respect compliance must be carefully monitored.[112]

Accountability requires that mechanisms for access to justice be developed.[113] Where there is a failure in the provision of human rights or a breach of rights norms, there must be systems to enable rights holders to make complaints and claim their rights.[114] This may include access to the court system, complaints mechanisms and compliance monitoring institutions.

In terms of higher education, accountability requires that legislation and policy reflect the international human rights obligations set out in Article 13 (see discussion in Chapter 1). Ultimate responsibility for ensuring the enjoyment of the right to higher education rests with the state. Where there is a failure to ensure the various aspects of the right to higher education are enjoyed, people must be able to access remedies through the court system or other appropriate institutions.

(c) Non-discrimination and Equality

The principles of non-discrimination and equality are expressly provided for in the ICESCR. Article 2(1) of the ICESCR provides that states parties 'undertake to guarantee that the rights enunciated in the [ICESCR] will be exercised without discrimination of any kind'.[115] Further, the human rights set out in the ICESCR, including the right to higher education, are stated as belonging to all people equally.[116]

Non-discrimination and equality, in a human rights-based approach, means that human rights must be provided to all people without 'distinction, exclusion or restriction' on any basis.[117] Primacy should be given to people who are

111. *International Covenant on Economic, Social and Cultural Rights*, opened for signature 19 December 1966, 993 UNTS 3 (entered into force 3 January 1976) art 2(1).

112. Australian Human Rights Commission, above n 89.

113. United Nations Children's Fund and United Nations Educational, Scientific and Cultural Organization (UNICEF and UNESCO), 'A Human Rights-Based Approach to Education for All' (UNICEF/UNESCO, 2007) 75.

114. Sandkull, above n 97, 3–4; see also United Nations Children's Fund and United Nations Educational, Scientific and Cultural Organization (UNICEF and UNESCO), 'A Human Rights-Based Approach to Education for All' (UNICEF/UNESCO, 2007) 75.

115. *International Covenant on Economic, Social and Cultural Rights*, opened for signature 19 December 1966, 993 UNTS 3 (entered into force 3 January 1976) art 2(2).

116. Ibid preamble, art 3, art 13(2)(c).

117. Rioux and Pinto, above n 93, 628.

particularly vulnerable to discrimination and face the biggest obstacles to the enjoyment of rights.[118] Thus, higher education must be equally accessible to all without discrimination, subject only to the caveat that the individuals have capacity. Policies and processes should also be in place to ensure access for marginalised groups.[119]

The key human rights provision in this respect is Article 13 of the ICESCR (see Chapter 1(C)(1)).[120] Article 13(1)(c) makes it clear that equality, and particularly equality of opportunity, underpins the human rights-based approach. Under this approach, the intrinsic value of education is prioritised over its instrumental value—it is not important whether access to education will result in greater job prospects or aid the economy; rather what is important is that all people have equal access to higher education.[121]

(D) Participation

As identified by Tobin, participation is an express principle of a human rights-based approach by virtue of a number of provisions set out in the ICCPR and the ICESCR.[122] In particular, the ICCPR provides for a right to take part in the conduct of public affairs,[123] to freedom of expression,[124] to freedom of association with others[125] and to freedom of peaceful assembly.[126] Further, Article 13(1) of the ICESCR provides that 'education shall enable all persons to participate effectively in a free society'.[127]

118. Australian Human Rights Commission, above n 89.

119. UNESCO, *World Conference on Higher Education: Framework for Priority Action for Change and Development in Higher Education* (9 October 1988) <http://www.unesco.org/education/educprog/wche/declaration_eng.htm#world%20declaration> art I(1)(a).

120. *International Covenant on Economic, Social and Cultural Rights*, opened for signature 19 December 1966, 993 UNTS 3 (entered into force 3 January 1976) art 13.

121. Robeyns, above n 27, 75; McCowan, *Education as a Human Right*, above n 3, 11.

122. Tobin, 'Understanding a Human Rights Based Approach', above n 90, 70–71.

123. *International Covenant on Civil and Political Rights*, opened for signature 19 December 1966, 999 UNTS 171 (entered into force 23 March 1976) art 25(a).

124. Ibid art 19(2).

125. Ibid art 22(1).

126. Ibid art 21.

127. *International Covenant on Economic, Social and Cultural Rights*, opened for signature 19 December 1966, 993 UNTS 3 (entered into force 3 January 1976) art 13(1).

The principle of participation requires that rights holders are included and able to participate in processes that affect their rights.[128] Being able to participate includes being able to express views on relevant matters and have those views taken into account. Participation is a particularly important principle in the context of higher education, and requires that students' views be sought out and taken into account in the development of policies, procedures and pedagogy.[129] Thus, according to UNICEF and UNESCO, students should be 'active contributors to their own learning, rather than passive recipients of education'.[130] Through meaningful participation, student engagement should be increased,[131] resulting in more profound learning and better student outcomes.

(E) Dignity

One of the underlying principles of a human rights-based approach is respect for the inherent dignity, or worth, of all human beings.[132] The importance of this principle is evident from the Charter of the United Nations,[133] the Universal Declaration of Human Rights,[134] the ICCPR,[135] and the ICESCR[136] as well as

128. United Nations Children's Fund and United Nations Educational, Scientific and Cultural Organization (UNICEF and UNESCO), 'A Human Rights-Based Approach to Education for All' (UNICEF/UNESCO, 2007) 10–11.

129. UNESCO, *World Conference on Higher Education: Framework for Priority Action for Change and Development in Higher Education* (9 October 1988) <http://www.unesco.org/education/educprog/wche/declaration_eng.htm#world%20declaration> art I(1)(k).

130. United Nations Children's Fund and United Nations Educational, Scientific and Cultural Organization (UNICEF and UNESCO), 'A Human Rights-Based Approach to Education for All' (UNICEF/UNESCO, 2007) 33–4.

131. Katherine Covell, 'School Engagement and Rights-Respecting Schools' (2010) 40(1) *Cambridge Journal of Education* 39, 40.

132. See Samantha Besson, 'Justifications', in Daniel Moeckli, Sangeeta Shah and Sandesh Sivakumaran (eds), *International Human Rights Law* (2nd ed, Oxford University Press, 2014) 34, at 46; Luís Roberto Barroso, 'Here, There, and Everywhere: Human Dignity in Contemporary Law and in the Transnational Discourse' (2012) 35 *Boston College International & Comparative Law Review* 331, at 360; Audrey Chapman, 'Human Dignity, Bioethics, and Human Rights' (2011) 3 *Amsterdam Law Forum* 3, at 3; Christopher McCrudden, 'Human Dignity and Judicial Interpretation of Human Rights' (2008) 19 *European Journal of International Law* 655, at 722–4.

133. *Charter of the United Nations* preamble.

134. *Universal Declaration of Human Rights*, GA Res 217A (III), UN GAOR, 3rd sess, 183rd plen mtg, UN Doc A/810 (10 December 1948), preamble, art 1, art 22, art 23.

135. *International Covenant on Civil and Political Rights*, opened for signature 19 December 1966, 999 UNTS 171 (entered into force 23 March 1976) preamble, art 1.

136. *International Covenant on Economic, Social and Cultural Rights*, opened for signature 19 December 1966, 993 UNTS 3 (entered into force 3 January 1976) preamble, art 13(1).

numerous other key international human rights treaties.[137] In the context of higher education, respect for dignity means that students should not be seen as a means to an end but as ends in themselves,[138] and thus higher education has intrinsic importance.

(F) Interdependence and Indivisibility

The principles of interdependence and indivisibility are derived from the Vienna Declaration and Programme of Action.[139] Indivisibility means that all human rights are integral to human dignity; all human rights are equal and cannot be ranked in importance.[140] The right to higher education, in this sense, is no more or less important than other rights, such as the right to freedom of thought, conscience and religion or the right to housing.[141] Further, the principle that human rights are interdependent is based on the reality that realisation of a right usually requires realisation of other rights.[142] For example, the right to higher education may depend on the realisation of the right to freedom of expression.[143]

137. See *International Convention on the Elimination of All Forms of Racial Discrimination*, opened for signature 21 December 1965, 660 UNTS 195 (entered into force 4 January 1969) preamble; *Convention on the Elimination of All Forms of Discrimination against Women*, opened for signature 1 March 1980, 1249 UNTS 13 (entered into force 3 September 1981) preamble; *Convention against Torture and Other Cruel, Inhuman or Degrading Treatment or Punishment*, opened for signature 10 December 1984, 1465 UNTS 85 (entered into force 26 June 1987) preamble; *Convention on the Rights of the Child*, opened for signature 20 November 1989, 1577 UNTS 3 (entered into force 2 September 1990) preamble, art 23(1), art 28(2), art 37(c), art 40(1); *International Convention on the Protection of the Rights of All Migrant Workers and Members of Their Families*, opened for signature 18 December 1990, 2220 UNTS 3 (entered into force 1 July 2003) art 17(1), art 70; *Convention on the Rights of Persons with Disabilities*, opened for signature 30 March 2007, 2515 UNTS 3 (entered into force 3 May 2008) art 1, art 3(a), art 8(1)(a), art 16(4), art 24(1)(a), art 25(d); *International Convention for the Protection of All Persons from Enforced Disappearance*, opened for signature 6 February 2007, 2716 UNTS 3 (entered into force 23 December 2010) art 19(2), art 24(5)(c).

138. Tobin, 'Understanding a Human Rights Based Approach', above n 90, 73.

139. UN General Assembly, *Vienna Declaration and Programme of Action*, GA Res 48/121, A/CONF.157/23 (12 July 1993) [I(5)]; Tobin, 'Understanding a Human Rights Based Approach', above n 90, 74.

140. United Nations Children's Fund and United Nations Educational, Scientific and Cultural Organization (UNICEF and UNESCO), 'A Human Rights-Based Approach to Education for All' (UNICEF/UNESCO, 2007) 10–11.

141. *International Covenant on Civil and Political Rights*, opened for signature 19 December 1966, 999 UNTS 171 (entered into force 23 March 1976) art 18; *International Covenant on Economic, Social and Cultural Rights*, opened for signature 19 December 1966, 993 UNTS 3 (entered into force 3 January 1976) art 11.

142. UNESCO, *The Human Rights-Based Approach: Statement of Common Understanding* (2004) UNICEF <http://www.unicef.org/sowc04/files/AnnexB.pdf> 92.

143. *International Covenant on Civil and Political Rights*, opened for signature 19 December 1966, 999 UNTS 171 (entered into force 23 March 1976) art 19.

(G) Cultural Sensitivity

International human rights must be operationalised in a way that is respectful of culture. That this is so is clear from the terms of the Vienna Declaration and Programme of Action.[144] It is also supported by the right set out in Article 15(1)(a) of the ICESCR to take part in cultural life.[145] In relation to higher education, this principle means that states must provide flexibility for higher education institutions to accommodate cultural difference. In particular, it should be taken into account in ensuring that higher education regulations do not discriminate on the basis of religion (see Chapter 1, part C(6)(a)).

3. Strengths of the Human Rights-Based Approach

(A) Normative Basis

The human rights-based approach is based on moral normative standards—in this case that all people are entitled to higher education provided that they have the requisite capacity. Although the market-based approach may also be said to have a normative basis, the particular nature of the human rights-based approach has important consequences. First, it entails using human rights as set out in international law as a framework for making ethical decisions.[146] Human rights themselves in this sense represent ethical standards. This can be contrasted with the market-based approach, which, for example, seeks to achieve 'the abolition of class, inequality, and privilege'[147] by focusing on ensuring the optimal operation of the market rather than on abolition itself. Second, the nature of human rights is that enjoyment of rights is unconditional.[148] Unlike under the market-based approach, economic, practical and other arguments cannot be used to deny provision of higher education. As stated by UNICEF and UNESCO, such an approach is more likely to encourage 'social cohesion, integration and stability', and develop 'respect for peace and non-violent conflict resolution'.[149]

144. UN General Assembly, *Vienna Declaration and Programme of Action*, GA Res 48/121, A/CONF.157/23 (12 July 1993) [I(5)].

145. *International Covenant on Economic, Social and Cultural Rights*, opened for signature 19 December 1966, 993 UNTS 3 (entered into force 3 January 1976) art 15(1)(a).

146. Jim Ife, *Human Rights from Below: Achieving Rights through Community Development* (Cambridge University Press, 2010) 124.

147. Esping-Andersen, above n 4, 9.

148. McCowan, *Education as a Human Right*, above n 3, 12–13.

149. United Nations Children's Fund and United Nations Educational, Scientific and Cultural Organization (UNICEF and UNESCO), 'A Human Rights-Based Approach to Education for All' (UNICEF/UNESCO, 2007) 12–13.

(b) Well Established Approach

The human rights-based approach is well established and provides a 'common language' and lens through which to view and approach societal issues, such as higher education.[150] As a result, this approach constitutes a powerful instrument that can be used to advocate for higher education.[151] In this respect, utilisation of well-established human rights language can lend legitimacy to an approach to higher education that might otherwise be criticised.[152] As asserted by Lundy and McEvoy, the human rights-based approach possesses a '"moral coinage" . . . [that] allows rights-holders to make claims for treatment which are not dependent on the goodwill, charity or inclination of those who can provide that help'.[153]

Further, the human rights-based approach is supported by an internationally accepted legal framework.[154] As Tomaševski asserts, the international nature of this approach 'provide[s] tools for identifying problems and a toolbox of global experiences in solving them'.[155] In this respect, in developing and implementing higher education law and policy, the human rights-based approach will enable states to identify issues and draw on the experiences of other states in developing solutions. Further, the international framework includes some monitoring and reporting mechanisms to ensure adequate progress towards the goal of securing the right to higher education.[156]

(c) Empowerment and Accountability

One of the key strengths of a human rights-based approach to higher education is empowerment.[157] Instead of being viewed as objects of charity, those demanding

150. Ibid 11; Robeyns, above n 27, 80.

151. Robeyns, above n 27, 80.

152. Andrea Cornwall and Celestine Nyamu-Musembi, 'Putting the "Rights-Based Approach" to Development into Perspective' (2004) 25(8) *Third World Quarterly* 1415, 1418.

153. Laura Lundy and Lesley McEvoy, 'Developing Outcomes for Educational Services: A Children's Rights-Based Approach' (2009) 1(1) *Effective Education* 43, 58. See also Manfred Nowak, 'The Right to Education—Its Meaning, Significance and Limitations' (1991) 9 *Netherlands Quarterly of Human Rights* 418, 425; Leah K McMillan, 'What's in a Right? Two Variations for Interpreting the Right to Education' (2010) 56 *International Review of Education* 531, 541; Ball, above n 80, 289.

154. Katarina Tomaševski, *Report Submitted by the Special Rapporteur*, UN Doc E/CN.4/2004/45 (15 January 2004) [19].

155. Ibid.

156. Sandkull, above n 97, 7. See also Tobin, 'Beyond the Supermarket Shelf', above n 107, 281–2.

157. United Nations Children's Fund and United Nations Educational, Scientific and Cultural Organization (UNICEF and UNESCO), 'A Human Rights-Based Approach to Education for All' (UNICEF/UNESCO, 2007) 12–13.

access to higher education are able to claim it as a right.[158] Accordingly, rights claimants are encouraged to take a more active role in pursuing their own well-being, which in turn may assist in building a greater sense of dignity,[159] and in the higher education context, may result in students being more engaged in their studies.[160] Further, rights language makes it clear that both states and the international community have an obligation to ensure the provision of rights, including through the allocation of sufficient resources.[161] In this way, the human rights-based approach emphasises accountability and transparency, making it more likely that rights may be realised.[162]

(D) Attention to Process

A further strength of the human rights-based approach to higher education is that it sees the process of achieving rights, and not just the end goal of rights enjoyment, as being important.[163] This is significant because it entails respect for all human rights, rather than just focusing on the end goal of ensuring access to quality higher education.

(E) Challenging the Power Imbalance

Finally, a key strength of the human rights-based approach to higher education is that it can be used to contest existing power structures.[164] By empowering people to claim a right to higher education, government and higher education institutions are obligated to consider the views of rights holders and work towards ensuring the provision of the right to higher education. As a result, higher education should no longer remain the preserve of a societal elite.

4. Weaknesses of the Human Rights-Based Approach

(A) Focus on Law

A key criticism of the human rights-based approach is that it is too focused on law. Jim Ife points out that although 'the work of lawyers, and the mechanisms

158. Paul Gready and Jonathan Ensor, 'Introduction' in Paul Gready and Jonathan Ensor (eds), *Reinventing Development? Translating Rights-Based Approaches from Theory into Practice* (Zed Books, 2005) 1, 23. See also McCowan, *Education as a Human Right*, above n 3, 12–13; Sandkull, above n 97, 7.

159. Anderson, above n 89, 109. See also McMillan, above n 153, 540.

160. Covell, above n 131, 40.

161. Sandkull, above n 97, 7.

162. Office of the UN High Commissioner for Human Rights, cited in Cornwall and Nyamu-Musembi, above n 152, 1417. See also Anderson, above n 89, 109; Sandkull, above n 97, 7.

163. McCowan, *Education as a Human Right*, above n 3, 12–13. See also Sandkull, above n 97, 7.

164. Sandkull, above n 97, 7. See also Ball, above n 80, 289.

of the law, are important for human rights', the law in itself is not sufficient to achieve human rights goals.[165] This is also true in the context of the right to higher education; the law is inadequate in isolation. Although legislation is important, the right to higher education requires the state to formulate appropriate policy, and to allocate appropriate resources to ensure enjoyment of the right.[166] This requires cooperation with higher education institutions, which must also bear some responsibility. An overreliance on law has had the unfortunate result of 'marginalis[ing] . . . other professions and occupations in human rights work'.[167]

The over-reliance on law is also problematic in terms of addressing human rights issues.[168] Although it would be possible to provide access to courts or tribunals for those seeking to claim a right to higher education, in reality it may not be a practical or attractive means of dispute resolution for relevant individuals.[169] As pointed out by Ife, law, in this sense, is 'a blunt instrument' in that it lacks an ability 'to deal with more subtle, complex or ambiguous situations in which human rights are daily denied or violated'.[170]

Such criticism should serve to highlight the importance of a human rights-based approach to higher education being multisectoral and interdisciplinary as well as utilising appropriate accountability mechanisms. Without the involvement of relevant sectors and disciplines—including government, law, higher education and those disciplines being taught within higher education institutions—a human rights-based approach is unlikely to be successful. To ensure that the right to higher education is protected, appropriate accountability mechanisms might include, for example, legislative compliance audits, regular mandatory reporting internally and externally and the establishment of complaints mechanisms.

(b) Lack of Support for the Right to Education

International human rights institutions have shown a tendency to avoid or ignore economic, social and cultural rights, including the right to higher education. This is possibly partly the result of the over-reliance on the legal discipline, as civil and political rights are generally more amenable to legal adjudication.[171] The other

165. Ife, above n 146, 75.

166. Ibid.

167. Ibid 111–112. See also Robeyns, above n 27, 77.

168. See Katarina Tomaševski, *Annual Report of the Special Rapporteur on the Right to Education*, UN Doc E/CN.4/2002/60 (7 January 2002) [7].

169. Gready and Ensor, above n 158, 8–9.

170. Ife, above n 146, 89.

171. Ibid 111–112.

possible reason is the continuing impact of the Cold War on human rights institutions. Tomaševski, former Special Rapporteur on the Right to Education, asserts that the Cold War 'has prevented the Commission from performing its key task of denouncing abuses' and that as a result breaches of the right to education 'continue unchallenged'.[172]

The right to higher education in particular is neglected. The international focus on the right to primary education, without mention of higher education, operates to undermine any recognised right to higher education and contributes to the shift in the perception of higher education as a traded service.[173] The lack of international support for the right to higher education is a significant weakness to the adoption of a human rights-based approach to higher education. Nevertheless, with sufficient domestic will, a human rights-based approach may still be successfully implemented, as is evident from consideration of the human rights-based approach case studies in Chapter 4.

(c) Translation into Policy

One criticism of the human rights-based approach to education is that its translation into policy does not accord with the ideals of the human rights norm. For example, it is claimed that the human rights-based approach, in practice, is concerned primarily with access and overlooks other important issues such as quality of education.[174] Further, it is argued that many policies and programs that purport to implement human rights norms are based on 'universalism', which regards teaching as 'essential to creating future human capital' and thus ignores the intrinsic importance of education.[175] Similarly, it is contended that once the key requirements of the right to education are met (eg, access, appropriate teaching staff and appropriate resources), 'a government might wash its hands and say that it did its duty, even if the real situation is far from optimal because of the complexity of social life'.[176] To the extent that these criticism are true, such policies and programs must be further developed or replaced, to ensure that the approach is truly based on and reflective of human rights standards.

172. Katarina Tomaševski, 'Has the Right to Education a Future within the United Nations? A Behind-the-Scene Account by the Special Rapporteur on the Right to Education 1998–2004' (2005) 5 *Human Rights Law Review* 205, 209.

173. Katarina Tomaševski, *Report Submitted by the Special Rapporteur*, UN Doc E/CN.4/2004/45 (15 January 2004) [7–8].

174. McMillan, above n 153, 541.

175. Ibid 538.

176. Robeyns, above n 27, 77, 82.

(D) Empty Words

A potential risk of the human rights-based approach is that states may use the human rights language without implementation of the human rights content. As Tomaševski notes, 'there is a risk that "rights" will become a weasel-word into which almost any contents can be fitted'.[177] Similarly, rights may be reduced to their legal content, while their moral, social and other aspects are ignored.[178] Thus, it is imperative that the principle of accountability accompanies any human rights-based approach, to ensure that it is what it claims to be.

(E) Conflict Producing

Finally, the human rights-based approach is also criticised on the basis that it sets people and rights organisations in opposition to the state, thereby producing conflict.[179] Although this is a real possibility, where it is agreed that the state is responsible for the provision of public services, the only alternative is to allow the state to escape accountability. Without holding the state responsible, there can be no assurance that people will be able to enjoy their rights, including the right to higher education.

5. Conclusion: Human Rights-Based Approach

Although a human rights-based approach to higher education lacks international support, where it is properly implemented in a domestic setting it holds great potential, as is demonstrated in Chapter 4 of this book. The approach provides a recognised, ethical framework for decision making, which could provide for greater equity and social justice in the higher education setting.

D. CONCLUSION

There are innumerable ways in which higher education systems can be framed. This chapter has considered two contrasting ideological frameworks, the market-based approach and the human rights-based approach. The key features of each approach, as well as their strengths and weaknesses, have been considered in order to attempt to contribute to a greater understanding of what might comprise the ideal higher education system.

177. Tomaševski, 'Removing Obstacles', above n 75, 22.

178. Robeyns, above n 27, 76.

179. Macpherson, above n 103, 276.

The importance of education, including higher education, is uncontested; 'education operates as a multiplier', increasing people's life chances and opportunities.[180] Yet recent perceptions of education as a means for capital creation and as an exportable service[181] have thrown higher education policy into the spotlight in its challenge to the concept of a 'right' to higher education.[182] Before conventional approaches to higher education are dismissed, however, the underpinning rationale behind such systems and the potential consequences of such a radical change should be considered.

Although both approaches considered here have some merit, the rights-based approach has a pronounced advantage over the market-based approach. The market-based approach fails to account for the reality that higher education is (at least in part) a public good.[183] As Michael Peters asserts, 'the state must play some role in the provision of [higher education] ..., otherwise [it] ... will be undersupplied'.[184] The market-based approach is also problematic in its reliance on stakeholders having information about service quality. In the higher education context, such information is difficult to produce, leading to the use of substitute indicators of quality, such as prestige. This can have the unwanted effects of increasing stratification of institutions and raising tuition fees.

In contrast, the human rights-based approach is able to recognise and respect individual dignity. The human rights-based approach positions students as 'subjects with entitlements' as opposed to consumers.[185] This sense of dignity that attaches to rights is reinforced through the concept of responsibilities, which is well explained by Ife: '[u]nderstanding rights and responsibilities together links us with each other in a network of rights and responsibilities: my rights require responsibilities of others; the rights of others impose responsibilities on me'.[186] The inclusive nature of such an approach brings people into relationship with each other; being premised on equity, it is more likely to lead to human happiness

180. Tomaševski, 'Removing Obstacles', above n 75, 9.

181. Katarina Tomaševski, *Progress Report of the Special Rapporteur on the Right to Education*, UN Doc E/CN.4/2000/6 (1 February 2000) [66].

182. See Devidal, above n 78, 93; Tomaševski, *Human Rights Obligations in Education: The 4-A Scheme*, above n 77, 55.

183. Giroux, above n 69, 432. See also Katarina Tomaševski, *Report Submitted by the Special Rapporteur*, UN Doc E/CN.4/2004/45 (15 January 2004) [16].

184. Peters, above n 10, 91. See also Katarina Tomaševski, *Report Submitted by the Special Rapporteur*, UN Doc E/CN.4/2004/45 (15 January 2004) [8].

185. Tobin, 'Beyond the Supermarket Shelf', above n 107, 278–9.

186. Ife, above n 146, 91.

and a harmonious society.[187] Further, the human rights-based approach is compelling because '[s]tates have voluntarily accepted the obligations imposed by the international human rights instruments'[188] from which the international human rights doctrine gains both moral and legal force.[189]

Yet the human rights-based approach also faces problems, the most significant being excessive demand for free higher education, propelled by the growing phenomenon of 'credentialism.'[190] Gareth Williams's argument, that free higher education together with credentialism may result in 'an ever longer and eventually a lifelong scramble for qualifications', is more than plausible.[191] Rather than discard the concept of rights for an uncompromising market-based approach, however, such issues can be addressed within the human rights-based approach.

Ultimately, this analysis is limited by its theoretical nature. Higher education policy frameworks do not exist in theory but in reality; they do not exist as a 'pure case'[192] but are a hybrid of different ideas and objectives. It remains necessary, then, to consider existing state higher education policies, analyse them in terms of the theoretical frameworks discussed above and draw some conclusions based on this evidence as to the merits of the market-based and human rights-based systems. This work will have the added benefit of 'raising public debate . . . [and] creating greater policy awareness',[193] as well as working for a re-legitimisation of the right to education as it applies to higher education.[194] Thus, Chapter 3 in Part Two of this book establishes a framework that can be used to evaluate state higher education policies in terms of their teaching and learning function. In Chapter 4 this framework will be drawn upon to consider existing state higher education policies.

187. See Ivan A Snook and Colin Lankshear, *Education and Rights* (Melbourne University Press, 1979) 35.

188. Tobin, 'Beyond the Supermarket Shelf', above n 107, 298.

189. See Ball, above n 80, 291; Kishore Singh, 'The Right to Education: International Legal Obligations' (2005) 1 *International Journal of Education Law and Policy* 103, 109; Australian Human Rights Commission, above n 89; Tobin, 'Beyond the Supermarket Shelf', above n 107, 278.

190. Williams, above n 77, 106–7.

191. Ibid.

192. Esping-Andersen, above n 4, 28–9.

193. Singh, above n 189, 118.

194. See Katarina Tomaševski, *Annual Report of the Special Rapporteur on the Right to Education*, UN Doc E/CN.4/2001/52 (11 January 2001) [84].

REFERENCE LIST

A. Articles/Books/Reports

Anderson, Kirsten, 'How Can a Rights-Based Approach to Development Programming Help to Achieve Quality Education? Evaluating the Education Guarantee Scheme in Madhya Pradesh' (2006) 2 *Asia-Pacific Journal on Human Rights and the Law* 75

Ball, Olivia, 'Conclusion' in Paul Gready and Jonathan Ensor (eds), *Reinventing Development? Translating Rights-Based Approaches from Theory into Practice* (Zed Books, 2005) 278

Barnett, Ronald, 'Editorial' (1996) 21(1) *Studies in Higher Education* 3

Barroso, Luís Roberto, 'Here, There, and Everywhere: Human Dignity in Contemporary Law and in the Transnational Discourse' (2012) 35 *Boston College International & Comparative Law Review* 331

Bennett, Daniel L, 'Myth Busting: The Laissez-Faire Origins of American Higher Education' (2014) 18(4) *The Independent Review* 503

Besson, Samantha, 'Justifications', in Daniel Moeckli, Sangeeta Shah and Sandesh Sivakumaran (eds), *International Human Rights Law* (2nd ed, Oxford University Press, 2014) 34

Brennan, John, and Rajani Naidoo, 'Higher Education and the Achievement (and/or Prevention) of Equity and Social Justice' (2008) 56(3) *Higher Education* 287

Brown, Roger, 'Introduction' in Roger Brown (ed), *Higher Education and the Market* (Routledge, 2011) 1

Brown, Roger, 'Markets and Non-Markets' in Roger Brown (ed), *Higher Education and the Market* (Routledge, 2011) 6

Brown, Roger, 'The Impact of Markets' in Roger Brown (ed), *Higher Education and the Market* (Routledge, 2011) 20

Brunner, José Joaquín, 'Chile: Challenges to Autonomy and Accountability in a Privatized Context' (2013) 3 *Leadership and Governance in Higher Education* 1

Chapman, Audrey, 'Human Dignity, Bioethics, and Human Rights' (2011) 3 *Amsterdam Law Forum* 3

Coomans, Fons, 'Content and Scope of the Right to Education as a Human Right and Obstacles to Its Realization' in Yvonne Donders and Vladimir Volodin (eds), *Human Rights in Education, Science and Culture: Legal Developments and Challenges* (UNESCO Publishing, 2007)

Cornwall, Andrea and Celestine Nyamu-Musembi, 'Putting the "Rights-Based Approach" to Development into Perspective' (2004) 25(8) *Third World Quarterly* 1415

Covell, Katherine, 'School Engagement and Rights-Respecting Schools' (2010) 40(1) *Cambridge Journal of Education* 39

Devidal, Pierrick, 'Trading Away Human Rights? The GATS and the Right to Education: A Legal Perspective' in Dave Hill and Ravi Kumar (eds), *Global Neoliberalism and Education and its Consequences* (Routledge, 2009) 73

Dill, David D, 'Higher Education Markets and Public Policy' (1997) 10(3)–(4) *Higher Education Policy* 167

Esping-Andersen, Gosta, *The Three Worlds of Welfare Capitalism* (Polity Press, 1990)

Fincher, Mark and Stephen Katsinas, 'Testing the Limits of the Price Elasticity of Potential Students at Colleges and Universities: Has the Increased Direct Cost to the Student Begun to Drive Down Higher Education Enrolment?' (2017) 39(1) *Journal of Higher Education Policy and Management* 31

Giroux, Henry A, 'Neoliberalism, Corporate Culture, and the Promise of Higher Education' (2002) 72(4) *Harvard Educational Review* 425

Goedegebuure, Leo, Frans Kaiser, Peter Maassen and Egbert de Weert, 'Higher Education Policy in International Perspective: An Overview' in Leo Goedegebuure, Frans Kaiser, Peter Maassen, Lyn Meek, Frans van Vught and Egbert de Weert (eds), *Higher Education Policy: An International Comparative Perspective* (Pergamon Press, 1993) 1

Gready, Paul and Jonathan Ensor, 'Introduction' in Paul Gready and Jonathan Ensor (eds), *Reinventing Development? Translating Rights-Based Approaches from Theory into Practice* (Zed Books, 2005) 1

Gunn, Andrew, 'The Role of Political and Policy Studies in Higher Education Policy Research' 1 *Theory and Method in Higher Education Research* 27

Harris, Neville, *Education, Law and Diversity* (Hart Publishing, 2007)

Hodgson, Douglas, *The Human Right to Education* (Ashgate, 1998)

Husen, Torsten, 'Open Admissions and Numerus Clausus—Causes and Consequences', in Gordon Roderick and Michael Stephens (eds), *Higher Education for All?* (Routledge, 2012) 187

Ife, Jim, *Human Rights from Below: Achieving Rights through Community Development* (Cambridge University Press, 2010)

Katz, Michael B, 'Public Education as Welfare' (Summer, 2010) *Dissent* 52

Klees, Stephen J, 'A Quarter Century of Neoliberal Thinking in Education: Misleading Analyses and Failed Policies' (2008) 6(4) *Globalisation, Societies and Education* 311

Lundy, Laura and Lesley McEvoy, 'Developing Outcomes for Educational Services: A Children's Rights-Based Approach' (2009) 1(1) *Effective Education* 43

Lynch, Kathleen, 'Equality in Education' (2001) 90(360) *Studies* 395

Lynch, Kathleen, 'Equality and Education: A Framework for Theory and Action' in Mary Ann Lyons and Fionnuala Waldron (eds), *Perspectives on Equality: The Second Seamus Heaney Lectures* (The Liffey Press, 2005) 121

Lynch, Kathleen, 'International League Tables and Rankings in Higher Education: An Appraisal' in Imelda Elliott, Michael Murphy, Alain Payeur and Raymond Duval (eds), *Mutations de L'Enseignement Supérieur et Internationalisation* (De Boeck, 2011) 19

Lynch, Kathleen, 'New Managerialism, Neoliberalism and Ranking' (2014) 13 *Ethics in Science and Environmental Politics* 141

Lynch, Kathleen and Claire O'Riordan, 'Inequality in Higher Education: A Study of Class Barriers' (1998) 19(4) *British Journal of Sociology of Education* 445

Lynch, Kathleen and John Baker, 'Equality in Education: An Equality of Condition Perspective' (2005) 3(2) *Theory and Research in Education* 131

Macpherson, Ian, 'The Rights-Based Approach to Adult Education: Implications for NGO-Government Partnerships in Southern Tanzania' (2009) 39(2) *Compare: A Journal of Comparative and International Education* 263

Marginson, Simon, 'The Impossibility of Capitalist Markets in Higher Education' (2013) 28(3) *Journal of Education Policy* 353

Maynard, Alan, 'Economic Aspects of State Intervention', in Gordon Roderick and Michael Stephens (eds), *Higher Education for All?* (Routledge, 2012) 112

McCowan, Tristan, 'The Growth of Private Higher Education in Brazil: Implications for Equity and Quality' (2004) 19(4) *Journal of Education Policy* 453

McCowan, Tristan, 'Expansion without Equity: An Analysis of Current Policy on Access to Higher Education in Brazil' (2007) 53 *Higher Education* 579

McCowan, Tristan, 'Higher Education and the Profit Incentive' in Dave Hill and Ravi Kumar (eds), *Global Neoliberalism and Education and Its Consequences* (Routledge, 2009) 54

McCowan, Tristan, 'Human Rights, Capabilities and the Normative Basis of "Education for All"' (2011) 9(3) *Theory and Research in Education* 283

McCowan, Tristan, *Education as a Human Right: Principles for a Universal Entitlement to Learning* (Bloomsbury Academic, 2013)

McMillan, Leah K, 'What's in a Right? Two Variations for Interpreting the Right to Education' (2010) 56 *International Review of Education* 531

McCrudden, Christopher, 'Human Dignity and Judicial Interpretation of Human Rights' (2008) 19 *European Journal of International Law* 655

Naidoo, Rajani, Avi Shankar and Ekant Veer, 'The Consumerist Turn in Higher Education: Policy Aspirations and Outcomes' (2011) 27(11–12) *Journal of Marketing Management* 1142

Nowak, Manfred, 'The Right to Education—Its Meaning, Significance and Limitations' (1991) 9 *Netherlands Quarterly of Human Rights* 418

Oketch, Moses, Tristan McCowan and Rebecca Schendel, 'The Impact of Tertiary Education on Development: A Rigorous Literature Review' (Literature Review, Department for International Development, April 2014)

Peters, Michael, 'Re-Thinking Education as a Welfare Right' (2002) 13(5) *School Field* 79

Rasmussen, Palle, Kathleen Lynch, Jacky Brine, Pepka Boyadjieva, Michael A Peters and Heinz Sunker, 'Education, Equality and the European Social Model' in Roger Dale and Susan Robertson (eds), *Globalisation & Europeanisation in Education* (Symposium Books, 2009) 159

Rioux, Marcia H and Paula C Pinto, 'A Time for the Universal Right to Education: Back to Basics' (2010) 31(5) *British Journal of Sociology of Education* 621

Robeyns, Ingrid, 'Three Models of Education: Rights, Capabilities and Human Capital' (2006) 4(1) *Theory and Research in Education* 69

Schendel, Rebecca and Tristan McCowan, 'Higher Education and Development: Critical Issues and Debates' in Tristan McCowan and Elaine Unterhalter (eds), *Education and International Development: An Introduction* (2015) 275

Schendel, Rebecca, Tristan McCowan and Moses Oketch, 'The Economic and Non-Economic Benefits of Tertiary Education in Low-Income Contexts' (2014) 77 *International Higher Education* 6

Schultz, Theodore W, 'Investment in Human Capital' (1961) 51(1) *American Economic Review* 1

Sen, Amartya, 'Human Development and Financial Conservatism' (1998) 26(4) *World Development* 733

Sinclair, Mark, 'Three Futures for University Provision: The Social Justice Market, Capitalism and Private For-Profit Universities' (2003) 25(2) *Journal of Higher Education Policy and Management* 161

Singh, Kishore, 'The Right to Education: International Legal Obligations' (2005) 1 *International Journal of Education Law and Policy* 103

Sleeman, J F, *The Welfare State: Its Aims Benefits and Costs* (George Allen & Unwin, 1973)

Snook, Ivan A and Colin Lankshear, *Education and Rights* (Melbourne University Press, 1979)

Steier, Francis A, 'The Changing Nexus: Tertiary Education Institutions, the Marketplace and the State' (2003) 57(2) *Higher Education Quarterly* 158

Tilak, Jandhyala B G, 'Financing of Higher Education: Traditional versus Modern Approaches' (2012) 2(1) *Yuksekogretim Dergisi Journal of Higher Education* 28

Tobin, John, 'Beyond the Supermarket Shelf: Using a Rights Based Approach to Address Children's Health Needs' (2006) 14 *The International Journal of Children's Rights* 275

Tobin, John, 'Understanding a Human Rights Based Approach to Matters Involving Children: Conceptual Foundations and Strategic Considerations' in Antonella Invernizzi and Jane Williams, *The Human Rights of Children: From Visions to Implementation* (Ashgate Publishing, 2011) 61

Tomaševski, Katarina, 'Globalizing What: Education as a Human Right or as a Traded Service?' (2005) 12(1) *Indiana Journal of Global Legal Studies* 1

Tomaševski, Katarina, 'Has the Right to Education a Future within the United Nations? A Behind-the-Scene Account by the Special Rapporteur on the Right to Education 1998–2004' (2005) 5 *Human Rights Law Review* 205

Tomaševski, Katarina, *Human Rights Obligations in Education: The 4-A Scheme* (Wolf Legal Publishers, 2006)

Tomlinson, Michael, 'The Impact of Market-Driven Higher Education on Student-University Relations: Investing, Consuming and Competing' (2016) 29 *Higher Education Policy* 149

Tooley, James, 'The "Neo-Liberal" Critique of State Intervention in Education: A Reply to Winch' (1998) 32(2) *Journal of Philosophy of Education* 267

Walker, Melanie, 'A Capital or Capabilities Education Narrative in a World of Staggering Inequalities?' (2012) 32 *International Journal of Educational Development* 384

Willemse, Nienke and Paul de Beer, 'Three Worlds of Educational Welfare States? A Comparative Study of Higher Education Systems across Welfare States' (2012) 22(2) *Journal of European Social Policy* 105

Williams, Gareth, 'The Problems of Financing Higher Education', in Gordon Roderick and Michael Stephens (eds), *Higher Education for All?* (Routledge, 2012) 106

Williams, Jeffrey, 'The Pedagogy of Debt' (2006) 33(4) *College Literature* 155

B. Cases/Constitutions/Legislation

Parliament of Finland, *Constitution of Finland* <http://web.eduskunta.fi/Resource.phx/parliament/relatedinformation/constitution.htx?lng=en>

Suomen perustuslaki 11.6.1999/731, 16 [Ministry of Justice (Finland) unofficial trans, *The Constitution of Finland 11 June 1999*, s 16 <http://www.finlex.fi/fi/laki/kaannokset/1999/en19990731.pdf>

C. Official international documents

Charter of the United Nations

Convention against Torture and Other Cruel, Inhuman or Degrading Treatment or Punishment, opened for signature 10 December 1984, 1465 UNTS 85 (entered into force 26 June 1987)

Convention on the Elimination of All Forms of Discrimination against Women, opened for signature 1 March 1980, 1249 UNTS 13 (entered into force 3 September 1981)

Convention on the Rights of Persons with Disabilities, opened for signature 30 March 2007, 2515 UNTS 3 (entered into force 3 May 2008)

Convention on the Rights of the Child, opened for signature 20 November 1989, 1577 UNTS 3 (entered into force 2 September 1990)

International Convention for the Protection of All Persons from Enforced Disappearance, opened for signature 6 February 2007, 2716 UNTS 3 (entered into force 23 December 2010)

International Convention on the Elimination of All Forms of Racial Discrimination, opened for signature 21 December 1965, 660 UNTS 195 (entered into force 4 January 1969)

International Convention on the Protection of the Rights of All Migrant Workers and Members of Their Families, opened for signature 18 December 1990, 2220 UNTS 3 (entered into force 1 July 2003)

International Covenant on Civil and Political Rights, opened for signature 19 December 1966, 999 UNTS 171 (entered into force 23 March 1976)

International Covenant on Economic, Social and Cultural Rights, opened for signature 19 December 1966, 993 UNTS 3 (entered into force 3 January 1976)

Tomaševski, Katarina, *Progress Report of the Special Rapporteur on the Right to Education,* UN Doc E/CN.4/2000/6 (1 February 2000)

Tomaševski, Katarina, *Annual Report of the Special Rapporteur on the Right to Education,* UN Doc E/CN.4/2001/52 (11 January 2001)

Tomaševski, Katarina, *Annual Report of the Special Rapporteur on the Right to Education,* UN Doc E/CN.4/2002/60 (7 January 2002)

Tomaševski, Katarina, *Report of the Special Rapporteur,* UN Doc E/CN.4/2003/9 (21 January 2003)

Tomaševski, Katarina, *Report Submitted by the Special Rapporteur,* UN Doc E/CN.4/2004/45 (15 January 2004)

UN General Assembly, *Vienna Declaration and Programme of Action,* GA Res 48/121, A/CONF.157/23 (12 July 1993)

Universal Declaration of Human Rights, GA Res 217A (III), UN GAOR, 3rd sess, 183rd plen mtg, UN Doc A/810 (10 December 1948)

D. Other

Australian Human Rights Commission, *Human Rights Based Approaches* <https://www.humanrights.gov.au/human-rights-based-approaches>

Sandkull, Olof, 'Strengthening Inclusive Education by Applying a Rights-based Approach to Education Programming' (Paper presented at the Inclusive and Supportive Education Congress Conference, Glasgow, Scotland, August 2005) 1

Tomaševski, Katarina, 'Removing Obstacles in the Way of the Right to Education' (Right to Education Primers No 1, 2001)

Tomaševski, Katarina, *Manual on Rights-Based Education: Global Human Rights Requirements Made Simple* (2004) UNESCO <http://unesdoc.unesco.org/images/0013/001351/135168e.pdf>

UNESCO, *World Conference on Higher Education: Framework for Priority Action for Change and Development in Higher Education* (9 October 1988) <http://www.unesco.org/education/ educprog/wche/declaration_eng.htm#world%20declaration>

UNESCO, *The Human Rights-Based Approach: Statement of Common Understanding* (2004) UNICEF <http://www.unicef.org/sowc04/files/AnnexB.pdf>

United Nations Children's Fund and United Nations Educational, Scientific and Cultural Organization ('UNICEF and UNESCO'), 'A Human Rights-Based Approach to Education for All' (UNICEF/UNESCO, 2007)

PART TWO

Evaluation of State Approaches

3

Evaluating Higher Education Policy and Legislation

A. INTRODUCTION

Higher education is important because it enables people to engage in deep learning and to contribute to society as citizens through employment; it also empowers them to advance their own lives.[1] It is particularly important for economic growth and should be supported as part of a sector-wide approach. Thus, although countries should allocate resources initially towards lower education stages, investment is also required at the higher education level.

The importance of higher education demands serious consideration as to how it is approached at all levels, from the pedagogy used by academics, to the courses institutions elect to run and the missions they adopt. Perhaps even more important, it also requires analysis of the overarching policy framework relating to the public higher education system. There are countless choices available to states in terms of how to approach higher education, and the choices that are made have significant consequences for the students who attend higher education institutions and the public benefits that flow from teaching and learning activities.

1. See generally David F Labaree, 'Public Goods, Private Goods: The American Struggle over Educational Goals' (1997) 34(1) *American Educational Research Journal* 39.

The Human Rights-Based Approach to Higher Education. Jane Kotzmann.
© Oxford University Press 2018. Published 2018 by Oxford University Press.

Although states must make decisions in relation to how to approach higher education, these decisions must be made within the constraints of international structures. In particular, trade agreements between states can have the effect of dictating the terms of access to higher education. Further, where such terms are tied to the provision of aid, choice in relation to higher education policy can be especially limited. Nevertheless, the reality of such developments underscores the need to think seriously about the approaches that are taken to higher education, at the state level and at the international level.

Deciding on the best approach to higher education, with the objective of achieving quality teaching and learning within a higher education system, requires consideration of the purposes of higher education. As Ronald Barnett notes, 'behind our sense of what constitutes quality, there lies—whether explicitly formed or held tacitly—a view as to the ends that higher education should serve'.[2] However, '[t]he purpose of higher education is a contested issue'[3] that, despite the proliferation of higher education ranking systems, has not been widely considered.[4] Therefore, rather than using ranking systems to inform higher education policy, policymakers need to reflect on the aims of higher education and evaluate higher education policy in light of those aims. To assist in this task, this chapter seeks to develop a conception of the purposes of higher education, as well as a framework for evaluating higher education policy, both in substance and effect, against those purposes.[5]

B. THE PURPOSES OF HIGHER EDUCATION

1. Introduction

Identifying the purposes of higher education is difficult for a number of reasons.[6] First, higher education is a social construction. This means that identifying its

2. Ronald Barnett, 'The Idea of Quality: Voicing the Educational' (1992) 46(1) *Higher Education Quarterly* 3, 5. See also Christopher Pollitt, 'Measuring University Performance: Never Mind the Quality, Never Mind the Width?' (1990) 44(1) *Higher Education Quarterly* 60, 65.

3. Kim Watty, 'Addressing the Basics: Academics' View of the Purpose of Higher Education' (2006) 33(1) *The Australian Educational Researcher* 23, 26.

4. Michael Allen, *The Goals of Universities* (Open University Press, 1988) 14. Although this reference is from 1988, the situation remains largely unchanged.

5. This chapter is concerned with the public provision of higher education, and references to 'higher education' should be interpreted accordingly.

6. Edward LeRoy Long, Jr, *Higher Education as a Moral Enterprise* (Georgetown University Press, 1992) 1. See also John Sizer, 'Assessing Institutional Performance and Progress' in Leslie Wagner (ed), *Agenda for Institutional Change in Higher Education* (SRHE, 1982) 33, 35–6. Note that the purposes of higher education identified in this chapter may potentially be extended to lower levels of education.

purposes 'is a political, and not a technical, problem'.[7] The purposes must be negotiated and decided by people, which is difficult because higher education can potentially be directed towards countless ends and people have different views on which ends are important.[8] For example, in their study of higher education institution mission statements, Christopher C Morphew and Matthew Hartley noted that common elements included, '[t]he notion of serving the local area . . . [c]ommitment to diversity . . . the importance of instilling civic duty . . . [and] the importance of a broad, liberal arts education'.[9]

Second, the purposes of higher education may legitimately differ between institutions.[10] Higher education institutions do not necessarily operate as one-stop-shops; instead, they may choose to focus on different disciplines and different objectives. For example, whereas one institution may elect to focus on developing a strong research capacity, another may choose to pursue policies for social inclusion. Although there is no necessity for an institution to choose only one purpose, it is legitimate for an institution to focus on particular aims.

Despite the difficulty of identifying the purposes of higher education, it is an important task. Without an understanding of the purposes to which higher education should be directed, it is impossible to meaningfully evaluate higher education policy. As David Billing asserts, '[b]efore we can judge institutions of higher education, we must make up our minds what they are for. Before they can judge themselves, institutions must decide what they are for'.[11] Similarly, Radford notes that '[t]he value of what is done in higher education, and the scope of its endeavours . . . are inextricably linked with conceptions of its purpose'.[12] As purposes may vary between institutions, the core aims that underpin a higher education system need to be established.[13]

7. Labaree, above n 1, 40–1.

8. Allen, above n 4, 13–14.

9. Christopher C Morphew and Matthew Hartley, 'Mission Statements: A Thematic Analysis of Rhetoric across Institutional Type' (2006) 77(3) *The Journal of Higher Education* 456, 464.

10. See Leo Goedegebuure, Frans Kaiser, Peter Maassen, Lynn Meek, Frans van Vught and Egbert de Weert, 'International Perspectives on Trends and Issues in Higher Education Policy' in Leo Goedegebuure, Frans Kaiser, Peter Maassen, Lyn Meek, Frans van Vught and Egbert de Weert (eds), *Higher Education Policy: An International Comparative Perspective* (Pergamon Press, 1993) 315, 317.

11. David Billing, 'Judging Institutions' in Graeme C Moodie (ed), *Standards and Criteria in Higher Education* (SRHE & NFER-Nelson, 1986) 65, 65.

12. John Radford, 'The Changing Purposes of Higher Education' in John Radford, Kjell Raaheim, Peter de Vries and Ruth Williams (eds), *Quantity and Quality in Higher Education* (Jessica Kingsley Publishers, 1997) 7, 7.

13. See R A Barnett, 'Institutions of Higher Education: Purposes and 'Performance Indicators' (1988) 14(1) *Oxford Review of Education* 97, 98.

Identifying a general set of aims for higher education should begin with an understanding of existing agreements as to what those purposes are. In this respect, the *World Declaration on Higher Education for the Twenty-First Century*, adopted at the World Conference on Higher Education at which 182 states were represented, provides that the mission of higher education is 'to contribute to the sustainable development and improvement of society as a whole' and includes responsibility to (among other things):

> a. educate highly qualified graduates and responsible citizens able to meet the needs of all sectors of human activity. . . .
> b. provide opportunities . . . for higher learning and for learning throughout life . . . to educate for citizenship and for active participation in society. . . .
> c. advance, create and disseminate knowledge through research. . . .
> d. help understand, interpret, preserve, enhance, promote and disseminate national and regional, international and historic cultures. . . .
> e. help protect and enhance societal values . . . [and]
> f. contribute to the development and improvement of education at all levels.[14]

As these aims are the product of broad consensus, they should inform any understanding of the purposes of higher education; thus they inform the purposes put forward in this chapter.

Although debate continues as to whether higher education should be undertaken 'for its own sake', or 'more properly dedicated to the preparation of people to serve society',[15] both ends can be pursued. Higher education (or education in general) cannot be provided purely for individual purposes, because if that were the case there would be no reason to provide it with public support or finance.[16] Higher education cannot be provided only for the public good, however, as ultimately it is the individual who must achieve it.[17] The reality that the

14. UNESCO, *World Conference on Higher Education: World Declaration on Higher Education for the Twenty-First Century: Vision and Action* (9 October 1998) [art 1].

15. Long, above n 7, 12. See also Allen, above n 4, 15–16, 20–2, 156.

16. See Harold T Shapiro, *A Larger Sense of Purpose: Higher Education and Society* (Princeton University Press, 2005) 90.

17. Ronald Barnett, *Improving Higher Education: Total Quality Care* (Open University Press, 1992) 33–4.

benefits of higher education are both private and public supports this assertion that higher education must operate for the individual for intrinsic and instrumental reasons as well as for society. Thus, Clark Kerr's concept of the 'multiversity . . . a concept of the university as having a multiplicity of purposes',[18] is adopted here. It is important to note that the common theme behind the asserted purposes of higher education is a commitment to 'what is morally right and fundamentally good'.[19] As a public institution, it would be illogical for higher education to operate without such commitment.

2. Education for Individual Transformation

An important purpose of higher education is to empower individuals through their own self-development.[20] For example, the mission statement for McMaster University cites a purpose of 'inspir[ing] critical thinking [and] personal growth';[21] Boston University's includes being 'committed to educating students to be reflective, resourceful individuals',[22] while the University of Virginia aims for the 'development of the full potential of talented students'.[23] Through education, students are exposed to knowledge and ideas, and through engagement with them they are likely to find that aspects of themselves strengthen and change. The purpose is thus one of transformation and encompasses a number of different aims, including exposure to academic knowledge, development of 'autonomy and integrity', and development of intellectual skills and perspectives.[24] In Barnett's words, this objective is 'educational in orientation and . . . concerned with the development of the minds of individual students'.[25]

18. Allen, above n 4, 20. See generally Clark Kerr, 'The Idea of a Multiversity' in Clark Kerr (ed), *The Uses of the University* (Oxford University Press, 2001) 1; Stefan Collini, *What Are Universities For?* (Penguin Books, 2012) 3–19.

19. Long, above n 7, xiii.

20. See P T Gibbs, 'Isn't Higher Education Employability?' (2000) 52(4) *Journal of Vocational Education and Training* 559, 560.

21. McMaster University, *University Mission Statement and Vision* <http://www.mcmaster.ca/univsec/reports_lists/mission.cfm>.

22. Boston University, *Mission Statement* <http://www.bu.edu/info/about/mission-statement/>.

23. University of Virginia, *Mission Statement* (18 April 2014) <http://www.virginia.edu/statementofpurpose/purpose.html>.

24. Barnett, 'The Idea of Quality', above n 2, 7–8 (emphasis altered).

25. Ibid 8–9.

The purpose of transformation is fundamental in that it is, and has always been, central to the concept of higher education.[26] It can also be considered fundamental to the extent that other concepts of purpose—for example, fitness for purpose or value for money—may be considered ways of achieving the transformative purpose rather than purposes in their own right.[27] Further, the perceived importance of the transformative purpose goes some way towards explaining the 'history of higher education being seen as something valuable in its own right'.[28]

Thus, what is valued according to the purpose of transformation is the extent to which students learn about themselves and the world, and gain different and deeper perspectives.[29] This learning includes intellectual abilities such as being able to use logic, make connections, argue, and engage in critical reflection.[30] It also includes aspects of character, including the development of morals and values.[31] The end goal of transformation should be students who are academically competent and are able to operate independently and be self-critical.[32]

3. Education for Social Mobility

Higher education may be directed towards the purpose of social mobility, enabling individuals to improve their life circumstances and extend their 'life chances'.[33] According to David F Labaree, the goal of social mobility 'argues that education is a commodity, the only purpose of which is to provide individual students with a competitive advantage in the struggle for desirable social positions'.[34] To this end, it 'asserts that schools should provide students with the educational credentials they need in order to get ahead'.[35] From this perspective,

26. See Watty, 'Addressing the Basics', above n 3, 34.

27. Lee Harvey, 'Quality Is Not Free! Quality Monitoring Alone Will Not Improve Quality' (1997) 3(2) *Tertiary Education and Management* 133, 140.

28. Ibid 139.

29. See Shapiro, above n 16, 7.

30. Ronald Barnett, 'Entry and Exit Performance Indicators: Some Policy and Research Issues' (1988) 13(1) *Assessment and Evaluation in Higher Education*, 16, 21.

31. Anne Colby and Thomas Ehrlich with Elizabeth Beaumont, Jennifer Rosner and Jason Stephens, 'Introduction: Higher Education and the Development of Civic Responsibility' in Thomas Ehrlich (ed), *Civic Responsibility and Higher Education* (Oryx Press, 2000) xxi, xxvii.

32. Barnett, 'Institutions of Higher Education', above n 13, 107–8.

33. Barnett, 'The Idea of Quality', above n 2, 5–6.

34. Labaree, above n 1, 42.

35. Ibid 50.

higher education is beneficial for the individual, because it enables the individual to improve his or her situation relative to others in society. For example, by obtaining a law degree, an individual is equipped to obtain a position as a lawyer, which is likely to result in the individual gaining a better salary and enjoying expanded career opportunities in the future.

In contemporary times, the goal of social mobility has been strongly emphasised by higher education institutions, students and society.[36] Kem Saichaie and Morphew note in their study of college and university websites that '[i]nstitutions in our sample emphasized their educational role as levers for individual advancement and enjoyment rather than as a broader instrument for improving communities and society' and that 'the messages . . . on their websites . . . promoted—nearly exclusively—contemporary social mobility aims'.[37] A cursory analysis of university mission statements supports this assertion. The University of Phoenix aims to 'enable students to develop knowledge and skills necessary to achieve their professional goals',[38] part of Oregon State University's mission is to produce 'graduates competitive in the global economy',[39] and Central Michigan University includes an aim 'to prepare students for productive careers'.[40]

This emphasis on the social mobility goal has led to the experience of credentialism, by virtue of which increasingly higher qualifications are required to do particular jobs.[41] To return to the example of the lawyer, to date the qualification required to obtain a position as a lawyer in Australia has been an undergraduate law degree. In the future, however, credentialism may result in a need to obtain both an undergraduate law degree and a specialist law master's degree, or a juris doctor (postgraduate) law degree, in order to be competitive in the job market. Although credentialism provides individuals with a means to get ahead in life, ultimately it simply preserves the existing hierarchy, as it is not possible for everyone to advance within a hierarchy. In this respect, Labaree explains that credentialism 'preserves the probability of social stasis and social reproduction,

36. See ibid 43.

37. Kem Saichaie and Christopher C Morphew, 'What College and University Websites Reveal about the Purposes of Higher Education' (2014) 85(4) *The Journal of Higher Education* 499, 522–3.

38. University of Phoenix, *Mission and Purpose* <http://www.phoenix.edu/about_us/about_university_of_phoenix/mission_and_purpose.html>.

39. Oregon State University, *Mission Statement* <http://oregonstate.edu/main/mission>.

40. Central Michigan University, *University Mission, Vision and Values* (2 December 2010) <https://www.cmich.edu/about/Pages/university_goals.aspx>.

41. See Labaree, above n 1, 71–3.

because the likelihood of getting ahead is limited by the social structure's pyramid shape'.[42]

There are two significant problems with directing higher education towards the goal of social mobility. The first is that placing the focus on the instrumental value of education, in the form of the credential available, diminishes the importance of learning and education itself.[43] In this context, Labaree observes that the social mobility purpose makes 'credentials a more important acquisition for students than knowledge and skills'.[44] If students are encouraged to focus on gaining qualifications, and getting the best possible results within qualifications, in order to get a job, the rational student response will be to look for the quickest and easiest ways to achieve the best qualifications, regardless of the learning achieved (or not achieved) in the process. The result is that education is reconceptualised as a commodity to be purchased for social advancement, and credentials become more highly valued than the learning itself.[45]

The second problem with adopting the social mobility goal for higher education is that it is underpinned by inequality. Ultimately, not everyone is able to be the best or to obtain the best jobs. As John Brennan and Rajani Naidoo identify, for higher education to enable individual social mobility there needs to be 'room at the top'.[46] Social mobility encourages individuals to seek to better their own life circumstances, but inevitably this is at the cost of the circumstances of others in society.

Advocates might argue that social mobility is about enabling equal opportunity, and awards the best life circumstances on the basis of merit. To the extent that education is equally accessible, there is some truth to this argument, and academic merit is certainly a better criterion to determine life circumstances than other individual characteristics that may be used, such as gender, race or age.[47] Where there is not equal access to higher education, however, merit-based entry can end up reproducing social class. In this respect, a lack of equality at the primary and secondary levels of education will also influence the ability of a prospective student to demonstrate 'merit'.

42. See ibid 72.

43. See ibid 55–6.

44. See ibid 72.

45. Ibid.

46. John Brennan and Rajani Naidoo, 'Higher Education and the Achievement (and/or Prevention) of Equity and Social Justice' (2008) 56(3) *Higher Education* 287, 290 (emphasis altered).

47. See Labaree, above n 1, 60.

The social mobility goal, however, shifts the focus of the individual from the enjoyment of education and its value in pursuing a personally desired life path, to a single-minded focus on competing for what society considers to be the best life circumstances. In this respect, it is not going too far to argue that social mobility 'is at core anti-educational',[48] and for this reason it should not be considered a valid objective for higher education.

4. Education for a Better Society

The transformation and social mobility goals both focus on the benefits of higher education for the individual and thus higher education as a private good, but higher education can also be conceived as a public good. In this respect, higher education should be endowed with public purposes.[49] Such purposes are evident in many university mission statements: for example, Griffith University aims to make a 'major contribution to society' and enable its students to 'make meaningful life-long contributions to their communities',[50] Aalto University aims to work 'towards a better world . . . support Finland's success and contribute to Finnish society',[51] and the University of Edinburgh aims to '[m]ake a significant, sustainable and socially responsible contribution to Scotland, the UK and the world'.[52]

An important public goal of higher education is the preparation of individuals as members of society, or education for citizenship.[53] From this perspective, it is important to educate students to fit in with a vision of what society should be.[54]

48. See ibid 68.

49. Shapiro, above n 16, 1.

50. Griffith University, *Mission Statement* <http://www.griffith.edu.au/about-griffith/governance/mission-statement>.

51. Aalto University, *Mission, Vision and Values* (20 March 2014) <http://www.aalto.fi/en/about/strategy/>.

52. The University of Edinburgh, *Mission* (5 April 2011) <http://www.ed.ac.uk/about/mission-governance/mission>.

53. See Shapiro, above n 16, 37–8; Labaree, above n 1, 42; Colby and Ehrlich, with Beaumont, Rosner and Stephens, above n 31, xxxiii; Carol Geary Schneider, 'Educational Missions and Civic Responsibility: Toward the Engaged Academy' in Thomas Ehrlich (ed), *Civic Responsibility and Higher Education* (Oryx Press, 2000) 98, 100; Linda J Sax, 'Citizenship Development and the American College Student' in Thomas Ehrlich (ed), *Civic Responsibility and Higher Education* (Oryx Press, 2000) 3, 3. See generally Tristan McCowan and Sonia Gomez, *Citizenship Education in Commonwealth Countries* (Commonwealth Secretariat, 2012).

54. Lee Benson and Ira Harkavy, 'Saving the Soul of the University: What Is to Be Done?' in Kevin Robins and Frank Webster (eds), *The Virtual University? Knowledge, Markets, and Management* (Oxford University Press, 2002) 169, 184.

Harold T Shapiro, for example, asserts that '[w]e must think . . . about what kind of person, what kind of skills, and what goals should characterize that society, and only then inquire just what type of education . . . contributes to these goals'.[55] Further, it should be noted that this goal requires higher education institutions to teach students for citizenship, at the same time as modelling citizenship values.[56]

According to Labaree, the social citizenship objective may be considered to comprise three distinct characteristics: 'the pursuit of citizenship training, equal treatment, and equal access'.[57] Education for citizenship, as noted above, is based on a notion of the ideal society, which higher education can assist in achieving by teaching for 'a common culture and a sense of shared membership in the community'.[58] Equal treatment may be valued as an aspect of the ideal society, and in the higher education context requires that all students be treated equally.[59] Further, in an ideal society, all people should be granted equal access to higher education, regardless of differentiating characteristics such as gender or physical ability.[60] As Brennan and Naidoo note, access goes beyond the question of private benefit, and is also concerned with public access to the knowledge produced by universities.[61]

In keeping with the notion of higher education for the creation of an ideal society, higher education should also work for social justice ends. Ira Harkavy asserts, for example, that '[i]f the schooling system does not powerfully accelerate social justice . . . then . . . universities must be performing poorly'.[62] Similarly, Kathleen Lynch, Margaret Crean and Marie Moran argue that 'universities have a particular remit to challenge injustice . . . [because they] are quintessentially public interest institutions'.[63] For this purpose, social justice principles should be used throughout higher education institutions and reflected in their processes

55. Shapiro, above n 16, 90.

56. Ibid 105–7.

57. See Labaree, above n 1, 44 (emphasis altered).

58. See ibid 45.

59. But note that equal does not necessarily mean the same.

60. See Labaree, above n 1, 46.

61. Brennan and Naidoo, above n 46, 288.

62. Ira Harkavy, 'The Role of Universities in Advancing Citizenship and Social Justice in the 21st Century' (2006) 1(1) *Education, Citizenship and Social Justice* 5, 8.

63. Kathleen Lynch, Margaret Crean and Marie Moran, 'Equality and Social Justice: The University as a Site of Struggle' in Michael W Apple, Stephen J Ball and Luis Armando Gandin (eds), *The Routledge International Handbook of the Sociology of Education* (Routledge, 2010) 296.

and decisions.[64] Thus, there must be a strong understanding of how to operationalise social justice principles so that they underpin an institution's operations.[65]

Related to the notion of higher education for social justice is the purpose of using higher education 'as a site of resistance'.[66] To achieve a society based on values of social justice, equality and fairness, it is important that there be a space for social comment and critique. Higher education is well equipped to provide this space given its nature as a site of critical thinking and research.[67] However, higher education institutions cannot be politically neutral; rather they must operate, in the words of Freire, for 'domestication or for freedom'.[68] As Lynch, Crean and Moran explain, they 'can indulge in banking education that controls and domesticates thinking in the practice of regurgitation and regulation, or they can engage in critical education that challenges both teacher and student to engage in praxis.'[69] By taking on the role of critic in research and by encouraging critical thinking in students, higher education institutions will contribute towards the realisation of a truly democratic society.[70]

Ultimately, discussion of higher education for the benefit of society is about attributing higher education with the aim of 'creation of a new society—non-violent and non-exploitative—consisting of highly cultivated, motivated and integrated individuals, inspired by love for humanity and guided by wisdom'.[71] This is the goal

64. Ibid 299.

65. Ibid.

66. Kathleen Lynch, 'Equality and Resistance in Higher Education' (1995) 5(1) *International Studies in Sociology of Education* 93, 106. See also Mags Crean and Kathleen Lynch, 'Resistance, Struggle and Survival: The University as a Site for Transformative Education' in Andrew O'Shea and Maeve O'Brien (eds), *Pedagogy, Oppression and Transformation in a 'Post-Critical' Climate* (Bloomsbury Publishing, 2011) 51. See generally Brennan and Naidoo, above n 46, 296–7.

67. Lynch, 'Equality and Resistance in Higher Education', above n 66, 106. See also Lynch, Crean and Moran, above n 63, 297; See generally Ronald Barnett and Carolina Guzman, 'The Human Rights University: A Feasible Utopia' in Claudia Brunner and Josefine Scherling (eds), *Bildung, Menschenrechte, Universitat. Menschenrechts-Bildung and Hochschulen im Wandel als gesellschaftliche Herausforderung* (Drava Verlag, 2012) 269–88.

68. Paulo Freire, quoted in Lynch, Crean and Moran, above n 63, 297. See generally Paulo Freire, *Pedagogy of the Oppressed* (Penguin, 1972).

69. Lynch, Crean and Moran, above n 63, 297.

70. See Long, above n 7, 13.

71. UNESCO, *World Conference on Higher Education: World Declaration on Higher Education for the Twenty-First Century: Vision and Action* (9 October 1998) [art 6(d)]. See also Harkavy, above n 62, 6. See generally Tristan McCowan, 'Educating Citizens for Participatory Democracy: A Case Study of Local Government Education Policy in Pelotas, Brazil' (2006) 26(5) *International Journal of Educational Development* 456.

agreed upon by the representatives at the World Conference on Higher Education and should therefore form the foundation for policy and practice in higher education. Although the goal is lofty, without a firm and aspirational goal, higher education institutions and systems are unlikely to create meaningful change in society.

5. Education for Employment and the Economy

Higher education has also traditionally had the purpose of educating individuals for subsequent employment, or in Barnett's words, 'the production of highly qualified manpower'.[72] This purpose is evident in many university mission statements. For example, Mississippi State University 'embraces its role as a major contributor to the economic development of the state',[73] Duke University's mission includes 'prepar[ing] future members of the learned professions',[74] and Yale University seeks to 'educate [students] . . . for leadership in scholarship . . . [and] the professions'.[75]

The economic purpose is considered the dominant role of higher education by many. For example, Philippe Laredo asserts that '[t]he central role of universities has long been to train students and to prepare them . . . for the professional activities they will later undertake'.[76] Similarly, research shows that the public values higher education primarily for its ability to prepare individuals for employment and thus have a positive impact on the economy.[77]

The view that higher education should train students for employment has prompted a movement for vocationalism in higher education. Proponents argue that higher education should respond to this instrumental purpose.[78] In particular, it has been argued that the traditional focus on academic subjects and

72. Barnett, 'The Idea of Quality', above n 2, 5–6. See also Barnett, 'Institutions of Higher Education', above n 13, 109.

73. Mississippi State University, *Vision and Mission Statements* <http://www.msstate.edu/web/mission.html>.

74. Duke University, *Mission Statement* (23 February 2001) <http://www.trustees.duke.edu/governing/mission.php>.

75. Yale University, *University Mission Statement* <http://www.yale.edu/about/mission.html>.

76. Philippe Laredo, 'Revisiting the Third Mission of Universities: Toward a Renewed Categorization of University Activities?' (2007) 20(4) *Higher Education Policy* 441, 441.

77. Geary Schneider, above n 53, 106.

78. Derek Glover, Sue Law and Andrea Youngman, 'Graduateness and Employability: Student Perceptions of the Personal Outcomes of University Education' (2002) 7(3) *Research in Post-Compulsory Education* 293, 293.

disciplines in the curriculum should be replaced with a focus on training and development of employment skills.[79]

This view of higher education may be labelled the social efficiency approach, which is based on the idea that education must prepare individuals for employment, as this is vital for the economic well-being of all individuals.[80] In this respect, what is important is the economy rather than higher education; governments should invest in higher education because of its economic benefit.[81] Jamil Salmi explains the point well: higher education is crucial because it 'helps countries build globally competitive economies by developing a skilled, productive, and flexible labor force and by creating, applying, and spreading new ideas and technologies'.[82] Further, in recent times, the concept of the knowledge-based economy has prompted an increased focus on higher education as a means for economic growth.

Although there is merit to the social efficiency goal, there is a danger in overemphasising it and ignoring the other purposes of higher education. If higher education is dedicated solely to producing productive, skilled people for the labour market, then this will inevitably influence what is taught in higher education institutions as well as how it is taught. A higher education system devoted primarily to social efficiency may assist in achieving economic growth, but is unlikely to contribute towards a society that has strong values or is socially just.[83]

6. Conclusion: Purposes of Higher Education

Higher education institutions are public institutions and must serve a number of purposes;[84] hence Kerr's concept of the 'multiversity' is particularly helpful.[85] These purposes may be usefully categorised as including individual

79. See Labaree, above n 1, 47.

80. See ibid 42.

81. Elaine El-Khawas, Robin DePieto-Jurand and Lauritz Holm-Nielsen, 'Quality Assurance in Higher Education: Recent Progress; Challenges Ahead' (LCSHD Paper Series No 23, World Bank, September 1998) 1. See also Roger King, 'What Is Higher Education For? Strategic Dilemmas for the Twenty-First Century University' (1995) 3(4) *Quality Assurance in Education* 14, 14; Allen, above n 4, 28.

82. Jamil Salmi, *The Challenge of Establishing World-Class Universities* (World Bank, 2009) 2.

83. See Tristan McCowan, 'The Elusive Notion of Quality in the Bologna Process' in Joao Menelau Paraskeva (ed), *Unaccomplished Utopia: Neoconservative Dismangling of Public Higher Education in the European Union* (Sense, 2010) 95, 95. See also, Gibbs, above n 20, 559–60.

84. McCowan, 'The Elusive Notion of Quality', above n 83, 103.

85. See Allen, above n 4, 20; Kerr, above n 18, 1; Collini, above n 18, 3–19.

transformation, the betterment of society and social efficiency. Whereas the betterment of society and social efficiency goals are public in nature, reflecting the status of higher education as a public good, the transformation goal is private, which recognises that ultimately it is the individual who must do the work to achieve higher education.[86]

Public policy should be developed to ensure that the higher education system takes a balanced approach towards these goals. As noted above, an overemphasis on the social efficiency goal can be potentially detrimental to the ability of higher education to instil values and contribute to justice in society. Similarly, overemphasis of the transformation and betterment of society goals is likely to result in a neglect of the social efficiency goal, and thus be a potential detriment to the economy and individual standard of living. The need to keep a balance among educational goals suggests the importance of ensuring that higher education institutions are operating in pursuit of these goals. It is essential, therefore, to have a framework for evaluating higher education policy.

C. EVALUATING HIGHER EDUCATION POLICY AND LEGISLATION

1. Introduction

Government policy and legislative frameworks relating to higher education have a significant influence on the higher education system and individual higher education institutions. This is because policy, together with legislation used to enact it, determines a range of aspects of higher education. Policy will dictate, for example, whether higher education is funded through taxpayer money or directly from students. It will also determine the extent to which higher education is regulated by government or subjected to market forces. Similarly, it is by virtue of policy that decisions are made on which institutions are able to operate in the higher education sector and which higher education functions are valued most.

To enable governments to adopt the best policy approaches, the approaches need to be able to be evaluated. Although this is a difficult and complex task[87] and cannot be 'absolutely objective',[88] it is the only way to ensure that policy decisions

86. See Labaree, above n 1, 51.

87. Adela Garcia-Aracil and Davinia Palomares-Montero, 'Examining Benchmark Indicator Systems for the Evaluation of Higher Education Institutions' (2009) 60 *Higher Education* 217, 219.

88. Nian Cai Liu and Ying Cheng, 'The Academic Ranking of World Universities' (2005) 30(2) *Higher Education in Europe* 127, 135.

are research based.[89] Further, it is also central to ensuring that changes to policy are directed at 'quality improvement'.[90] In this context, it should be noted that the aim of evaluating higher education policy is to 'generate increased efforts to improve the educational system'.[91] In tandem with this aim, identifying the signs of effective higher education policy should also operate to enable the provision of 'better information about the quality of education' in our higher education systems for 'policymakers, educators and the public'.[92]

This section endeavours to identify some relevant signs of effective higher education policy, which will enable a comparison between state policy approaches to higher education.[93] In this respect, the analysis will consider both the substance of policy and some of its effects. Although it may be desirable to undertake an evaluation of the effects of policy detached from substance, the nature of the purposes of higher education teaching and learning make this an extremely difficult, perhaps impossible, task. The signs identified below have been chosen as they are reflective of particular purposes of higher education, together represent a methodologically pluralistic approach, and are measurable. In identifying these signs, it is not contended that they will conclusively indicate whether a particular policy approach meets or is likely to meet the aims of higher education teaching and learning. Rather, the signs that are identified should be taken as pointers that are suggestive of a system which enables the achievement of those purposes. It is acknowledged that an assumption that these signs are comparable across states does underpin the analysis.[94]

In identifying signs of a successful higher education system, a methodologically pluralistic approach is taken in order to gain a detailed, comprehensive understanding of the impact of policy on higher education systems and their ability to achieve all of their aims.[95] This discussion therefore includes reference

89. See Graeme C Moodie, 'Fit for What?' in Graeme C Moodie (ed), *Standards and Criteria in Higher Education* (SRHE & NFER-Nelson, 1986) 1, 2.

90. See Heather Fry, 'Quality Judgements and Quality Improvement' (1995) 49(1) *Higher Education Quarterly* 59, 76.

91. J Douglas Willms, 'The Challenge of Developing New Educational Indicators' (1995) 17(1) *Educational Evaluation and Policy Analysis* 113, 115.

92. Rolf K Blank, 'Developing a System of Education Indicators: Selecting, Implementing and Reporting Indicators' (1993) 15(1) *Educational Evaluation and Policy Analysis* 65, 77.

93. See Linda Hantrais, *International Comparative Research: Theory, Methods and Practice* (Palgrave Macmillan, 2009) 120.

94. See ibid 67.

95. See ibid 95–117. See generally Pollitt, above n 2, 77.

to both numerical and non-numerical signs,[96] and 'draw[s] upon and seek[s] to utilize the fullest range of information and evidence that can reasonably be accumulated'.[97] This analysis is based on the promotion of particular values;[98] in particular it is underpinned by the belief that higher education is 'a place for universal learning, for challenging received orthodoxies, and for promoting social justice and equality'.[99]

2. Preliminary Comments

(a) Measuring the System

The approach taken here is to focus on the quality of the higher education system rather than individual higher education institutions. The analysis is therefore relevant to its intended purpose—enabling a comparison of systems[100]—and at the same time meets 'a longstanding need to shift discussion from the existing rankings of the world's best universities to the standing of the whole higher education system in each country'.[101] This change in discourse is important. As Simon Marginson and Marijk van der Wende note, 'the national identity of [higher education] . . . continues to be more important in the eyes of the world than the institutional identity of the individual [institutions]'.[102] Further, in accordance with the principles of equality and social justice that inform this discussion, what is important is that all people are afforded the opportunity to enjoy quality education, rather than only a select few.[103]

96. See Barnett, 'Institutions of Higher Education', above n 13, 109–10; Barnett, *Improving Higher Education,* above n 17, 108–9.

97. Barnett, *Improving Higher Education,* above n 17, 115–116. See also Barnett, 'The Idea of Quality', above n 2, 13.

98. See Barnett, 'The Idea of Quality', above n 2, 10.

99. Kathleen Lynch, 'Control by Numbers: New Managerialism and Ranking in Higher Education' (2014) *Critical Studies in Education* 190, 202.

100. See generally Simon Marginson and Marijk van der Wende, 'To Rank or to Be Ranked: The Impact of Global Rankings in Higher Education' (2007) 11(3–4) *Journal of Studies in International Education* 306, 321.

101. Ross Williams, Anne Leahy, Gaétan de Rassenfosse and Paul Jensen, 'U21 Ranking of National Higher Education Systems' (Project Report, Melbourne Institute of Applied Economic and Social Research, May 2015) 8.

102. Marginson and van der Wende, above n 100, 307.

103. Tony Sheil, 'Moving beyond University Rankings: Developing a World Class University System in Australia' (2010) 52(1) *Australian Universities' Review* 69, 70.

(B) The Inadequacy of Existing Rankings

A plethora of different ranking systems for higher education exist. In theory, it should be possible to group institutional rankings by country and draw conclusions about the value of the different national approaches to higher education, or alternatively to simply reference existing system rankings. This is not possible, however, because the rankings carry significant limitations to the extent that they may be considered 'practically worthless'.[104]

Rankings of higher education institutions are widely criticised for a number of reasons.[105] First, there are significant methodological problems with institutional rankings.[106] Marginson and van der Wende note, for example, that when 'criteria such as research and student selectivity are adopted as the base of a holistic ranking of institutions . . . the terms of interinstitutional competition are defined by credentialism, not the formative role of higher education'.[107]

Further, rankings only position institutions against 'one model of institution, that of the comprehensive research intensive university, and for the most part are tailored to science-strong and English-speaking universities'.[108] Thus, institutions that adopt different models or missions, focus on different disciplines or operate in countries where English is not a first language are marginalised by institutional rankings.[109] Similarly, the most important ranking systems place little or no emphasis on the quality of teaching within institutions,[110] meaning that any educational purposes that are served through teaching are not reflected in the

104. Collini, above n 18, 17.

105. See Jamil Salmi, 'The Road to Academic Excellence: Lessons of Experience' in Philip G Altbach and Jamil Salmi (eds), *The Road to Academic Excellence: The Making of World-Class Research Universities* (World Bank, 2011) 324. See also Kathleen Lynch, 'New Managerialism, Neoliberalism and Ranking' (2014) 13 *Ethics in Science and Environmental Politics* 141, 141; Kathleen Lynch, 'Neo-Liberalism and Marketisation: The Implications for Higher Education' (2006) 5(1) *European Educational Research Journal* 1, 6; Kathleen Lynch, 'International League Tables and Rankings in Higher Education: An Appraisal' in Imelda Elliott, Michael Murphy, Alain Payeur, Raymond Duval (eds), *Mutations de L'Enseignement Supérieur et Internationalisation* (De Boeck, 2011) 19, 30.

106. See Marginson and van der Wende, above n 100, 321; Jamil Salmi and Alenoush Saroyan, 'League Tables as Policy Instruments: Uses and Misuses' (2007) 19(2) *Higher Education Management and Policy* 24, 43–5.

107. Marginson and van der Wende, above n 100, 320.

108. Ibid 306. See also Liu and Cheng, above n 88, 133; Sheil, above n 103, 72; Sarah S Amsler and Chris Bolsmann, 'University Ranking as Social Exclusion' (2012) 33(2) *British Journal of Sociology of Education*, 283, 287; Lynch, 'Control by Numbers', above n 99, 196.

109. See Marginson and van der Wende, above n 100, 321, 326.

110. Ibid 309–11.

rankings. Lynch sums up the impact of these problems well, noting that 'rankings denigrate by exclusion those activities that cannot be counted in the ordering of things'.[111]

Second, rankings encourage a focus on the characteristics of higher education that can be represented numerically, thus bypassing '[t]he actual value of institutions—as *educational* institutions'.[112] The use of numerical performance indicators is widely questioned. Barnett, for example, argues that '[t]o believe that we can say something of real insight about the quality of an educational process by describing it in numerical terms is an illusion'.[113] Focusing on the numerical indicators themselves, rather than seeing them as information that may prompt further investigation,[114] results in a tendency to overlook the important aspects of education, such as 'the character of the educational processes', in favour of quantitative measures.[115] As Lynch notes, within such an approach, '[q]uestions regarding the value, purpose and politics of higher education and rankings get swept aside [and] . . . [s]ocial justice debates about access, participation and outcomes from higher education are side-lined'.[116] Similarly, the role of the 'public intellectual' is overlooked and thus devalued.[117]

Fourth, institutional rankings focus attention on so-called 'world-class universities' and in so doing, divert attention from 'more fundamental tertiary education needs'.[118] Most ranking systems only rank a very small number of institutions,[119] and therefore cannot be considered a true indicator of the world's best institutions. Further, it takes significant resources, time and energy to build a world-class university such as those that top most ranking systems. Directing these resources to the pursuit of an elite level of research excellence can 'harm an individual university or an academic system'.[120] Ultimately, the impact is felt by

111. Lynch, 'Control by Numbers', above n 99, 199.

112. Barnett, 'Institutions of Higher Education', above n 13, 101–2. See generally Liu and Cheng, above n 88, 132; El-Khawas, DePieto-Jurand and Holm-Nielsen, above n 81, 9.

113. Barnett, 'The Idea of Quality', above n 2, 12.

114. Barnett, 'Entry and Exit Performance Indicators' above n 30, 23–5.

115. Barnett, 'Institutions of Higher Education', above n 13, 101–2.

116. Lynch, 'Control by Numbers', above n 99, 201.

117. Ibid.

118. Salmi, above n 82, 13. See also Sheil, above n 103, 72.

119. See Laredo, above n 76, 453–4; Lynch, 'Control by Numbers', above n 99, 196.

120. Philip G Altbach, 'The Costs and Benefits of World Class Universities' (2004) Jan/Feb *Academe* 20.

people; although a small elite will be able to enjoy a perceived world-class higher education, the majority will need to make sacrifices to enable this to happen.

Although system rankings, as distinct from institutional rankings, also exist, they suffer from some of the same limitations. Tony Sheil notes, for example, that the QS SAFE rankings 'rely on existing results for individual institutions to evaluate 40 national higher education systems'.[121] Thus, given that these system rankings emerge from institutional rankings, the same limitations attach to the outcome. While the Lisbon Council University Systems Ranking (the Lisbon rankings) ranks systems on the basis of its own established criteria, it too, adopts a 'one-size-fits-all approach', overlooking the differences in higher education missions.[122] Further, like most institutional rankings, the Lisbon rankings fail to incorporate any measures of quality in teaching,[123] thus failing to assess the extent to which higher education purposes related to teaching and learning are achieved in different systems. Similarly, although the Universitas 21 rankings do incorporate measures of teaching and assess systems against identified criteria, little explanation is provided in relation to how these criteria were established or how they link with the purposes of higher education teaching and learning.[124]

Finally, perhaps the most important criticism of existing ranking systems is that they omit any in-depth discussion of the purposes of higher education. As discussed above, there is a clear link between notions of purpose and excellence in higher education,[125] and ultimately these concepts are subjective. Most ranking systems neglect to discuss this connection and focus on discourse around excellence without indicating what purposes the supposed excellence relates to.[126] The Lisbon rankings, for example, briefly note that 'our universities and tertiary education systems exist to educate and prepare people to be fully-functioning, well-developed members of our advanced, post-industrial society', before proceeding to identify six criteria for measuring excellence.[127] Although there is nothing

121. Sheil, above n 103, 74–5.

122. Ibid.

123. Ibid.

124. See Williams, Leahy, de Rassenfosse and Jensen, above n 101.

125. Barnett, 'The Idea of Quality', above n 2, 5. See also Pollitt, above n 2, 65.

126. See Times Higher Education, *Times Higher Education World University Rankings 2014–2015* <http://www.timeshighereducation.co.uk/world-university-rankings/2014-15/world-ranking>; Center for World-Class Universities at Shanghai Jiao Tong University, *Methodology*, Academic Ranking of World Universities since 2003 <http://www.shanghairanking.com/ARWU-Methodology-2014.html>.

127. Peer Ederer, Philipp Schuller and Stephan Willms, 'University Systems Ranking: Citizens and Society in the Age of Knowledge' (Policy Brief, The Lisbon Council, 2008) 2–3.

objectionable about this expressed purpose, there is a lack of clarity around what exactly the study counts as the proper purposes of higher education, and how these translate to appropriate measures of excellence. As a result of this omission in rankings, important discussions about purpose, including 'questions of social justice, transformative education, or even the politics, philosophy or sociology of education' are neglected.[128]

3. Signs of a Successful Higher Education System

This section refers to signs rather than indicators because '[i]ndicators are defined as selected statistics intended to inform policymakers, educators, and the public about the condition of the education system',[129] but the signs outlined here include both quantitative and qualitative information. Further, as a result of the clear link between educational purposes and excellence,[130] the signs identified here are directed specifically to determining whether a particular identified purpose is being achieved. A summary of the identified signs is contained in Appendix A.

(a) Signs of Individual Transformation

The educational goal of transformation is directed towards prompting change in students. This goal is generally poorly assessed (or not assessed at all) in existing rankings, owing to the difficulty involved in assessing change in large numbers of students and the complexity involved in assessing teaching quality.[131] Nevertheless, as Barnett notes, higher education 'is essentially an educative process'; thus it is crucial to be able to evaluate the education provided and its impact on students.[132]

It is possible to assess the extent of student transformation by making 'observations and judgments about . . . states of mind and intellectual achievements'.[133]

128. Amsler and Bolsmann, above n 108, 292.

129. Blank, above n 92, 66. Similarly, Rowley defines performance indicators in higher education as 'authoritative, quantitative measures of key attributes of the activities of institutions and their component units'. Jennifer Rowley, 'Measuring Quality in Higher Education' (1996) 2(3) *Quality in Higher Education* 237, 242.

130. Barnett, 'The Idea of Quality', above n 2, 5. See also Pollitt, above n 2, 65.

131. See generally McCowan, 'The Elusive Notion of Quality', above n 83, 98.

132. Barnett, 'The Idea of Quality', above n 2, 16–17. See also El-Khawas, DePieto-Jurand and Holm-Nielsen, above n 81, 12.

133. Barnett, *Improving Higher Education,* above n 17, 138–9.

Given the difficulty of seeking to assess each student's transformation, however, an easier way to collect approximate data regarding student change is through student surveys. Where questions asked of students are relevant, student survey data can assist in measuring the extent to which an institution is enabling student transformation. However, such data are not perfect: students are not necessarily aware of their own transformation, and the transformation may be realised after the survey is undertaken.

Teaching quality is a key factor involved in student learning, but it is difficult to assess as it can take many forms. Some common factors are nevertheless considered important.[134] There is general agreement that quality teaching is characterised by personalised learning.[135] Thus, the extent to which an institution's processes enable personalisation can be used as a sign of teaching quality. Further, providing formal education is not free and thus '[a] necessary condition for a well performing higher education system is that it is adequately resourced'.[136] In this respect, the amount of resources per student can provide some indication of teaching quality.[137] Finally, in order for institutions to have the flexibility to improve and develop courses, it is important that they have sufficient autonomy from government regulation to do so.[138]

Although it is difficult to directly assess teaching quality, it is much more straightforward to assess commitment to teaching, in other words, 'the value that an institution of higher education [or a higher education system] attaches to teaching and learning'.[139] According to John R Baird, 'the most important feature of higher education which must be changed in order that teaching and learning improve is the relative status of teaching and research';[140] thus indicators of a commitment to teaching should serve as a good proxy for quality teaching. In considering this aspect, what should be considered are 'varieties of institutional policy

134. See Tristan McCowan, 'The Growth of Private Higher Education in Brazil: Implications for Equity and Quality' (2004) 19(4) *Journal of Education Policy* 453, 462.

135. See John R Baird, 'Quality: What Should Make Higher Education "Higher"?' (1988) 7(2) *Higher Education Research and Development* 141, 143.

136. Williams, Leahy, de Rassenfosse and Jensen, above n 101, 9.

137. Ibid.

138. Salmi and Saroyan, above n 106, 52.

139. Barnett, *Improving Higher Education,* above n 17, 138–9 (emphasis altered).

140. Baird, above n 135, 147. Note that although this remark dates from 1988, the situation remains unchanged. See, eg, Emmaline Bexley, Richard James and Sophie Arkoudis, 'The Australian Academic Profession in Transition: Addressing the Challenge of Reconceptualising Academic Work and Regenerating the Academic Workforce' (Report, Department of Education, Employment and Workplace Relations, September 2011) in relation to the Australian context.

and practice which tell in support of an institution's claim to take teaching quality seriously'.[141] This may include the educational aims and policies adopted by the institution, the extent to which teaching staff undertake research activities that are relevant to teaching, regularity and nature of course monitoring and review, provision for development of staff teaching capacity, the relevance of teaching capacity and qualification for appointments and promotions, and the extent to which institutional documentation evidences value placed on teaching.[142]

(B) Signs of Improving Society

One of the purposes of higher education is to improve society. A key aspect of this goal is citizenship education,[143] which involves 'citizenship training, equal treatment, and equal access'.[144] To the extent that this goal relates to quality of teaching and learning, it is poorly measured by existing rankings for the reasons described above. Many rankings do, however, measure aspects of equity and access in higher education. The Lisbon rankings, for example, include criteria on inclusiveness and access in higher education.[145]

Measuring citizenship education must begin with a consideration of what kind of society is considered desirable.[146] In a democracy, this can often be ascertained through reference to state higher education policy. Once the state's vision of an ideal society is understood, measuring the state's success in teaching for citizenship will require an analysis of the extent to which these values are embedded in teaching and learning processes and curricula. Further, because teaching for citizenship also requires modelling citizenship values, the analysis will also require consideration of the extent to which state higher education institutions integrate citizenship values into their structures and processes. This approach has the benefit of attributing value to the 'self-definitions' of the state higher education

141. Barnett, *Improving Higher Education,* above n 17, 150.

142. Ibid 140–8. See also in relation to quality of academic staff, Brian Wilson, 'Quality in Universities, Sir Robert Menzies Oration, 4 October 1995' (1996) 18(2) *Journal of Higher Education Policy and Management* 149, 156; Watty, 'Addressing the Basics', above n 3, 25. See also in relation to the importance of critical reflection, Barnett, 'The Idea of Quality', above n 2, 15.

143. See Shapiro, above n 16, 37–38; Labaree, above n 1, 42; Colby and Ehrlich, with Beaumont, Rosner and Stephens, above n 31, xxxiii; Geary Schneider, above n 53, 100; Sax, above n 53, 3; Tristan McCowan, 'Can Schools Make Good Citizens?' in Richard Bailey (ed), *The Philosophy of Education: An Introduction* (Continuum, 2010) 86.

144. See Labaree, above n 1, 44 (emphasis altered).

145. Ederer, Schuller and Willms, above n 127, 3.

146. See Shapiro, above n 16, 90.

sector and its institutions; the unique way in which they define their own goals and vision is 'subjected to critical assessment'.[147]

One particular aspect of teaching for citizenship that should be considered is the extent to which connections between higher education institutions and the local community are fostered. As Harkavy asserts, '[w]hen colleges and universities give very high priority to actively solving strategic, real world, problems in their local community, a much greater likelihood exists that they will significantly advance citizenship, social justice and the public good'.[148]

To gauge the existence of connections to the local community, consideration should be given to the connections among curricula, assessment and local community issues, the relevance of higher education research to solving community problems and any communication channels between higher education institutions and the community. Also relevant will be a broader notion of connectivity, as 'focusing on solving *universal* problems that are manifested in their local communities' will enhance international collaboration and understanding.[149]

Citizenship training also requires equal treatment and equal access in higher education. As L David Weller asserts, '[e]quitable practices of fair and just treatment are crucial in promoting quality education'.[150] Measuring equal treatment should begin with ensuring that there is no discrimination in higher education, and that policies and practices are in place to protect peoples' rights to equal treatment. Further, equal treatment applies not only within higher education institutions, but also between them. Rigorous accreditation requirements should be in place to ensure that all institutions meet appropriate standards, even though they may focus on different disciplines and objectives.[151] Further, higher education funding should be distributed widely, rather than being concentrated on so-called elite institutions, to ensure the capacity of institutions to provide a comparable quality of teaching and research.[152]

Equal access to higher education requires that all people are able to participate in higher education on equal terms. To assess the extent of access, consideration

147. Barnett, *Improving Higher Education,* above n 17, 112.

148. Harkavy, above n 62, 33–4.

149. Ibid.

150. L David Weller, 'The Equity Factor: A Vital Part of the Quality Equation' (1995) 3(4) *Quality Assurance in Education* 44, 44.

151. See Sheil, above n 103, 75.

152. See Rosemary Deem, Ka Ho Mok and Lisa Lucas, 'Transforming Higher Education in Whose Image? Exploring the Concept of the "World-Class" University in Europe and Asia' (2008) 21 *Higher Education Policy* 83, 91.

must be given to government policy as well as institutional admission policies and practices to ensure students are not prevented from admission on discriminatory grounds, for example, as a result of characteristics such as race, gender, language, geographic location, 'financial hardship'[153] or other statuses such as being a refugee, migrant or internally displaced person.[154] It should be noted that admission is a process that covers all the years of enrolment.[155] To ensure that financial hardship does not prevent people from accessing higher education, higher education must be provided free by the state or fees charged and subsidies provided in a way that ensures equal access. Arrangements that allow students to delay payment of their fees without accruing interest on their debt, as well as comprehensive scholarship programs, may assist.

In connection with the overarching aim of improving society, higher education must also be directed towards social justice. Efforts towards this goal may take many different forms. As noted above, directing higher education activities towards addressing local and global issues will improve social justice outcomes.[156] Further, the extent to which traditionally marginalised groups participate in higher education should be considered. In this respect, 'the retention and success of students in their studies' is critical 'for under-represented student groups, [and] increasing diversity'.[157] This is because non-completion has negative implications in the form of 'personal impact and loss of life chances . . . financial implications for students (and their families), and for society and the economy'.[158] Social justice will also be served by ensuring that there is a wide 'choice of alternative forms of higher education', as higher education improves life outcomes and a wider range of choice will improve participation rates.[159] Finally, some states are wealthier than others, and in keeping with the aim of social justice, consideration should be given to the extent to which states engage in international assistance and cooperation in relation to higher education.

153. United Nations Educational, Scientific and Cultural Organization, 'World Education Report' (Report, UNESCO, 2000) 70.

154. See Right to Education Project, 'The Right to Education: Indicators' (May 2013).

155. United Nations Educational, Scientific and Cultural Organization, 'World Education Report' (Report, UNESCO, 2000) 70.

156. Harkavy, above n 62, 33–4.

157. Glenda Crosling, Margaret Heagney and Liz Thomas, 'Improving Student Retention in Higher Education' (2009) 51(2) *Australian Universities' Review* 9, 9.

158. Ibid.

159. Williams, Leahy, de Rassenfosse and Jensen, above n 101, 14.

Finally, higher education institutions must also enjoy autonomy to be able to challenge and oppose others in society.[160] In Lynch's terminology, this involves using higher education 'as a site of resistance'.[161] To assess the extent to which institutions act autonomously, consideration should be given to the existence of any 'direct government interference' in higher education,[162] as well as the extent to which academics enjoy freedom to teach and research. Also relevant will be the actual teaching and research activities of higher institutions, and the extent to which they can be considered to challenge authority for social justice purposes.[163] In this respect, the pedagogical practices of institutions may be considered in terms of whether they promote a banking model of education or critical education.[164]

(c) Signs of Social Efficiency

Higher education is also designed to improve social efficiency, that is, to educate people for employment and to improve the economy.[165] This aspect is generally well represented in existing rankings, as it tends to lend itself to measurement through numerical indicators. The Lisbon rankings, for example, measure '[t]he ability of a country's educational system to produce graduates with skills relevant for the country's labour market' and attractiveness of the higher education system to foreign students.[166] Similarly, the Shanghai Jiao Tong University rankings consider 'Nobel Laureates, Fields Medalists, Highly Cited Researchers . . . [and] papers published in Nature or Science' as well as 'papers indexed by Science Citation Index-Expanded (SCIE) and Social Science Citation Index (SSCI)'.[167]

In assessing the extent to which higher education is able to prepare students for employment, a number of factors may be considered. First, the correlation between higher education courses and types of employment, or the extent to

160. Although 'academic autonomy of itself does not necessarily deliver much by way of equity and social justice and indeed may itself be part of processes of elite reproduction', it is a necessary condition for enabling critical discussion to take place. See Brennan and Naidoo, above n 46, 298. See also Lynch, 'New Managerialism, Neoliberalism and Ranking', above n 105, 141.

161. Lynch, 'Equality and Resistance in Higher Education', above n 66, 106.

162. Williams, Leahy, de Rassenfosse and Jensen, above n 101, 14.

163. See Lynch, Crean and Moran, above n 63, 297.

164. See Freire, above n 68.

165. See Geary Schneider, above n 53, 106; Williams, Leahy, de Rassenfosse and Jensen, above n 101, 19.

166. Ederer, Schuller and Willms, above n 127, 3–4.

167. Center for World-Class Universities at Shanghai Jiao Tong University, above n 126.

which courses are vocationally oriented, will be relevant. Graduation rates will also be relevant in that completion is often required for employment. Similarly, the employability prospects of graduates compared with non-graduates should give insight into the extent to which higher education adds value from an employment perspective (although accepting that this may simply reflect credential inflation). In addition, the existence of significant skills shortages in the economy, resulting in a need to employ foreign workers, can indicate a misalignment between higher education and the employment sector.

Higher education is also intended to provide a public economic benefit. The preparedness of graduates to enter straight into employment will be relevant in measuring this benefit, as their entry into employment supplies human capital, in turn assisting economic growth. It is also important to consider the quality of research undertaken within the system, as research influences teaching and therefore impacts on the extent to which graduates gain cutting-edge knowledge and skills that may then be brought into the employment context.[168] Further, the extent to which the higher education system is 'well connected with the rest of the nation's society and is linked internationally in education and research' is critical in that connectedness indicates the 'absorption of new discoveries and ideas', which will assist the economy.[169] Connectedness can be identified through the number of international students in higher education as well as research collaboration between domestic and international academics.[170]

D. METHODOLOGY FOR EVALUATING SYSTEMS

1. Introduction

This section sets out a detailed and specific methodology for measuring the signs identified in the previous section. Although these signs could be measured in many different ways, particular measures have been selected for ease of analysis, availability and comparability of data, variety in methodological approach (eg, inclusion of both quantitative and qualitative measures), and complementarity. By complementarity it is meant that measures relating to a particular higher education purpose will, together, provide a well-rounded picture as to the extent that that objective may be being achieved. The methodology outlined below will be used in Chapter 4 to analyse higher education policies from six different states in order to determine the relative attractiveness of a human rights-based

168. See Brennan and Naidoo, above n 46, 296.

169. Williams, Leahy, de Rassenfosse and Jensen, above n 101, 16.

170. Ibid.

approach to higher education policy as compared to a market-based approach to higher education policy.

It is acknowledged that some of the measures identified below involve measuring concepts in different ways as between different states. For example, in relation to the first measure, 'student survey responses' (see 2(a) below), the surveys completed in each state do not ask identical questions. Nevertheless, to the extent that directly comparable data is not available or not possible, this methodology explains what is being compared and makes the case for its comparability.

The scales utilised for each measure have been developed to distinguish between the ranges of state conditions. For example, in relation to the measure 'personalised learning' (see 2(b) below), OECD state ratios of students to teaching staff range from 10 (Norway) to 45 (Greece) (although the second highest ratio is only 22 (Czech Republic)), with the average ratio being 17.[171] Thus, the scale utilised is based on bands of 2 percentage points: up to and including 14; 15–16; 17–18; 19–20; above 20. Where signs are qualitative in nature, an assessment rubric has been developed to clarify what is being considered and what constitutes 'very good', 'good', etc (for example, see 'commitment to teaching and learning' at 2(e) below).

2. Individual Transformation

(a) Student Survey Responses

To identify the extent of individual student transformation, the main student surveys conducted within each national system will be considered. Those survey items relevant to individual student transformation will be analysed. Survey responses are ranked according to the percentages of students who agree with individual transformation statements (Table 3.1).

Table 3.1. Assessment Criteria for Student Survey Responses

Rating	Percentage of students who agree with individual transformation statements in student surveys
Very good	Above 80 per cent
Good	Above 70–80 per cent
Average	Above 60–70 per cent
Poor	Above 50–60 per cent
Very poor	Up to 50 per cent

171. Organisation for Economic Cooperation and Development (OECD), 'Education at a Glance 2016: OECD Indicators' (OECD, 2016) 403.

Table 3.2. Assessment Criteria for Personalised Learning

Rating	Ratio of students to teaching staff
Very good	Student-teacher ratio of up to and including 14
Good	Student-teacher ratio of 15–16
Average	Student-teacher ratio of 17–18
Poor	Student-teacher ratio of 19–20
Very poor	Student-teacher ratio above 20

(b) Personalised Learning

In order to gain a snapshot of the processes conducive to personalised learning being utilised in a particular state's higher education system, the ratio of students to teaching staff in bachelor's, master's, doctoral or equivalent degrees will be considered.[172] Although the staff-student ratio is only one measure of the potential for individualised learning, and may not correlate with the use of appropriate teaching pedagogies, it can indicate the extent to which academics are able to individualise their teaching. The relevant criteria for assessing this sign is based on the Organisation for Economic Co-operation and Development (OECD) average student-teacher ratio of 17 (Table 3.2).

(c) Resources per Student

To assess the extent of resources provided to higher education students, the analysis will identify public and private expenditure on higher education as a percentage of gross domestic product (GDP),[173] and expenditure per higher education student in bachelor's, master's and doctoral degrees in dollar terms.[174] The overall ranking of this sign is based on the combination of these factors, with systems close to the OECD average figures rated as average (Table 3.3).

(d) Institutional Autonomy

For the purposes of this analysis, autonomy refers to the closeness of the relationship between the state and the higher education system and its institutions.[175] To

172. Data will be drawn from OECD published information which provides a ratio of students to teaching staff across advanced research programmes, tertiary-type A programmes and tertiary-type B programmes. See ibid.

173. Ibid 206.

174. Ibid 192.

175. See Walter Berka, 'The Legal and Philosophical Meaning of Autonomy in Education' in Walter Berka, Jan De Groof and Hilde Penneman (eds), *Autonomy in Education: Yearbook of the European Association for Education Law and Policy* (Kluwer Law International, 2000) vol 3, 3, 8.

Table 3.3. Assessment Criteria for Resources per Student

Rating	Expenditure on higher education	Expenditure per student
Very good	2.2 per cent of GDP or more	above $20,000
Good	1.8 per cent–2.1 per cent of GDP	$17,001 to $20,000
Average	1.4 per cent–1.7 per cent of GDP	$14,001 to $17,000
Poor	1.0 per cent–1.3 per cent of GDP	$11,001 to $14,000
Very poor	below 1.0 per cent of GDP	$11,000 or less

measure institutional autonomy, consideration is given to the aspects of autonomy relevant to teaching and learning. These are 'freedom to teach . . . to enrol and to hire':[176]

- Freedom to teach is considered in relation to the capacity of higher education institutions to design academic content;
- Freedom to enrol is considered in relation to the capacity of higher education institutions to select students; and
- Freedom to hire is considered in relation to the capacity of higher education institutions to decide on recruitment procedures.[177]

Although institutional autonomy is necessary in order to allow institutions the freedom to improve the 'quality and relevance' of courses,[178] the importance of government regulation in ensuring quality should not be overlooked and is taken into account in this analysis. The relevant criteria for assessing this sign are set out in Table 3.4.

(e) Commitment to Teaching and Learning

To measure the extent to which a higher education system is committed to teaching and learning, this analysis primarily focuses on the extent to which academic recruitment and promotion policies emphasise the importance of teaching and learning. The relevant criteria for assessing this sign are set out in Table 3.5.

176. Greg Craven, 'Pyne's Fine Words Fell on Deaf Ears', *The Australian* (Australia), 12 March 2014. See also Universities Australia, 'An Agenda for Australian Higher Education 2013–2016' (Statement, 2013, Universities Australia) 50; Universities Australia, 'Submission to the Review of Higher Education Regulation' (Submission, Universities Australia, June 2013).

177. See generally Thomas Estermann, Terhi Nokkala and Monika Steinel, 'University Autonomy in Europe II: The Scorecard' (Project Report, European University Association, 15 November 2011).

178. Salmi and Saroyan, above n 106, 52.

Table 3.4. Assessment Criteria for Institutional Autonomy

Rating	Extent of institutional autonomy
Very good	High levels of autonomy in relation to freedom to teach, enrol and hire; strong, sector-wide quality assurance mechanisms.
Good	High levels of autonomy in relation to freedom to teach, enrol and hire, with some limitations; strong quality assurance mechanisms in place.
Average	Autonomy generally granted in relation to freedom to teach, enrol and hire, but significant state control retained; quality assurance mechanisms in place.
Poor	Autonomy granted in relation to some aspects of freedom to teach, enrol or hire, but significant state control retained; weak quality assurance mechanisms.
Very poor	Little autonomy granted in relation to freedom to teach, enrol and hire, sector mainly subject to state control; no quality assurance mechanisms.

Table 3.5. Assessment Criteria for Commitment to Teaching and Learning

Rating	Policy emphasis on importance of teaching and learning
Very good	Sector-wide requirements in place to ensure academic recruitment and promotion places high emphasis on the capacity of academics to teach.
Good	Academic recruitment and promotion policies generally place strong emphasis on capacity of academics to teach.
Average	Variability in institutional practice in relation to the extent to which recruitment and promotion policies place emphasis on capacity of academics to teach.
Poor	Some emphasis in recruitment and promotion policies on capacity of academics to teach, but other criteria of significantly more importance.
Very poor	Minimal or no emphasis in recruitment and promotion policies on capacity of academics to teach.

3. Improving Society

(a) Integration of Values

To measure the extent to which values are integrated throughout the higher education teaching and learning sector, this analysis will focus on identification of values at the macro level. This is because national values must be identified

Table 3.6. ASSESSMENT CRITERIA FOR INTEGRATION OF VALUES

Rating	Extent of integration of values
Very good	Values very clearly identified at macro level.
Good	Values reasonably clearly identified at macro level.
Average	Identification of some values at macro level.
Poor	Values somewhat unclear at macro level.
Very poor	Values very unclear/not identified at macro level.

before they can be integrated throughout higher education. The relevant criteria for assessing this sign are set out in Table 3.6.

(B) TEACHING FOR CITIZENSHIP

To measure the extent to which a state's higher education policy is directed towards educating individuals for citizenship, a review of three university websites from each state will be undertaken. Institutions will be selected for review on the basis that they provide information concerning the institution's strategic plan/vision/mission and/or information as to why students should choose to study at the institution. The review will seek to identify strategic direction and focus in relation to teaching for citizenship. Although it is acknowledged that the declared goals of universities do not always translate into practice, it is submitted that the act of declaring goals does provide some evidence as to what ends higher education institutions consider to be important and thus are likely to pursue. Thus, the relevant criteria for assessing this sign are set out in Table 3.7.

(C) EQUAL OPPORTUNITY

As the OECD notes, educational opportunities can 'promote inclusive growth and reduce inequalities in societies through improved employment opportunities, higher earnings and overall wealth'[179] as well as improve the general well-being of individuals.[180] Providing equal opportunities to access higher education can therefore improve socio-economic circumstances and social harmony.[181] One way in which equal opportunity in access to higher education can be measured is through analysis of intergenerational mobility in education.[182] Individuals

179. OECD, 'Education at a Glance 2016', above n 171, 74.

180. OECD, 'Education at a Glance 2014: OECD Indicators' (OECD, September 2014) 84.

181. OECD, 'Education at a Glance 2016', above n 171, 74–5.

182. As measured by the OECD. See ibid 74–89.

Table 3.7. Assessment Criteria for Teaching for Citizenship

Rating	Emphasis in relation to teaching for citizenship
Very good	All reviewed websites indicated strong strategic direction and focus in relation to teaching for citizenship.
Good	Two or three reviewed websites indicated strategic direction and focus in relation to teaching for citizenship.
Average	One or two reviewed websites indicated strategic direction and/or focus in relation to teaching for citizenship.
Poor	One reviewed website indicated strategic direction and/or focus in relation to teaching for citizenship.
Very poor	No reviewed websites indicated any strategic direction or focus in relation to teaching for citizenship.

whose parents have lower educational attainment are generally less likely to access higher education. Increased intergenerational mobility is indicative of more equal opportunity to access higher education. This analysis will rank countries based on intergenerational mobility in higher education, by parents' educational attainment.[183] Two measures will be considered:

- the percentage of 25–44 year-old non-students accessing tertiary education where their parents have upper secondary or post-secondary non-tertiary education compared with where parents have below upper secondary education; and
- the percentage of 25-44 year-old non-students accessing tertiary education where their parents have tertiary education compared with where parents have upper secondary or post-secondary non-tertiary education.[184]

The assessment criteria (Table 3.8) are based on OECD average likelihoods, where:

- the difference in percentage of 25–44 year-old non-students accessing tertiary education where their parents have upper secondary or post-secondary non-tertiary education compared with where parents have below upper secondary education is 16 per cent; and

183. In this respect, OECD data for tertiary education is used as a proxy for higher education. Analysis is limited to individuals whose parents are native-born, as immigration policies can impact mobility where parents are foreign-born. See ibid.

184. See ibid 85–7.

Table 3.8. Assessment Criteria for Equal Opportunity

Rating	Percentage of 25–44 year-old non-students accessing tertiary education where their parents have upper secondary or post-secondary non-tertiary education compared with where parents have below upper secondary education	Percentage of 25–44 year-old non-students accessing tertiary education where their parents have tertiary education compared with where parents have upper secondary or post-secondary non-tertiary education
Very good	8 per cent and below	20 per cent and below
Good	9–13 per cent	21–25 per cent
Average	14–18 per cent	26–30 per cent
Poor	19–23 per cent	31–35 per cent
Very poor	23 per cent and over	36 per cent and over

- the difference in percentage of 25–44 year-old non-students accessing tertiary education where their parents have tertiary education compared with where parents have upper secondary or post-secondary non-tertiary education is 28 per cent.

(d) Freedom for Teaching and Research

For the purposes of this analysis, freedom for teaching and research refers to the 'freedom of the individual scholar in his/her teaching and research to pursue truth wherever it seems to lead without fear of punishment or termination of employment for having offended some political, religious or social orthodoxy'.[185]

To measure individual academic freedom for teaching and research, this analysis will adopt the approach taken by Karran, Beiter and Appiagyei-Atua.[186] The analysis will utilise a five-point scale to assess the extent of constitutional and legislative compliance with aspects of the UNESCO *Recommendation concerning the Status of Higher-Education Teaching Personnel* (1997).[187] The criteria for assessing this sign are set out in Table 3.9.

185. Leo Goedegebuure, Frans Kaiser, Peter Maassen and Egbert de Weert, 'Higher Education Policy in International Perspective: An Overview' in Leo Goedegebuure, Frans Kaiser, Peter Maassen, Lyn Meek, Frans van Vught and Egbert de Weert (eds), *Higher Education Policy: An International Comparative Perspective* (Pergamon Press, 1993) 1, 8.

186. See Terence Karran, Klaus Beiter and Kwadwo Appiagyei-Atua, 'Measuring Academic Freedom in Europe: A Criterion Referenced Approach' (2017) 1(2) *Policy Reviews in Higher Education* 209, 212–13.

187. UNESCO, *Recommendation concerning the Status of Higher-Education Teaching Personnel*, in Records of the General Conference, 29th sess (21 October to 12 November 1997) 26–36.

Table 3.9. Assessment Criteria for Freedom for Teaching and Research

Rating	Freedom for teaching and research
Very good	Provisions on academic freedom are in full compliance with generally agreed criteria, showing that academic freedom serves as a guiding principle within universities, such that it forms 'general principles' in the higher education legislation, or is referred to in various contexts throughout the legislation.
Good	Provisions exist showing that academic freedom serves as a guiding principle for activity in higher education, but there are a few minor deficits when provisions are assessed in the light of generally agreed criteria on academic freedom.
Average	A general statement is made on academic freedom, but without the necessary elaboration or concretization of this statement elsewhere in the higher education legislation or, where provisions exist addressing academic freedom, they reveal some serious deficits when assessed against generally agreed criteria on academic freedom.
Poor	A general statement is made on academic freedom but there is an absence of elaboration plus limitations or deficiencies (eg, freedom for research is mentioned but not for teaching), or, where provisions exist addressing academic freedom, they reveal major substantial deficits when assessed against generally agreed criteria on academic freedom.
Very poor	There is no reference to academic freedom at all in the Constitution or in higher education legislation.

SOURCE: Adapted from Terence Karran, Klaus Beiter and Kwadwo Appiagyei-Atua, 'Measuring Academic Freedom in Europe: A Criterion Referenced Approach' (2017) 1(2) *Policy Reviews in Higher Education* 209, 213, published by Taylor & Francis Ltd (see www.tandfonline.com).

COPYRIGHT CREDIT: Terence Karran, Klaus Beiter and Kwadwo Appiagyei-Atua, 'Measuring Academic Freedom in Europe: A Criterion Referenced Approach' (2017) 1(2) *Policy Reviews in Higher Education* 209, 212–213.

(e) International Assistance

To measure the extent to which states engage in international assistance in relation to higher education, this analysis will consider the proportion of official development aid that each state dedicates to education. Note that research indicates that expenditure on basic education has better returns than expenditure on tertiary education.[188] Further, obtaining basic education is generally a prerequisite to

188. See Janet Hunt, 'Aid and Development' in Damien Kingsbury, Joe Remenyi, John McKay and Janet Hunt (eds), *Key Issues in Development* (Palgrave Macmillan, 2004) 67, 76.

Table 3.10. Assessment Criteria for International Assistance

Rating	DAC member country average of official development assistance directed towards education, as a percentage of total official development assistance
Very good	> 10 per cent
Good	> 8 per cent to 10 per cent
Average	> 6 per cent to 8 per cent
Poor	> 4 per cent to 6 per cent
Very poor	Below or equal to 4 per cent

gaining access to higher education. Accordingly, rather than focus on the proportion of aid provided by each state specifically to higher education, this analysis focuses on the overall education aid budget as a percentage of total aid.

The relevant criteria for assessing this sign are based on the OECD Development Assistance Committee (DAC) member country average of official development assistance directed towards education, as a percentage of total official development assistance.[189] The criteria for assessing this sign are set out in Table 3.10.

4. Social Efficiency

(a) Vocational Orientation

Measuring the vocational orientation of higher education courses is a difficult exercise. Even though a distinction is often drawn between vocational and higher education, in reality all higher education courses involve a degree of vocationalism.[190] For the purpose of considering the vocational orientation of higher education, this analysis will focus on particular factors to identify the extent of vocational orientation of the national higher education system. These factors are the extent of implementation of work experience/internship-type programmes and employability skills into higher education courses, and feedback from graduates and employers as to the adequacy of higher education programme outcomes in the context of employability.

Table 3.11 sets out the criteria for assessing this sign.

189. See OECD, *DAC Global Relations* <http://www.oecd.org/dac/dac-global-relations/>; OECD, *Aid (ODA) by Sector and Donor [DAC5]* (30 April 2015) <http://stats.oecd.org/Index.aspx?datasetcode=TABLE5>.

190. See Andrew Norton, 'Mapping Australian Higher Education 2014–15' (Report No 2014-11, Grattan Institute, October 2014) 9–10.

Table 3.11. Assessment Criteria for Vocational Orientation

Rating	Extent of vocational orientation
Very good	Sector-wide program for integration of work experience/internship programmes and employability skills into higher education courses; high graduate and employer satisfaction with graduate skills.
Good	Generally widespread integration of work experience/internship programmes and employability skills into higher education courses; generally positive graduate and employer satisfaction with graduate skills.
Average	Some utilisation of work experience/internship programmes in higher education programmes and some efforts made towards teaching employability skills; comparable levels of satisfaction and dissatisfaction on part of graduates and employers in relation to graduate skills.
Poor	Awareness of value of work experience/internship programmes in higher education programmes and of teaching employability skills, but limited implementation; general dissatisfaction of graduates and employers in relation to graduate skills.
Very poor	No or very little implementation of work experience/internship programmes or teaching of employability skills in higher education programmes; high levels of graduate and employer dissatisfaction with graduate skills evident.

(b) Graduation Rates

In terms of social efficiency, it is imperative that higher education students complete their degrees. Employment selection criteria are often framed around completion of qualifications; thus although students who complete only a portion of a degree may assist in meeting individual transformation and social betterment goals, they are unlikely to contribute significantly to social efficiency. This is highlighted by the OECD, which reports tertiary graduation rates as a measure that 'illustrate[s] a country's capacity to provide future workers with advanced and specialised knowledge and skills'.[191]

In relation to this sign, graduation rates are indicated by the OECD reported tertiary graduation rates. These are defined as representing 'the estimated percentage of an age cohort that is expected to graduate over their lifetime'.[192]

191. OECD, 'Education at a Glance 2016', above n 171, 60.

192. Ibid 61.

Table 3.12. Assessment Criteria for Graduation Rates

Rating	First-time tertiary graduation rates—percentage of an age cohort that is expected to graduate over their lifetime (adjusted to exclude international student participation)
Very good	50 per cent or above
Good	Between 47 per cent and 49 per cent
Average	Between 44 per cent and 46 per cent
Poor	Between 41 per cent and 43 per cent
Very poor	40 per cent or below

Graduation rates in relation to first-time tertiary study will be considered.[193] Further, an adjusted graduation rate without international student participation will be considered (where data is available). This is because the inclusion of international students can artificially inflate graduation rates.[194] International students are often considered first-time graduates irrespective of previous education, and 'as they have crossed borders with the intention to study and not necessarily to work or to stay in the country, they might increase the absolute number of graduates within the population.'[195]

The criteria for assessing this measure are based on the average OECD first-time tertiary graduation rate (excluding international student participation) of 45.[196] Table 3.12 sets out the assessment criteria for this sign.

(c) Employability Prospects and Skills Shortages

As the OECD asserts, '[t]he economies of OECD countries depend upon a supply of high-skilled workers.'[197] Thus, one measure of the extent to which a higher education system is contributing to the goal of social efficiency is the employability prospects of graduates as well as any skills shortages existing in the economy. For the purposes of this analysis, this sign will be measured using data provided by the OECD in relation to employment rates by educational attainment (looking specifically at graduates of bachelor's or equivalent degrees),[198]

193. Ibid 68.

194. Ibid 62.

195. OECD, 'Education at a Glance 2014', above n 180, 78.

196. OECD, 'Education at a Glance 2016', above n 171, 68.

197. Ibid 90.

198. See ibid 103.

Table 3.13. Assessment Criteria for Employability Prospects and Skills Shortages

Rating	Employment rate	Existence of skills shortages
Very good	Employment rates for higher education graduates of 87 per cent or more	No significant or very limited skills shortages
Good	Employment rates for higher education graduates of between 84 and 86 per cent	Some skills shortages
Average	Employment rates for higher education graduates of between 81 and 83 per cent	Some significant skills shortages
Poor	Employment rates for higher education graduates of between 78 and 80 per cent	Widespread significant skills shortages
Very poor	Employment rates for higher education graduates of 77 per cent or less	Widespread, ongoing significant skills shortages

together with any evidence of skills shortages in the relevant economy. Ratings will be assigned in accordance with the criteria in Table 3.13, which are based around the OECD average employment rate for higher education graduates being 82 per cent.[199]

It is important to note the limitations of these measures. Although high employment rates for tertiary-educated people may indicate a well-functioning higher education system, it may instead be reflective of a very strong economy. In this context, Andrew Norton notes that '[w]hile universities help prepare their students for the labour market, broader economic trends and conditions are the main shorter-term influences on outcomes'.[200] Other factors may also impact on employability. Further, evidence of skills shortages is often provided by business-led surveys, which are by nature selective. For this reason, this analysis endeavours to take a holistic approach, and uses these measures as only one of a number of measures of an effective higher education system.

199. Ibid.

200. Norton, 'Mapping Australian Higher Education 2014–15', above n 190, 76.

(D) Research Quality

The quality of academic research is important for teaching and learning because it can be used to inform teaching and therefore influence the quality of graduates.[201] Research is intended to contribute to progress and innovation, to making society a better place and to increasing societal knowledge. Yet research quality is a problematic concept for a number of reasons. As Jamil Salmi and Alenoush Saroyan state in relation to university rankings, 'there is no commonly accepted static definition of quality that would fit all institutions'.[202] Further, numeric rankings fail to take into account 'longer term health, social or economic benefits that research might bring'.[203]

Nevertheless, research-led teaching is a critical means of ensuring that higher education graduates attain cutting-edge knowledge and skills and therefore should be taken into account in evaluating a state policy approach to higher education teaching. To this end, the approach taken here, for the purposes of state higher education policy comparison, is to draw on the measure of 'depth of world class universities in a country' as measured by the U21 Ranking of National Higher Education Systems. This measure is based on the Shanghai Jiao Tong University Academic Ranking of World Universities (ARWU). The ARWU, like all ranking systems, is problematic. It operates to compare the research performance of 'comprehensive research intensive universit[ies]' and favours English-speaking institutions, institutions that are strong in scientific research, and American universities.[204] Nevertheless, unlike many other ranking systems, the ARWU focuses solely on research performance.[205] Further, it is supported by other measures of research output[206] and 'there is a broad correlation between a nation's overall economic capacity and the standing of its research universities', making it an appropriate measure in the context of social efficiency.[207] Care is taken not to rely on

201. See generally, Lynden Griggs, 'Foreword—Special Issue on the Research/Teaching Nexus' (2012) 22(2) *Legal Education Review* 237; Marina Nehme, 'The Nexus between Teaching and Research: Easier Said Than Done' (2012) 22(2) *Legal Education Review* 241.

202. Salmi and Saroyan, above n 106, 46.

203. Kylie M Smith, Ellie Crookes and Patrick A Crookes, 'Measuring Research "Impact" for Academic Promotion: Issues from the Literature' (2013) 35(4) *Journal of Higher Education Policy and Management* 410, 410.

204. Marginson and van der Wende, above n 100, 306, 311. See also Amsler and Bolsmann, above n 108, 287; Salmi and Saroyan, above n 106, 590.

205. Marginson and van der Wende, above n 100, 309; Liu and Cheng, above n 88, 133.

206. Marginson and van der Wende, above n 100, 316.

207. Ibid 314.

Table 3.14. Assessment Criteria for Research Quality

Rating	'Depth of world class universities in a country' as measured by the U21 Ranking of National Higher Education Systems
Very good	80–100
Good	60–80
Average	40–60
Poor	20–40
Very poor	0–20

this measure alone[208] and to draw upon it only for the particular purpose of contributing to a holistic assessment of state higher education policy.[209]

Following the approach of the U21 Rankings, the measure of world class universities in a country is calculated as a weighted average of the number of state institutions in the ARWU top 500, divided by country population.[210] The assessment criteria are set out in Table 3.14.

(e) Global Connectivity

As asserted in the Universitas 21 rankings, '[t]he worth of a national higher education system is enhanced if it is well connected with the rest of the nation's society and is linked internationally in education and research.[211] Quality teaching and research, as well as the absorption of new ideas and discoveries, are likely to bring significant benefits to the economy. To measure global connectivity the following factors will be considered:

- the proportion of international students in tertiary education, and
- the proportion of domestic students enrolled in tertiary education abroad.[212]

208. See Liu and Cheng, above n 88, 132.

209. See Marginson and van der Wende, above n 100, 321. In relation to the ARWU Rankings, see Shanghai Jiao Tong University, *Academic Ranking of World Universities: Statistics*, Shanghai Ranking <http://www.shanghairanking.com/ARWU-Statistics-2014.html>. In relation to the U21 Rankings, see Universitas, *Measure 4: Output*, Universitas 21 <http://www.universitas21.com/article/projects/details/157/measure-4-output>.

210. Universitas, above n 209.

211. Williams, Leahy, de Rassenfosse and Jensen, above n 101, 16.

212. OECD, 'Education at a Glance 2016', above n 171, 341.

Table 3.15. Assessment Criteria for Global Connectivity

Rating	Proportion of international students in tertiary education	Proportion of domestic students enrolled in tertiary education abroad
Very good	above 10 per cent	above 3 per cent
Good	8–10 per cent	2.1–3 per cent
Average	5–7 per cent	1.1–2 per cent
Poor	2–4 per cent	0.1–1 per cent
Very poor	below 2 per cent	0

The assessment criteria for this measure are based on the OECD total proportion of international students in higher education as 6 per cent, and the OECD total proportion of domestic students enrolled in tertiary education abroad as 1.6 per cent.[213] Table 3.15 sets out the relevant assessment criteria.

E. CONCLUSION

Although few question the importance of higher education, its purposes continue to be relatively unconsidered. In spite of this, a plethora of systems designed to rank higher education institutions, and less frequently systems, exist. Rankings purport to judge the quality of higher education institutions, yet omit any in-depth discussion of the purposes that this quality is supposed to be in relation to.

In light of this omission, this chapter has sought to develop an understanding of what is likely to constitute effective higher education policy, in light of considered purposes of higher education. This analysis will enable consideration of the merit of particular state higher education policies and comparison with other state higher education policies. Rather than facilitating a ranking of institutions or systems, this analysis is intended to enable considered evaluation, with the purpose of improving higher education.

Given its centrality and importance in society, higher education has the potential to lead and contribute beyond its contribution to the economy, which is only one aspect of society. Ultimately, higher education should lead society towards comprehensive improvement, from assisting individual transformation to independence, to bettering society in terms of citizenship, equality, social justice, and the economy.[214] The next chapter draws upon the evaluative framework

213. Ibid 339–41.

214. See generally UNESCO, *World Conference on Higher Education: World Declaration on Higher Education for the Twenty-First Century: Vision and Action* (9 October 1998) [art 6(d)]. See also Harkavy, above n 62, 6.

developed in this chapter to consider six different state higher education policies. Systems reflecting the market-based and human rights-based approaches to higher education are selected, enabling the drawing of conclusions as to which of these approaches is more likely to assist a state to meet the purposes of higher education teaching and learning.

REFERENCE LIST

A. Articles/Books/Reports

Allen, Michael, *The Goals of Universities* (Open University Press, 1988)

Altbach, Philip G, 'The Costs and Benefits of World Class Universities' (2004) Jan/Feb *Academe* 20

Amsler, Sarah S, and Chris Bolsmann, 'University Ranking as Social Exclusion' (2012) 33(2) *British Journal of Sociology of Education* 283

Baird, John R, 'Quality: What Should Make Higher Education "Higher"?' (1988) 7(2) *Higher Education Research and Development* 141

Barnett, R A, 'Institutions of Higher Education: Purposes and 'Performance Indicators' (1988) 14(1) *Oxford Review of Education* 97

Barnett, Ronald, 'Entry and Exit Performance Indicators: Some Policy and Research Issues' (1988) 13(1) *Assessment and Evaluation in Higher Education*, 16

Barnett, Ronald, 'The Idea of Quality: Voicing the Educational' (1992) 46(1) *Higher Education Quarterly* 3

Barnett, Ronald, *Improving Higher Education: Total Quality Care* (Open University Press, 1992)

Barnett, Ronald and Carolina Guzman, 'The Human Rights University: A Feasible Utopia' in Claudia Brunner and Josefine Scherling (eds), *Bildung, Menschenrechte, Universitat. Menschenrechts-Bildung and Hochschulen im Wandel als gesellschaftliche Herausforderung* (Drava Verlag, 2012) 269

Benson, Lee and Ira Harkavy, 'Saving the Soul of the University: What Is to Be Done?' in Kevin Robins and Frank Webster (eds), *The Virtual University? Knowledge, Markets, and Management* (Oxford University Press, 2002) 169

Berka, Walter, 'The Legal and Philosophical Meaning of Autonomy in Education' in Walter Berka, Jan De Groof and Hilde Penneman (eds), *Autonomy in Education: Yearbook of the European Association for Education Law and Policy* (Kluwer Law International, 2000) vol 3, 3

Bexley, Emmaline, Richard James and Sophie Arkoudis, 'The Australian Academic Profession in Transition: Addressing the Challenge of Reconceptualising Academic Work and Regenerating the Academic Workforce' (Report, Department of Education, Employment and Workplace Relations, September 2011)

Billing, David, 'Judging Institutions' in Graeme C Moodie (ed), *Standards and Criteria in Higher Education* (SRHE & NFER-Nelson, 1986) 65

Blank, Rolf K, 'Developing a System of Education Indicators: Selecting, Implementing and Reporting Indicators' (1993) 15(1) *Educational Evaluation and Policy Analysis* 65

Brennan, John and Rajani Naidoo, 'Higher Education and the Achievement (and/or Prevention) of Equity and Social Justice' (2008) 56(3) *Higher Education* 287

Colby, Anne and Thomas Ehrlich with Elizabeth Beaumont, Jennifer Rosner and Jason Stephens, 'Introduction: Higher Education and the Development of Civic Responsibility' in Thomas Ehrlich (ed), *Civic Responsibility and Higher Education* (Oryx Press, 2000) xxi

Collini, Stefan, *What Are Universities For?* (Penguin Books, 2012)

Crean, Mags and Kathleen Lynch, 'Resistance, Struggle and Survival: The University as a Site for Transformative Education' in Andrew O'Shea and Maeve O'Brien (eds), *Pedagogy, Oppression and Transformation in a 'Post-Critical' Climate* (Bloomsbury Publishing, 2011) 51

Crosling, Glenda, Margaret Heagney and Liz Thomas, 'Improving Student Retention in Higher Education' (2009) 51(2) *Australian Universities' Review* 9

Deem, Rosemary, Ka Ho Mok and Lisa Lucas, 'Transforming Higher Education in Whose Image? Exploring the Concept of the "World-Class" University in Europe and Asia' (2008) 21 *Higher Education Policy* 83

Ederer, Peer, Philipp Schuller and Stephan Willms, 'University Systems Ranking: Citizens and Society in the Age of Knowledge' (Policy Brief, The Lisbon Council, 2008)

El-Khawas, Elaine, Robin DePieto-Jurand and Lauritz Holm-Nielsen, 'Quality Assurance in Higher Education: Recent Progress; Challenges Ahead' (LCSHD Paper Series No 23, World Bank, September 1998)

Estermann, Thomas, Terhi Nokkala and Monika Steinel, 'University Autonomy in Europe II: The Scorecard' (Project Report, European University Association, 15 November 2011)

Freire, Paulo, *Pedagogy of the Oppressed* (Penguin, 1972)

Fry, Heather, 'Quality Judgements and Quality Improvement' (1995) 49(1) *Higher Education Quarterly* 59

Garcia-Aracil, Adela and Davinia Palomares-Montero, 'Examining Benchmark Indicator Systems for the Evaluation of Higher Education Institutions' (2009) 60 *Higher Education* 217

Geary Schneider, Carol, 'Educational Missions and Civic Responsibility: Toward the Engaged Academy' in Thomas Ehrlich (ed), *Civic Responsibility and Higher Education* (Oryx Press, 2000) 98

Gibbs, P T, 'Isn't Higher Education Employability?' (2000) 52(4) *Journal of Vocational Education and Training* 559

Glover, Derek, Sue Law and Andrea Youngman, 'Graduateness and Employability: Student Perceptions of the Personal Outcomes of University Education' (2002) 7(3) *Research in Post-Compulsory Education* 293

Goedegebuure, Leo, Frans Kaiser, Peter Maassen and Egbert de Weert, 'Higher Education Policy in International Perspective: An Overview' in Leo Goedegebuure, Frans Kaiser, Peter Maassen, Lyn Meek, Frans van Vught and Egbert de Weert (eds), *Higher Education Policy: An International Comparative Perspective* (Pergamon Press, 1993) 1

Goedegebuure, Leo, Frans Kaiser, Peter Maassen, Lynn Meek, Frans van Vught and Egbert de Weert, 'International Perspectives on Trends and Issues in Higher Education Policy' in Leo Goedegebuure, Frans Kaiser, Peter Maassen, Lyn Meek,

Frans van Vught and Egbert de Weert (eds), *Higher Education Policy: An International Comparative Perspective* (Pergamon Press, 1993) 315

Griggs, Lynden, 'Foreword—Special Issue on the Research/Teaching Nexus' (2012) 22(2) *Legal Education Review* 237

Hantrais, Linda, *International Comparative Research: Theory, Methods and Practice* (Palgrave Macmillan, 2009)

Harkavy, Ira, 'The Role of Universities in Advancing Citizenship and Social Justice in the 21st Century' (2006) 1(1) *Education, Citizenship and Social Justice* 5

Harvey, Lee, 'Quality Is Not Free! Quality Monitoring Alone Will Not Improve Quality' (1997) 3(2) *Tertiary Education and Management* 133

Hunt, Janet, 'Aid and Development' in Damien Kingsbury, Joe Remenyi, John McKay and Janet Hunt (eds), *Key Issues in Development* (Palgrave Macmillan, 2004) 67

Karran, Terence, Klaus Beiter and Kwadwo Appiagyei-Atua, 'Measuring Academic Freedom in Europe: A Criterion Referenced Approach' (2017) 1(2) *Policy Reviews in Higher Education* 209

Kerr, Clark, 'The Idea of a Multiversity' in Clark Kerr (ed), *The Uses of the University* (Oxford University Press, 2001)

King, Roger, 'What Is Higher Education For? Strategic Dilemmas for the Twenty-First Century University' (1995) 3(4) *Quality Assurance in Education* 14

Labaree, David F, 'Public Goods, Private Goods: The American Struggle over Educational Goals' (1997) 34(1) *American Educational Research Journal* 39

Laredo, Philippe, 'Revisiting the Third Mission of Universities: Toward a Renewed Categorization of University Activities?' (2007) 20(4) *Higher Education Policy* 441

Liu, Nian Cai and Ying Cheng, 'The Academic Ranking of World Universities' (2005) 30(2) *Higher Education in Europe* 127

Long, Edward LeRoy, Jr, *Higher Education as a Moral Enterprise* (Georgetown University Press, 1992)

Lynch, Kathleen, 'Equality and Resistance in Higher Education' (1995) 5(1) *International Studies in Sociology of Education* 93

Lynch, Kathleen, 'Neo-Liberalism and Marketisation: The Implications for Higher Education' (2006) 5(1) *European Educational Research Journal* 1

Lynch, Kathleen, 'International League Tables and Rankings in Higher Education: An Appraisal' in Imelda Elliott, Michael Murphy, Alain Payeur, Raymond Duval (eds), *Mutations de L'Enseignement Supérieur et Internationalisation* (De Boeck, 2011) 19

Lynch, Kathleen, 'Control by Numbers: New Managerialism and Ranking in Higher Education' (2014) 56(2) *Critical Studies in Education* 190

Lynch, Kathleen, 'New Managerialism, Neoliberalism and Ranking' (2014) 13 *Ethics in Science and Environmental Politics* 141

Lynch, Kathleen, Margaret Crean and Marie Moran, 'Equality and Social Justice: The University as a Site of Struggle' in Michael W Apple, Stephen J Ball and Luis Armando Gandin (eds), *The Routledge International Handbook of the Sociology of Education* (Routledge, 2010) 296

Marginson, Simon and Marijk van der Wende, 'To Rank or to Be Ranked: The Impact of Global Rankings in Higher Education' (2007) 11(3–4) *Journal of Studies in International Education* 306

McCowan, Tristan, 'The Growth of Private Higher Education in Brazil: Implications for Equity and Quality' (2004) 19(4) *Journal of Education Policy* 453

McCowan, Tristan, 'Educating Citizens for Participatory Democracy: A Case Study of Local Government Education Policy in Pelotas, Brazil' (2006) 26(5) *International Journal of Educational Development* 456

McCowan, Tristan, 'Can Schools Make Good Citizens?' in Richard Bailey (ed), *The Philosophy of Education: An Introduction* (Continuum, 2010) 86

McCowan, Tristan, 'The Elusive Notion of Quality in the Bologna Process' in Joao Menelau Paraskeva (ed), *Unaccomplished Utopia: Neoconservative Dismangling of Public Higher Education in the European Union* (Sense, 2010) 95

McCowan, Tristan and Sonia Gomez, *Citizenship Education in Commonwealth Countries* (Commonwealth Secretariat, 2012)

Moodie, Graeme C, 'Fit for What?' in Graeme C Moodie (ed), *Standards and Criteria in Higher Education* (SRHE & NFER-Nelson, 1986) 1

Morphew, Christopher C and Matthew Hartley, 'Mission Statements: A Thematic Analysis of Rhetoric across Institutional Type' (2006) 77(3) *The Journal of Higher Education* 456

Nehme, Marina, 'The Nexus between Teaching and Research: Easier Said than Done' (2012) 22(2) *Legal Education Review* 241

Norton, Andrew, 'Mapping Australian Higher Education 2014–15' (Report No 2014-11, Grattan Institute, October 2014)

Organisation for Economic Cooperation and Development, 'Education at a Glance 2014: OECD Indicators' (OECD, September 2014)

Organisation for Economic Cooperation and Development, 'Education at a Glance 2016: OECD Indicators' (OECD, 2016)

Pollitt, Christopher, 'Measuring University Performance: Never Mind the Quality, Never Mind the Width?' (1990) 44(1) *Higher Education Quarterly* 60

Radford, John, 'The Changing Purposes of Higher Education' in John Radford, Kjell Raaheim, Peter de Vries and Ruth Williams (eds), *Quantity and Quality in Higher Education* (Jessica Kingsley Publishers, 1997) 7

Rowley, Jennifer, 'Measuring Quality in Higher Education' (1996) 2(3) *Quality in Higher Education* 237

Saichaie, Kem and Christopher C Morphew, 'What College and University Websites Reveal about the Purposes of Higher Education' (2014) 85(4) *The Journal of Higher Education* 499

Salmi, Jamil, *The Challenge of Establishing World-Class Universities* (World Bank, 2009)

Salmi, Jamil, 'The Road to Academic Excellence: Lessons of Experience' in Philip G Altbach and Jamil Salmi (eds), *The Road to Academic Excellence: The Making of World-Class Research Universities* (World Bank, 2011) 324

Salmi, Jamil and Alenoush Saroyan, 'League Tables as Policy Instruments: Uses and Misuses' (2007) 19(2) *Higher Education Management and Policy* 24

Sax, Linda J, 'Citizenship Development and the American College Student' in Thomas Ehrlich (ed), *Civic Responsibility and Higher Education* (Oryx Press, 2000) 3

Shapiro, Harold T, *A Larger Sense of Purpose: Higher Education and Society* (Princeton University Press, 2005)

Sheil, Tony, 'Moving beyond University Rankings: Developing a World Class University System in Australia' (2010) 52(1) *Australian Universities' Review* 69

Sizer, John, 'Assessing Institutional Performance and Progress' in Leslie Wagner (ed), *Agenda for Institutional Change in Higher Education* (SRHE, 1982) 33

Smith, Kylie M, Ellie Crookes and Patrick A Crookes, 'Measuring Research 'Impact' for Academic Promotion: Issues from the Literature' (2013) 35(4) *Journal of Higher Education Policy and Management* 410

United Nations Educational, Scientific and Cultural Organization, 'World Education Report' (Report, UNESCO, 2000) 70

Watty, Kim, 'Addressing the Basics: Academics' View of the Purpose of Higher Education' (2006) 33(1) *The Australian Educational Researcher* 23

Weller, L David, 'The Equity Factor: A Vital Part of the Quality Equation' (1995) 3(4) *Quality Assurance in Education* 44

Williams, Ross, Anne Leahy, Gaétan de Rassenfosse and Paul Jensen, 'U21 Ranking of National Higher Education Systems' (Project Report, Melbourne Institute of Applied Economic and Social Research, May 2015)

Willms, J Douglas, 'The Challenge of Developing New Educational Indicators' (1995) 17(1) *Educational Evaluation and Policy Analysis* 113

Wilson, Brian, 'Quality in Universities, Sir Robert Menzies Oration, 4 October 1995' (1996) 18(2) *Journal of Higher Education Policy and Management* 149

B. Official international documents

UNESCO, *Recommendation Concerning the Status of Higher-Education Teaching Personnel*, in Records of the General Conference, 29th sess (21 October to 12 November 1997)

UNESCO, *World Conference on Higher Education: World Declaration on Higher Education for the Twenty-First Century: Vision and Action* (9 October 1998)

C. Other

Aalto University, *Mission, Vision and Values* (20 March 2014) <http://www.aalto.fi/en/about/strategy/>

Boston University, *Mission Statement* <http://www.bu.edu/info/about/mission-statement/>

Center for World-Class Universities at Shanghai Jiao Tong University, *Methodology*, Academic Ranking of World Universities since 2003 <http://www.shanghairanking.com/ARWU-Methodology-2014.html>

Central Michigan University, *University Mission, Vision and Values* (2 December 2010) <https://www.cmich.edu/about/Pages/university_goals.aspx>

Craven, Greg, 'Pyne's Fine Words Fell on Deaf Ears', *The Australian* (Australia), 12 March 2014

Duke University, *Mission Statement* (23 February 2001) <http://www.trustees.duke.edu/governing/mission.php>

Griffith University, *Mission Statement* <http://www.griffith.edu.au/about-griffith/governance/mission-statement>

McMaster University, *University Mission Statement and Vision* <https://www.mcmaster.ca/presidentsoffice/mission.html>

Mississippi State University, *Vision and Mission Statements* <http://www.msstate.edu/web/mission.html>

OECD, *Aid (ODA) by Sector and Donor [DAC5]* (30 April 2015) <http://stats.oecd.org/Index.aspx?datasetcode=TABLE5>

OECD, *DAC Global Relations* <http://www.oecd.org/dac/dac-global-relations/>

Oregon State University, *Mission Statement* <http://oregonstate.edu/main/mission>

Right to Education Project, 'The Right to Education: Indicators' (May 2013)

Scimago Institutions Rankings, *Research Rankings* (2014) <http://www.scimagoir.com/research.php>

Shanghai Jiao Tong University, *Academic Ranking of World Universities: Statistics*, Shanghai Ranking <http://www.shanghairanking.com/ARWU-Statistics-2014.html> Universitas, *Measure 4: Output*, Universitas 21 <http://www.universitas21.com/article/projects/details/157/measure-4-output>

Suber, Peter, *A Very Brief Introduction to Open Access* (29 December 2004) Earlham College <http://legacy.earlham.edu/~peters/fos/brief.htm>

The University of Edinburgh, *Mission* (5 April 2011) <http://www.ed.ac.uk/about/mission-governance/mission>

Times Higher Education, *Times Higher Education World University Rankings 2014–2015* <http://www.timeshighereducation.co.uk/world-university-rankings/2014-15/world-ranking>

UNESCO, *Open Access to Scientific Information* <http://www.unesco.org/new/en/communication-and-information/access-to-knowledge/open-access-to-scientific-information/>

Universities Australia, 'An Agenda for Australian Higher Education 2013–2016' (Statement, 2013, Universities Australia) 50

Universities Australia, 'Submission to the Review of Higher Education Regulation' (Submission, Universities Australia, June 2013)

University of Phoenix, *Mission and Purpose* <http://www.phoenix.edu/about_us/about_university_of_phoenix/mission_and_purpose.html>

University of Virginia, *Mission Statement* (18 April 2014) <http://www.virginia.edu/statementofpurpose/purpose.html>

Yale University, *University Mission Statement* <http://www.yale.edu/about/mission.html>

Yousafzai, Malala, *Malala Yousafzai's Speech at the United Nations*, A World at School <http://www.aworldatschool.org/pages/the-text-of-malala-yousafzais-speech-at-the-united-nations>.

4

Practical Approaches to Higher Education

A. INTRODUCTION

Numerous different higher education systems operate in the contemporary world. No two states are the same, and higher education systems should be adapted to a state's particular environment and context.[1] Nevertheless, in developing higher education policy in any particular state, it would be remiss of policy-makers to ignore the existence of foreign higher education systems. Such systems can provide valuable evidence as to the impact of particular policy frameworks, including whether they are likely to have the desired effects, as well as any unforeseen adverse consequences.[2] Ensuring that higher education policy is research or evidence based in this way is likely to result in the development of more effective higher education systems.[3]

1. See Linda Hantrais, *International Comparative Research: Theory, Methods and Practice* (Palgrave Macmillan, 2009) 137.

2. See ibid.

3. See Anthony Welch, 'Evidence-Based Policy: Epistemologically Specious, Ideologically Unsound' in Helen Proctor, Patrick Brownlee and Peter Freebody (eds), *Controversies in Education: Orthodoxy and Heresy in Policy and Practice* (Springer, 2015) 63, 69. In relation to current policy development

The Human Rights-Based Approach to Higher Education. Jane Kotzmann.
© Oxford University Press 2018. Published 2018 by Oxford University Press.

It should be noted, however, that the phrase 'research based' is not used in the sense of 'evidence-based policy' outlined by Welch.[4] The approach being encouraged here is open to different methodologies and different forms of knowledge, and places values at the core of policy development. This is evidenced by the normative nature of the discussion, as well as the type of information considered; both quantitative and qualitative evidence is drawn upon. Further, the potential for a research based approach is demonstrated by Welch's discussion of Diane Ravitch's position, who 'was persuaded by the evidence that . . . testing and choice are undermining education'.[5] Although it is always possible that research and evidence may be ignored or misused in the political policy-making process, it must be hoped that they can be of some influence, as was seen in Ravitch's case.

Although foreign higher education systems can be analysed individually for evidence on which to base policy development, consideration of the similarities and differences between systems, as well as trends that emerge from analysis of multiple systems, is likely to yield more value. Examining the impact, for example, of higher education fee deregulation in multiple foreign states will provide more information on the associated strengths and weaknesses of such change than analysis of a single foreign state policy. In particular, to identify strengths and weaknesses associated with differences in ideology underpinning higher education systems, analysis of multiple systems, viewed in light of their underpinning ideology, is required.

This chapter seeks to analyse higher education policy in six states, with the purpose of determining whether a human rights-based approach to higher education policy, in comparison with a market-based approach, might better enable states to meet the purposes of higher education. States were chosen as the relevant unit of analysis due to the likelihood of having distinct policy regimes.[6] The selection of countries was based first on the countries belonging to the OECD, as relevant information is available via the OECD Education at a Glance report series, which assists comparability.[7] A subset of OECD countries were then selected on the basis of those countries being able to be seen as representative of the market-based approach or the human rights-based approach outlined in

practices in Australia, see Tom Clark, 'Under No Circumstances Resolve the Main Problem: Higher Education Policy Overview in Australia' (2004) 46(2) *Australian Universities Review* 12, 13.

4. See Hantrais, above n 1, 125; Welch, above n 3, 63.

5. See ibid 73.

6. See Hantrais, above n 1, 51.

7. See ibid.

Chapter 2.[8] Three states were chosen to represent each approach. This was to ensure that each case study was sufficiently similar to the policy approach, at the same time as ensuring a sufficient number of case studies to discount the possibility of anomalous results.[9] The selected countries are Chile, England and the United States in relation to the market-based approach, and Finland, Iceland and Sweden in relation to the human rights-based approach.

In terms of the analysis of the higher education policy in each state, each state's system is categorised on the basis of its ideological underpinnings, as being either reflective of a market-based approach to higher education or a human rights-based approach. Each policy framework is then evaluated in relation to its likely impact in enabling the state to meet the purposes of higher education.[10] This is established by reference to the signs, and associated measures, of a successful higher education system identified in Chapter 3.

Although it is acknowledged that the measures of a successful higher education policy may vary in the extent to which they indicate the attainment of a purpose of higher education, they are accorded equal weighting in this discussion. This approach facilitates an easier comparison between states and also reflects the reality that attempting to weight the different signs would be a subjective process. Further, given that this analysis seeks to generally identify the merits of one policy approach over another, numerical accuracy is not essential.

The methodology for measuring the signs of a successful higher education system was outlined in Chapter 3. The evaluation for each sign results in a ranking of 'very good', 'good', 'average', 'poor' or 'very poor' with associated scores (5–1) attached (see Appendix B). This provides the means for calculating an overall numerical country ranking, by adding together all country scores and then calculating the total score as a percentage of the available points. For example, in relation to Chile, the scores achieved for the relevant measures add up to 34 out of 60, which as a percentage equals 57 per cent (see Appendix B, Table B-1). The

8. This approach may be classified as a 'classification-of-cases-design . . . where cases are selected which represent a specific type of cases': see Anna Kosmützky, 'The Precision and Rigor of International Comparative Studies in Higher Education' (2016) 2 *Theory and Method in Higher Education Research* 199, 204. Note that information of this nature is frequently updated. This chapter is written on the basis of the information available at the time of writing. As indicated, this analysis relies heavily on OECD data. Although it is acknowledged that the OECD is not a neutral observer of higher education, the data it collects is very recent and assists comparability. Further, it is acknowledged that different conditions may exist in low and middle-income countries as compared to OECD countries. This does constitute a limitation of the research.

9. See Hantrais, above n 1, 56.

10. In relation to this methodology, see Andrew Gunn, 'The Role of Political and Policy Studies in Higher Education Policy Research' 1 *Theory and Method in Higher Education Research* 27, 30.

numerical aspect of the analysis enables comparison between states and frameworks (for a summary of the resulting country comparison see Appendix C). On the basis of this examination, conclusions are drawn as to the value of the market-based and human rights-based approaches to higher education policy.

B. MARKET-BASED APPROACHES

1. Chile

(a) Political Context and Approach

Chile's higher education system was the subject of significant reforms under military government in the 1980s,[11] which were 'based on the premise that education was a marketable good'.[12] As a result of these reforms, higher education became subject to market forces, which meant that fees increased and universities competed for students.[13] Accordingly, higher education in Chile has become extremely expensive, and students are left with significant debts which are subject to high interest rates.[14] In response, numerous mass student protests have taken place in Santiago and other major cities over the years.[15] Protestors oppose the poor quality and prohibitive costs of higher education and the inequality of educational opportunity, and demand free public higher education.[16] Many of these protests have been peaceful, however, many others have seen violence and the use of tear gas and water cannons against protestors.[17] Although current

11. José Joaquín Brunner, 'Chile's Higher Education: Between Market and State' (1993) 25(1) *Higher Education* 35, 35.

12. Emilio Rodríguez-Ponce, 'Time for Change in Chilean Higher Education', *University World News* (online), 20 December 2013 <http://www.universityworldnews.com/article.php?story=20131219150048533>.

13. Ibid.

14. *Chile: Students Protest to Demand Universal Education* (21 June 2017) teleSUR <http://www.telesurtv.net/english/news/Chile-Students-Protest-to-Demand-Universal-Education-20170621-0010.html>.

15. See Lorenzo Cini and César Guzmán-Concha, 'Student Movements in the Age of Austerity: The Cases of Chile and England' (2017) *Social Movement Studies* 1, 4–5; *Chile Police, Students Clash amid Rally for Free Education* (22 June 2017) PressTV <http://presstv.ir/Detail/2017/06/22/526138/Chile-protest-higher-education-fee>.

16. *Chile Police, Students Clash amid Rally for Free Education*, above n 15; *Chile: Students Protest to Demand Universal Education*, above n 14; Rodríguez-Ponce, above n 12.

17. *Chile Police, Students Clash amid Rally for Free Education*, above n 15; Lisa Nikolau, *Chile Continues Debate over Inequality in Higher Education* (3 January 2017) Humanosphere

president Michelle Bachelet has promised educational reform, to date the promise remains unfulfilled.[18]

Although Chile may be on the brink of implementing radical higher education reforms,[19] its current system is best characterised as reflective of a market-based approach to higher education. Higher education institutions compete with each other for students[20] and research is funded according to competition principles.[21] Moreover, institutions charge fees on a market basis: 'the most expensive are the private universities, while technical institutes are the least expensive'.[22] Fees are also relatively high: in 2011 the average annual tuition fee for first-degree programmes in public institutions was $5,885 (or $6,924 in government-dependent private institutions and $6,230 in independent private institutions) and for second- and further-degree programmes it was $6,345 (or $8,757 in government-dependent private institutions and $8,357 in independent private institutions).[23] Although public loans, scholarships and grants were available in 2011, 50 per cent of students did not benefit from any financial assistance and 82 per cent did not receive scholarships or grants in support of tuition fees.[24]

Chile's higher education system is also highly privatised. In 2013, 62 per cent of funding was sourced from private rather than public sources,[25] reflective of one of

<http://www.humanosphere.org/basics/2017/01/chile-continues-debate-over-inequality-in-higher-education/>.

18. *Chile Police, Students Clash amid Rally for Free Education*, above n 15; *Thousands of Chilean Students Take to Streets Demanding Education Reform* (11 April 2017) teleSUR <http://www.telesurtv.net/english/news/Thousands-of-Chilean-Students-Take-to-Streets-Demanding-Education-Reform-20170411-0022.html>; Nikolau, above n 17.

19. See Ignacio Sanchez Diaz, *Higher Education Reform Debated in Chile* (2 January 2017) Inside Higher Ed <https://www.insidehighered.com/blogs/world-view/higher-education-reform-debated-chile>; Ray Polglaze, 'Chile: Students Set to Win Free Higher Education', *Green Left Weekly* (online), 1 April 2014 <https://www.greenleft.org.au/node/56187>; 'Chile to Have Free Higher Education by 2016', *TeleSUR* (online), 4 December 2014 <http://www.telesurtv.net/english/news/Chile-to-Have-Free-Higher-Education-by-2016-20141204-0049.html>.

20. Ibid.

21. Brunner, 'Chile's Higher Education', above n 11, 35.

22. Jane Leer, 'Higher Education in Chile: A Study of Youth Perceptions' (2011) 1(1) *Penn State Journal of International Affairs* 27, 28.

23. Note that more recent information is not available. See OECD, 'Education at a Glance 2014: OECD Indicators' (OECD, 2014) 271.

24. Ibid 273.

25. Organisation for Economic Cooperation and Development (OECD), 'Education at a Glance 2016: OECD Indicators' (OECD, 2016) 218.

the purposes of the 1980s reforms, being to 'force . . . institutions to diversify their funding sources'.[26] A shift in the proportion of higher education institutions from public to private has also occurred. According to José Joaquín Brunner, following the 1980s reforms, 'Higher Education became private-dominant in the non-university levels and has now a dual public/private nature at the university level'.[27]

The Chilean higher education system evidences a distinct lack of government intervention. Government spending on higher education is conspicuously low at $2,866 per student, compared to the OECD average of $9,719.[28] Further, Jane Leer's research indicates that Chilean youths' perceive that 'market-based expansion . . . ha[s] . . . sacrificed quality and integrity for profit',[29] resulting in 'major discrepancies . . . in the value of a degree from different institutions'.[30] This suggests a lack of government regulation in relation to accreditation and quality.

Although the Chilean *Constitution* does recognise a right to education, in relation to higher education, the right is limited to promotion of the 'development of education at all levels; stimulat[ion of] scientific and technological research, artistic creation, and the protection and increase of the cultural patrimony of the Nation'.[31] This provision has not manifested in recognition of a right to higher education. This is evident in that tuition fees, where they are not offset by financial assistance, constitute a barrier to higher education for the less wealthy. In relation to the Chilean system, Leer notes that 'educational expansion has mostly benefited higher income earners and reinforced the socioeconomic hierarchy'.[32] Thus, a right to higher education, in the form of an equal right of all people to higher education, is not presently recognised in Chile.

(B) Evaluation

(i) Individual Transformation

Student Survey Responses

Chile does not currently conduct a national student survey of higher education students. This is evident from the OECD's recommendation in 2013 that

26. Brunner, 'Chile's Higher Education', above n 11, 36 (emphasis altered).

27. Ibid 35.

28. OECD, 'Education at a Glance 2016', above n 25, 221.

29. Leer, above n 22, 31.

30. Ibid 28.

31. *Constitution of the Republic of Chile 1980*, ch 3 art 19(10) [Anna I Vellvé Torras, Adela Staines and Jefri J Ruchti trans, *Chile's Constitution of 1980 with Amendments through 2012* (William S Hein & Co, 2012)].

32. Leer, above n 22, 29.

Chile introduce a 'student survey to gather information on students' experiences in relation to teaching and learning', which 'would allow institutions to benchmark nationally—or even internationally—the processes experienced by students'.[33] Given the lack of data in relation to this sign, a ranking of 'not applicable' is given.

Personalised Learning

Unfortunately, data is not available in relation to Chile's ratio of students to teaching staff in higher education institutions.[34] Accordingly, this criterion is ranked 'not applicable'.

Resources per Student

In 2013, Chile spent an amount equivalent to 2.4 per cent of GDP on tertiary education institutions.[35] This is significantly higher than the OECD average spend of 1.5 per cent of GDP.[36] Nevertheless, this does not translate to high spending per student. In 2013, Chile spent $7,642 per student, compared to the OECD average of $15,772.[37] On the basis of this analysis, Chile is ranked 'average' in relation to this criterion.

Institutional Autonomy

In Chile, the higher education sector enjoys significant autonomy.[38] Higher education institutions enjoy academic freedom,[39] including the freedom to design their own curricula, subject to some professional accreditation requirements.[40] Similarly, higher education institutions are able to set their own admission policies,[41] subject to the requirement that candidates hold a secondary school leavers

33. OECD, 'Reviews of National Policies for Education: Quality Assurance in Higher Education in Chile 2013' (Review, OECD, 2013) 95.

34. OECD, 'Education at a Glance 2016', above n 25, 403.

35. Ibid 206.

36. Ibid.

37. Ibid 192.

38. Reehana Raza, 'Examining Autonomy and Accountability in Public and Private Tertiary Institutions' (Report, Human Development Network and World Bank, November 2009) 25.

39. José Joaquín Brunner, 'Chile: Challenges to Autonomy and Accountability in a Privatized Context' (2013) 3 *Leadership and Governance in Higher Education* 1, 14.

40. Ibid 2, 11; Raza, above n 38, 24.

41. Brunner, 'Chile' above n 39, 11.

certificate.[42] Nevertheless, autonomy in this respect can be limited where institutions elect to enter particular government schemes.[43] Autonomy also exists for Chilean higher education institutions in relation to staff recruitment.[44]

Although higher education institutions in Chile enjoy 'ample autonomy', consistent sector-wide quality assurance mechanisms are lacking.[45] Initiatives directed towards autonomy have been implemented from the 1990s, and in particular 'quite recently and often suddenly, higher education institutions . . . are becoming subject to various kinds of accountability'.[46] These initiatives include licensing requirements and self-assessment process requirements, as well as an external accreditation system that is voluntary, but which institutions must undergo if they wish to receive public financing.[47] Nevertheless, these measures are challenged by the lack of impartiality of the accrediting body, its ineffectiveness in identifying prohibited behaviour, and general criticism of the quality assurance system,[48] which 'is not working nearly as well as it should'.[49] Thus, Chile is ranked 'average' in relation to this criterion.

Commitment to Teaching and Learning

In Chile, there is no national framework governing academic career structures.[50] Instead, higher education institutions are able to establish their own career

42. Ibid 2, 15.

43. Raza, above n 38, 24.

44. Brunner, 'Chile' above n 39, 10.

45. Ibid 2, 12–13. See also *Improving Quality at Higher Education Institutions in Chile* (24 November 2016) United Nations Educational, Scientific and Cultural Organization/International Institute for Educational Planning <http://www.iiep.unesco.org/en/improving-quality-higher-education-institutions-chile-3786>.

46. Brunner, 'Chile' above n 39, 2, 7–9, 18. See also OECD and World Bank, 'Tertiary Education in Chile' (Reviews of National Policies for Education, OECD and World Bank, 2009) 15–16.

47. Brunner, 'Chile' above n 39, 2, 11–12; Raza, above n 38, 25; Daniel Uribe and Juan Salamanca, 'Country Background Report—Chile: OECD Thematic Review of Tertiary Education' (Country Background Report, Higher Education Division, Ministry of Education, June 2007) 71–6.

48. Brunner, 'Chile' above n 39, 25. See also OECD and World Bank, 'Tertiary Education in Chile', above n 46, 15–16.

49. OECD, 'Quality Assurance in Higher Education in Chile' (Reviews of National Policies for Education, OECD, November 2012) 9.

50. Paulo Santiago, Karine Tremblay, Ester Basri and Elena Arnal, 'Tertiary Education for the Knowledge Society' (Report vol 2, OECD, 2008) 157.

structures, including decisions in relation to appointment and promotion.[51] Criteria for promotion include years of experience, student evaluations and the faculties' scientific output.[52] To the extent that student evaluations can be considered a measure of teaching, teaching quality is generally taken into account. Policy directed towards the improvement of teaching quality, however, is primarily focused on increasing the number of academics that have doctoral degrees,[53] suggesting that research is a more important factor in recruitment and promotion decisions than teaching. Chile is thus ranked 'poor' in relation to this criterion.

(ii) Improving Society

Integration of Values

The Chilean *Constitution* identifies some values intended to inform the Chilean higher education system. These include that education is directed towards the development of the individual and that the system operates on the basis of freedom of education.[54] Further, the Chilean *General Law on Education 2009* identifies the following values as inspiring the Chilean educational system: universality and permanent education, quality of education, equity of the educational system, autonomy, diversity, responsibility, participation, flexibility, transparency, integration, sustainability and interculturality.[55] These values are therefore very clearly identified at the macro level, and on the basis of this analysis, Chile is ranked 'very good' in relation to this criterion.

Teaching for Citizenship

To gauge the extent to which the Chilean higher education system is focused on teaching for citizenship, a review of the following three Chilean university websites was undertaken:

- Universidad Arturo Prat
- Universidad de Antofagasta
- Universidad de Los Lagos

51. Ibid 157, 159. See also OECD and World Bank, 'Tertiary Education in Chile', above n 46, 53; Uribe and Salamanca, above n 47, 51.

52. Uribe and Salamanca, above n 47, 51.

53. Ibid 53.

54. *Constitution of the Republic of Chile 1980*, ch 3 art 19(10–11) [Anna I Vellvé Torras, Adela Staines and Jefri J Ruchti trans, *Chile's Constitution of 1980 with Amendments through 2012* (William S Hein & Co, 2012)].

55. *Establish the General Law of Education* (2 July 2010) Biblioteca del Congreso Nacional de Chile <https://www.leychile.cl/Navegar?idNorma=1006043#free0> art 3 [Google Chrome trans].

These institutions were selected on the basis of relevant information being available in the English language.

The Universidad Arturo Prat's Strategic Plan indicates some emphasis on teaching for citizenship. Pursuant to the University's vision, it is '[c]ommitted to the continuous training of technicians, professionals and postgraduates capable of contributing [t]hrough the generation, transfer and learning of knowledge, to economic, social and cultural development'.[56] This vision is not clear from website information directed to students, however, with the only mention of citizenship being the credibility the University's 'State character' will bring to 'the world of work'.[57]

The Universidad de Antofagasta's vision and mission indicates an emphasis on teaching for citizenship. Its vision includes forming 'socially responsible professionals with solid training', while its mission includes '[t]he training of people as professionals and the development of human talent at a continuous and advanced level, with the imprint of responsibility towards society and sustainable development'.[58]

The Universidad de Los Lagos also demonstrates some commitment to teaching for citizenship. Its mission includes 'training professionals and technicians with solid knowledge, pluralism and commitment to their environment'.[59]

Thus, although all surveyed websites demonstrate some direction towards teaching for citizenship, the message is not strongly conveyed to students. Consequently, Chile is ranked 'good' in relation to this criterion.

Equal Opportunity, Equal Treatment and Equity

In Chile, the percentage of 25–44 year-old non-students accessing tertiary education where their parents have below upper secondary education is 12 per cent, compared with 37 per cent where their parents have upper secondary or post-secondary non-tertiary education.[60] This is a difference of 25 per cent, significantly higher than the OECD average of 16 per cent.[61] The percentage of

56. Universidad Arturo Prat, *Strategic Definitions: Vision* (2014) Universidad Arturo Prat <http://www.unap.cl/mk/pei/files/assets/basic-html/page10.html> [Google Chrome trans].

57. Universidad Arturo Prat, *The University I Want,* Universidad Arturo Prat <http://www.unap.cl/admision/2017/unap.html> [Google Chrome trans].

58. Universidad de Antofagasta, *Plan de Desarrollo Estrategico Convenio Plurianual 2016–2020,* Universidad de Antofagasta <http://intranetua.uantof.cl/plan_desarrollo/> [Google Chrome trans].

59. Universidad de Los Lagos, *University,* Universidad de Los Lagos <http://www.ulagos.cl/contenido03.php?id=1> [Google Chrome trans].

60. OECD, 'Education at a Glance 2016', above n 25, 85–6.

61. Ibid.

25–44 year-old non-students accessing tertiary education where their parents have tertiary education is 77 per cent, a 40 per cent increase over where their parents have upper secondary or post-secondary non-tertiary education. The difference of 40 per cent is markedly higher than the OECD average difference of 28 per cent.[62] Thus, Chile is ranked 'very poor' for this criterion.

Freedom for Teaching and Research

Article 11 of the Chilean *Constitution* provides for a right to academic freedom. This Article states '[f]reedom of education has no other limitations but those imposed by morals, good customs, public order and national security'.[63] Further, '[o]fficially recognized education cannot be oriented to propagating any type of political-partisan tendency'.[64] Pursuant to Article 3 of the *General Law of Education,* '[t]he Chilean educational system is built on the basis of the rights guaranteed in the Constitution, as well as in the international treaties ratified by Chile and in force and, in particular, the right to education and freedom of education'.[65]

These constitutional and legislative provisions provide a clear general statement and guiding principle for higher education, although further elaboration of the principle would be desirable. Accordingly, Chile is ranked 'good' in relation to this criterion.

International Assistance

Unfortunately, data in relation to the proportion of official development aid dedicated to education compared with total official development aid is not available for Chile.[66] Accordingly, this criterion is ranked 'not applicable'.

62. Ibid 86–7.

63. *Constitution of the Republic of Chile 1980,* ch 3 art 19(11) [Anna I Vellvé Torras, Adela Staines and Jefri J Ruchti trans, *Chile's Constitution of 1980 with Amendments through 2012* (William S Hein & Co, 2012)]. But note a different translation references the 'freedom of teaching', see *Fixes the Refunded, Coordinated and Systematized Text of the Political Constitution of the Republic of Chile* (4 May 2017) Biblioteca del Congreso Nacional de Chile <https://www.leychile.cl/Navegar?idNorma=242302> ch 3 art 19(11) [Google Chrome trans].

64. *Constitution of the Republic of Chile 1980,* ch 3 art 19(11) [Anna I Vellvé Torras, Adela Staines and Jefri J Ruchti trans, *Chile's Constitution of 1980 with Amendments through 2012* (William S Hein & Co, 2012)].

65. *Establish the General Law of Education* (2 July 2010) Biblioteca del Congreso Nacional de Chile <https://www.leychile.cl/Navegar?idNorma=1006043#free0> [Google Chrome trans].

66. OECD, *Aid (ODA) by Sector and Donor [DAC5]* (30 April 2015) <http://stats.oecd.org/Index.aspx?datasetcode=TABLE5>.

(iii) Social Efficiency

Vocational Orientation

Although a clear awareness of the importance of work-integrated learning and the teaching of employability skills is evident in Chile, significant room for improvement remains. The Chilean Ministry of Education has identified the development of 'society's advanced human capital' as one of the important functions of the country's higher education system.[67] Yet although some disciplines have adopted initiatives to improve the 'labour market relevance' of courses, such initiatives remain 'discipline-based rather than institutionally driven'.[68] The Chilean curriculum is considered rigid and outdated, based largely on theoretical classroom learning and lacking emphasis on practical skills.[69] Further, an OECD and World Bank review in 2009 indicated that employers lacked 'regular, systematic input into universities' curriculum content, teaching practices, or institutional governance'.[70]

Students and employers appear to be dissatisfied with the capacity of the Chilean higher education system to prepare graduates for employment. Student survey respondents indicated a low level of confidence in the system of higher education, with the average response to a question relating to preparation for employment rated at 3.79 out of 10.[71] Further, students considered that the system lacked 'quality and integrity'[72] and felt that many students 'end up paying for degrees that are "useless" after graduation—degrees that provide them with no real skills, knowledge, nor credibility in the job market'.[73] These concerns are echoed by employer feedback, which indicates 'significant misgivings about the relevance of the knowledge, competencies, and skills that university graduates bring to the labour market'.[74] In relation to this criterion, Chile is ranked 'poor'.

67. Uribe and Salamanca, above n 47, 7.

68. OECD and World Bank, 'The Bío Region, Chile' (Review of Higher Education in Regional and City Development, OECD-World Bank, August 2009) 6. See also Uribe and Salamanca, above n 47, 20.

69. See OECD and World Bank, 'Tertiary Education in Chile', above n 46, 27; Uribe and Salamanca, above n 47, 11.

70. OECD and World Bank, 'Tertiary Education in Chile', above n 46.

71. Leer, above n 22, 30.

72. Ibid 31.

73. Ibid.

74. OECD and World Bank, 'Tertiary Education in Chile', above n 46 (emphasis altered).

Graduation Rates
In 2014, Chile's first-time tertiary graduation rate (excluding international students) was 51 per cent.[75] The OECD average rate was 45 per cent.[76] Overall, this results in a ranking of 'very good' for this sign.

Employability Prospects and Skills Shortages
In Chile, the employment rate for 25–64 year-olds who have completed a bachelor's or equivalent degree is 85 per cent, higher than the OECD average of 82 per cent.[77] Nevertheless, skills shortages resulting from a strong economy and jobs growth exist.[78] Although some of these shortages are in non-higher-education related areas, such as electricians and welders,[79] many of them are in professions requiring higher education qualifications. For example, significant shortages exist for mining professionals, health professionals, accountants and auditors, engineers and information technology professionals.[80] This skills mismatch is, however, reported to be easing.[81] Chile is ranked 'average' in relation to this criterion.

Research Quality
Chile has one university listed in the top 500[82] and a population of 18 million.[83] The U21 Ranking for Chile is 5.6. This result is 'very poor'.

Global Connectivity
Chile's higher education student population has very limited contact with the global higher education community. In 2014, 0 per cent of higher education students in Chile were international students.[84] Similarly, only 0.8 per cent of

75. OECD, 'Education at a Glance 2016', above n 25, 68.

76. Ibid.

77. Ibid 103.

78. Mary Anne Thompson, *Employment Outlook: Chile* (1 April 2014) Going Global <http://www.goinglobal.com/articles/1160/>.

79. Ibid.

80. Ibid.

81. Hays, *Hays Global Skills Index 2016: Chile* <http://www.hays-index.com/countries/chile/>.

82. Shanghai Jiao Tong University, *Academic Ranking of World Universities: Statistics*, Shanghai Ranking <http://www.shanghairanking.com/ARWU-Statistics-2016.html>.

83. *Chile Population*, Trading Economics <http://www.tradingeconomics.com/chile/population>.

84. OECD, 'Education at a Glance 2016', above n 25, 339.

national tertiary students in Chile in 2014 were enrolled abroad.[85] Chile is thus ranked 'very poor' in relation to this criterion.

2. England

(a) Political Context and Approach

England has undertaken significant reforms to its higher education system in recent years.[86] Reforms implemented from 2012 'put the market at [higher education's] ... heart'[87] and are reflective of a market-based model.[88] The primary function of the reforms was to implement the recommendations of the Browne Review[89] by transferring the costs of higher education from the state to students, and implementing a loan scheme so that students would only be required to repay loans after they started earning a wage.[90] Further reforms were proposed in 2016, and the *Higher Education and Research Act 2017* passed Parliament in April 2017.[91] The controversial and highly scrutinised Act is expected to enable universities participating in the Teaching Excellence Framework and meeting

85. Ibid 341.

86. See generally Cini and Guzmán-Concha, above n 15, 2–3. Note that as '[h]igher education is a devolved matter in Scotland, Wales and Northern Ireland' (Department for Business, Innovation & Skills, *Higher Education: Students at the Heart of the System* (White Paper, 2011) ii), the focus of this discussion is on evaluating English higher education policy. To the extent that relevant data is available specifically in relation to England, such data is utilised in this analysis. To the extent, however, that data specifically in relation to England is not available, but data in relation to the UK is available, this analysis considers the data relating to the UK as an indicator for the English system.

87. John Holmwood and Gurminder K Bhambra, 'The Attack on Education as a Social Right' (2012) 111(2) *The South Atlantic Quarterly* 392, 392.

88. See ibid 393; Michael Tomlinson, 'The Impact of Market-Driven Higher Education on Student-University Relations: Investing, Consuming and Competing' (2016) 29 *Higher Education Policy* 149.

89. See Lord John Browne, Michael Barber, Diane Doyle, David Eastwood, Julia King, Rajay Naik and Peter Sands, *Securing a Sustainable Future for Higher Education: An Independent Review of Higher Education Funding & Student Finance* (Review, 12 October 2010).

90. Ron Johnston, 'England's New Scheme for Funding Higher Education through Student Fees: "Fair And Progressive"?' (2013) 84(2) *The Political Quarterly* 200, 200.

91. Rachel Pells, *Universities Given Permission to Increase Tuition Fees Every Year* (28 April 2017) The Independent <http://www.independent.co.uk/news/education/education-news/university-tuition-fees-uk-rise-increase-every-year-government-higher-education-courses-study-a7707291.html>.

minimum eligibility requirements to increase their fees in line with inflation until 2020.[92]

The English higher education reforms have been subject to a 'visceral revulsion of the electorate at seeing education turned into a commodity'.[93] Student and lecturer protests were staged against the reforms, perceived as an 'ideologically led market experiment'.[94] A number of English higher education institutions also boycotted the annual national student satisfaction survey in protest against tuition fee increases.[95] Jeremy Corbyn, leader of the Labour Party, promised to abolish tuition fees in the lead up to the recent election, which resulted in a hung Parliament.[96] English students have been reported to be graduating with higher levels of debt than in any other English-speaking country,[97] and higher education institution applications have dropped by 4 per cent.[98]

92. Andrew Gunn, *Six Things You Need to Know about the Higher Education Bill* (4 April 2017) The Conversation <http://theconversation.com/six-things-you-need-to-know-about-the-higher-education-bill-74945>; David Morris, *Be It Enacted: The Higher Education and Research Act* (27 April 2017) Wonkhe <http://wonkhe.com/blogs/be-it-enacted-the-higher-education-and-research-act-2017/>.

93. Stefan Collini, *Voters Should Be Enraged by Higher Education Profiteering* (6 June 2017) The Guardian <https://www.theguardian.com/education/2017/jun/06/higher-education-profiteering-tuition-fees-universities>. See also Ariane de Gayardon, *England Embraces the Delusion of Free Tuition* (14 July 2017) University World News <http://www.universityworldnews.com/article.php?story=20170712153136573>.

94. Rebecca Ratcliffe, *Students and Lecturers March against Tories' Education Bill* (20 November 2016) The Guardian <https://www.theguardian.com/world/2016/nov/19/students-lecturers-march-tories-education-bill-brexit-eu>.

95. Max Ramsay, *Oxford University Students Are Latest to Boycott Student Survey in Protest over Tuition Fee Hikes* (12 January 2017) The Independent <http://www.independent.co.uk/student/news/oxford-university-students-protest-tuition-fees-hike-boycott-student-survey-satisfaction-tef-sorana-a7523781.html>.

96. De Gayardon, above n 93; Jon Stone, *Jeremy Corbyn: Scrap Tuition Fees and Give Students Grants Again, Says Labour Leadership Contender* (16 July 2017) The Independent <http://www.independent.co.uk/news/uk/politics/scrap-tuition-fees-and-give-students-grants-again-says-labours-jeremy-corbyn-10392769.html>.

97. Aftab Ali, *Graduate Debt in England Higher than Any Other English-Speaking Country* (28 April 2016) The Independent <http://www.independent.co.uk/student/student-life/finances/graduate-debt-in-england-higher-than-any-other-english-speaking-country-a7004666.html>.

98. David Green, *It's Time to Radically Rethink University Tuition Fees* (13 July 2017) The Guardian <https://www.theguardian.com/higher-education-network/2017/jul/13/its-time-to-radically-rethink-university-tuition-fees>; Simon Baker, *Applications to UK Universities down 4 Per Cent, Says UCAS* (13 July 2017) Times Higher Education <https://www.timeshighereducation.com/news/applications-uk-universities-down-4-cent-says-ucas>.

Under the English higher education system, higher education institutions are able to set their own fees, up to a maximum fee currently capped at £9,250 per year for 2017–2018.[99] By enabling fee differentiation, it was expected 'that universities would compete for students through their fee-setting'.[100] Although '[a]lmost all universities opted to charge the maximum',[101] Andy Adcroft, Jon Teckman and Robert Willis argue that variable tuition fees will 'exacerbate' competitive forces, which will shape and influence higher education in the UK.[102] Average annual tuition fees charged in England are relatively high, at $9,019 for students in government-dependent private institutions in 2013/2014.[103] These are offset to some extent by public support including loans and reduced interest rates.[104]

Competition is also present in other aspects of the English higher education system. At present, 'numerous information sources exist to help British students make their choice' in relation to the higher education institution they wish to attend.[105] These include student-experience surveys and league tables.[106] Nevertheless, it is unclear the extent to which league tables, which rank universities, actually assist students to make choices in relation to higher education[107] and 'a continuing asymmetry of information [persists] ... despite the growth of such information'.[108] Competition in the English system is also present in

99. *Higher Education (Higher Amount) (England) Regulations 2010* (UK) No 3020 <http://www.nationalarchives.gov.uk/doc/open-government-licence/>, s 4; UCAS, *Undergraduate Tuition Fees and Student Loans*, UCAS <https://www.ucas.com/ucas/undergraduate/finance-and-support/undergraduate-tuition-fees-and-student-loans>; John Morgan, *University Tuition Fee Cap of £9,250 Confirmed for 2017–18* (21 July 2016) Times Higher Education <https://www.timeshighereducation.com/news/university-tuition-fee-cap-of-nine-thousand-two-hundred-and-fifty-pounds-confirmed-for-2017-2018>.

100. Johnston, above n 90, 201.

101. Ibid 200.

102. Andy Adcroft, Jon Teckman and Robert Willis, 'Is Higher Education in the UK Becoming More Competitive?' (2010) 23(6) *International Journal of Public Sector Management* 578, 585.

103. OECD, 'Education at a Glance 2016', above n 25, 243. Although note that these figures are based on the academic year 2010/2011, prior to implementation of the 2012 higher education reforms which had the effect of doubling and in some cases tripling university fees—at 261.

104. See ibid 249.

105. Anneliese Dodds, 'The British Higher Education Funding Debate: The Perils of "Talking Economics"' (2011) 9(3) *London Review of Education* 317, 319. See also Adcroft, Teckman and Willis, above n 102, 582.

106. Dodds, above n 105, 319.

107. Ibid 320.

108. Ibid 319.

the form of competition for 'research funds and commercial sponsorship and consultancies'.[109]

The English higher education system is far removed from a rights-based approach. Although, as John Holmwood and Gurminder K Bhambra assert, 'liberal market policy regimes like [that of England] express classic liberal rights of citizenship',[110] they do not tend to embrace social and economic rights such as the right to education. Further, acceptance of social rights in English government policy has declined; '[t]he UK is readily characterized as having shifted from an institutionalized social rights model to a neoliberal, market-based model'.[111] Accordingly, the human right to higher education is not provided for in English higher education legislation or policy. Aspects of a rights-based approach are apparent, however. Public spending on tertiary education institutions per student is above the OECD average.[112] Policies are also in place to promote equality of opportunity in higher education. For example, under the 2012 reforms, universities that wish to charge more than £6,000 per annum must have an approved Access Agreement, which sets out how the university will widen access to higher education.[113] Overall, however, the ability of higher education institutions to set their own fees together with the heavy focus on 'user-pays' indicates that the English system best represents the market-based approach.

(B) Evaluation

(i) Individual Transformation

Student Survey Responses

The National Student Survey (NSS) is the main student survey undertaken in the UK. The NSS is 'a census of nearly half a million students across the UK' and has been conducted on an annual basis since 2005.[114] Nevertheless, the NSS has been criticised for being 'based on typical customer surveys in which students

109. Patrick Ainley, 'The New "Market-State" and Education' (2004) 19(4) *Journal of Education Policy* 497, 506.

110. Holmwood and Bhambra, above n 87, 393.

111. Ibid.

112. OECD, 'Education at a Glance 2016', above n 25, 221.

113. See Department for Business, Innovation & Skills, *Higher Education,* above n 86, 56; Johnston, above n 90, 207.

114. *About the NSS,* The National Student Survey <http://www.thestudentsurvey.com/about.php>.

rate items rather than how they feel they have engaged with their programme'.[115] In relation to measurement of student transformation, three statements included in the NSS concerned with 'personal development' are relevant.[116] In terms of the statement 'the course has helped me present myself with confidence', 78.5 per cent of students in higher education institutions 'definitely' or 'mostly' agreed with the statement in 2015, compared with 78 per cent in 2016.[117] For the statement 'my communication skills have improved', 79.5 per cent of students 'definitely' or 'mostly' agreed with the statement in both 2015 and 2016.[118] Similarly stable results are seen in relation to the statement 'as a result of the course, I feel confident in tackling unfamiliar problems', to which 79.5 per cent of students 'definitely' or 'mostly' agreed in 2015 and 2016.[119] Although more limited than other state student surveys, these results appear to paint a generally positive picture of student transformation in English higher education and results in a ranking of 'good' for England in relation to this criterion.

Personalised Learning

The ratio of students to teaching staff in bachelor's, master's, doctoral or equivalent level degrees in the UK is 17.[120] This figure is equivalent to the OECD average of 17.[121] England is thus ranked 'average' in relation to this criterion.

Resources per Student

In the UK, the proportion of spending on higher education equates to 1.8 per cent of GDP, higher than the OECD average of 1.5 per cent of GDP.[122] In terms of annual expenditure per higher education student in 2013, the UK spent $25,744

115. James Williams, 'What Do Students Deserve? Concerns Mount over Quality of Expanding Higher Education', *The Conversation* (online), 28 May 2014 <http://theconversation.com/what-do-students-deserve-concerns-mount-over-quality-of-expanding-higher-education-27041>.

116. *National Student Survey*, The National Student Survey <www.thestudentsurvey.com/content/NSS2015_Questionnaire.pdf>.

117. Note that results are averages of full-time and part-time student results. *National Student Survey Results 2016* (5 October 2016) Higher Education Funding Council for England <http://www.hefce.ac.uk/lt/nss/results/2016/>.

118. Ibid.

119. Ibid.

120. OECD, 'Education at a Glance 2016', above n 25, 403.

121. Ibid.

122. Ibid 206.

per student, which favourably compares with the OECD average of $15,772.[123] On the basis of this analysis, England is ranked 'very good' in relation to this criterion.

Institutional Autonomy

The UK higher education sector enjoys significant levels of autonomy. Higher education institutions are independent legal entities and are not owned or run by the state.[124] In relation to teaching, curricular content is freely determined by higher education institutions, although this is subject to professional accreditation requirements.[125] Similarly, academics enjoy autonomy in relation to research.[126] Higher education institutions are free to set their own student admission criteria and procedures,[127] and are unrestricted in their ability to recruit staff.[128]

Quality in UK higher education is monitored through sector-wide quality assurance mechanisms. Higher education institutions are required to undergo institutional accreditation.[129] The Quality Assurance Agency for Higher Education is an independent body responsible for publishing and maintaining a quality code for higher education and undertaking external reviews of higher education institutions.[130] On the basis of this discussion, England achieves a ranking of 'very good' for this criterion.

123. Ibid 192.

124. Steve Baskerville, 'A Guide to UK Higher Education and Partnerships for Overseas Universities' (Research Series 11, UK Higher Education International Unit, July 2013) 11.

125. Thomas Estermann, Terhi Nokkala and Monika Steinel, 'University Autonomy in Europe II: The Scorecard' (Project Report, European University Association, 15 November 2011) 52; Hilde Penneman, 'Synoptic Review of the Country Reports' in Walter Berka, Jan De Groot and Hilde Penneman (eds), *Autonomy in Education: Yearbook of the European Association for Education Law and Policy* (Kluwer Law International, 2000) vol 3, 41, 61–2; Hilde Penneman, 'Autonomy in Education: Review of the Country Reports' in Walter Berka, Jan De Groot and Hilde Penneman (eds), *Autonomy in Education: Yearbook of the European Association for Education Law and Policy* (Kluwer Law International, 2000) vol 3, 29, 34.

126. Baskerville, above n 124, 11.

127. Estermann, Nokkala and Steinel, above n 125, 46–7; Baskerville, above n 124, 11.

128. Estermann, Nokkala and Steinel, above n 125, 38.

129. European University Association, *United Kingdom* <http://www.university-autonomy.eu/countries/united-kingdom/>.

130. Quality Assurance Agency, *About Us* <http://www.qaa.ac.uk/about-us>.

Commitment to Teaching and Learning

In the UK, higher education institutions have the legal autonomy to make their own hiring and promotional decisions, and there is no national framework for academic career structures.[131] In general, however, applicants require a doctorate degree for entry-level lecturer positions,[132] and both teaching and research performance are relevant to decisions in relation to promotion.[133] Nevertheless, although achievement in teaching is relevant to promotion, there has been widespread concern in recent years that the higher education reward system favours the research criterion.[134] This is particularly so in the context of the introduction of the Research Assessment Exercise, the outcomes of which determine the amount of public funding that higher education institutions receive.[135] Although most institutions have adopted policies designed to value and reward teaching, they do not yet have a significant impact on academic career progression.[136] Thus, in relation to this criterion, England is ranked 'poor'.

(ii) Improving Society

Integration of Values

Despite the existence of national policies and legislation, the values underpinning the English higher education system are somewhat unclear and must be inferred from a variety of sources. The government's higher education participation policy indicates a strong importance attached to equality of opportunity and fairness. It asserts that '[a]nyone with the ability who wants to go to university should have the chance to do so, whatever their economic or social background'.[137] This

131. Santiago, Tremblay, Basri and Arnal, above n 50, 149.

132. European University Institute, *United Kingdom, Academic Structure* (24 October 2014) <http://www.eui.eu/ProgrammesAndFellowships/AcademicCareersObservatory/AcademicCareersbyCountry/UnitedKingdom.aspx>.

133. Ibid.

134. Rebecca Turner and David Gosling, 'Rewarding Excellent Teaching: The Translation of a Policy Initiative in the United Kingdom' (2012) 66(4) *Higher Education Quarterly* 415, 416.

135. Santiago, Tremblay, Basri and Arnal, above n 50, 160.

136. Annette Cashmore, Chris Cane and Robert Cane, 'Rebalancing Promotion in the HE Sector: Is Teaching Excellence Being Rewarded?' (HEA Research Series, The Higher Education Academy, 3 July 2013) 36. See also Turner and Gosling, above n 134, 415.

137. Department for Business, Innovation & Skills, *2010 to 2015 Government Policy: Higher Education Participation* (8 May 2015) <https://www.gov.uk/government/publications/2010-to-2015-government-policy-higher-education-participation/2010-to-2015-government-policy-higher-education-participation>.

value is reinforced via the 'National Strategy for Access and Student Success in Higher Education'.[138] Further, the government's access to higher education policy indicates that financial sustainability, innovation and quality are also values that inform the English higher education system.[139] On the basis of this discussion, England is ranked 'poor' in relation to this criterion.

Teaching for Citizenship

To gauge the extent to which the English higher education system is focused on teaching for citizenship, a review of the following three English university websites was undertaken:

- University of Lancaster
- The Open University
- University of Bath

Lancaster University's strategic plan evinces a clear focus on teaching for citizenship. The University's values include 'engaging actively to change the world, through our teaching'[140] and its strategic priority in relation to teaching is expressed as being directed to 'transform people's lives and society through teaching and student experience'.[141] This focus is not evident from the reasons that the University provides to students to choose Lancaster, however, aside from employability prospects.[142]

The Open University 'Strategic Plan 2012–2017: Securing the Mission' suggests little focus on teaching for citizenship.[143] Similarly, the University's website does not demonstrate significant focus in this respect.[144]

The University of Bath's 'University Strategy 2013–2016' indicates a strong focus on teaching for citizenship. Part of the University's vision includes having

138. Department for Business, Innovation and Skills, 'National Strategy for Access and Student Success in Higher Education' (Strategy, Office for Fair Access and Higher Education Funding Council for England, April 2014).

139. Department for Business, Innovation & Skills, *2010 to 2015 Government Policy,* above n 137.

140. Lancaster University, 'Our Strategy for 2020' (Strategic Plan, Lancaster University) 3.

141. Ibid 6.

142. Lancaster University, *Five Great Reasons* <http://www.lancaster.ac.uk/study/why-lancaster/>.

143. The Open University, 'Strategic Plan 2012–2017: Securing the Mission' (Strategic Plan, The Open University, 2015).

144. See The Open University, *What It's Like to Study* <http://www.open.ac.uk/courses/what-study-like>.

'global impact through our alumni',[145] while its mission includes 'deliver[ing] world-class . . . teaching, educating our students to become future leaders and innovators'.[146] Further, the University cites excellence in education as including enhancing student 'future employability and broader contributions to society'.[147] Nevertheless, this focus is not evident in the University's website information concerning its ranking and reputation.[148]

On the basis of this discussion, England is ranked as 'average' for this criterion.

Equal Opportunity, Equal Treatment and Equity

In England, the percentage of 25–44 year-old non-students accessing tertiary education where their parents have below upper secondary education is 17 per cent, compared with 42 per cent where their parents have upper secondary or post-secondary non-tertiary education.[149] This is a difference of 25 per cent, significantly higher than the OECD average of 16 per cent.[150] The percentage of 25–44 year-old non-students accessing tertiary education where their parents have tertiary education is 72 per cent, a 30 per cent increase over where their parents have upper secondary or post-secondary non-tertiary education. This difference is similar to the OECD average of 28 per cent.[151] Thus, England is ranked 'poor' for this criterion.

Freedom for Teaching and Research

The UK has no written constitution, and thus does not protect academic freedom by such means.[152] The UK also has no specific piece of legislation relating to higher education.[153] Some limited protection for academic freedom is found

145. University of Bath, 'University Strategy 2013–2016: A World-Class University in a World Heritage City' (Strategic Plan, University of Bath, 2013) 2.

146. Ibid 3.

147. Ibid 6.

148. University of Bath, *Rankings and Reputation* <http://www.bath.ac.uk/about/rankings/index.html>.

149. OECD, 'Education at a Glance 2016', above n 25, 85–6.

150. Ibid.

151. Ibid 86–7.

152. Terence Karran, Klaus Beiter and Kwadwo Appiagyei-Atua, 'Measuring Academic Freedom in Europe: A Criterion Referenced Approach' (2017) 1(2) *Policy Reviews in Higher Education* 209, 233.

153. Ibid 234.

in the *Education Reform Act 1988*.[154] On this basis, England is ranked 'poor' in relation to this criterion.[155]

International Assistance

In 2015, the UK directed approximately 7 per cent of total official development aid towards education.[156] This is comparable with the DAC member country average of 6.8 per cent[157] and results in a rating for this criterion of 'average'.

(iii) Social Efficiency

Vocational Orientation

In the UK, opportunities for supported work experience and internships within higher education programmes are widespread, although a lack of available data makes evaluation difficult.[158] Relevant strategies include integration of 'sandwich placements' (year-long placements integrated within higher education courses),[159] and other work experience and internship opportunities.[160] Research indicates there has been some decline in the extent of sandwich placements and a decrease in work-experience-type opportunities generally.[161] There is no system-wide framework for integration of these types of vocational programmes, and there is a recognised 'need to increase opportunities for students to acquire relevant work experience during their studies'.[162] Nevertheless, business and industry do often have input into curriculum matters,[163] and many higher education

154. *Education Reform Act 1988* (UK) c IV, s 202(1)–(2); ibid.

155. Note that this ranking accords with the ranking of 5 per cent given in Karran, Beiter and Appiagyei-Atua, above n 152, 229.

156. OECD, *Aid (ODA) by Sector and Donor [DAC5]*, above n 66.

157. Ibid.

158. Oakleigh Consulting Limited and Career Development Organisation, 'Increasing Opportunities for High Quality Higher Education Work Experience: Report to HEFCE by Oakleigh Consulting Ltd and CRAC' (Report, Oakleigh Consulting Limited and Career Development Organisation, July 2011) i.

159. Australian Workforce and Productivity Agency, 'Work Integrated Learning: AWPA Scoping Paper' (Scoping Paper, Australian Workforce and Productivity Agency, undated) 8.

160. Oakleigh Consulting Limited and Career Development Organisation, above n 158, i.

161. Ibid ix–x.

162. Sir Tim Wilson, 'A Review of Business-University Collaboration' (Review, February 2012) 1.

163. Ibid 2.

institutions incorporate the teaching of employability skills within the higher education curriculum.[164]

In relation to satisfaction with higher education in terms of vocational direction, students and employers indicate general overall satisfaction. Surveys conducted by the Confederation of British Industry (CBI) indicated 'a widespread confidence among students that they are developing employability skills while at university'.[165] Nevertheless, a significant number of students indicated that they did not feel they had developed numeracy, business and customer awareness skills.[166] Surveys of employers indicated a similar view, with employers generally satisfied that the graduates they had recruited possessed most employability skills, but many indicating dissatisfaction with graduates' business and customer awareness and self-management skills.[167] Dissatisfaction is more evident in the European Commission's study, in which 52 per cent of employers identified a shortage of applicants with the right skills and capabilities as being a key reason for difficulty filling vacancies.[168] This is to some extent supported by the reported incidence of skill mismatch in the UK of 36.9 per cent.[169] On the basis of this discussion, England is ranked 'good' in relation to this criterion.

Graduation Rates

In 2014, the UK's first-time tertiary graduation rate (excluding international students) was 42 per cent, lower than the OECD average rate of 45 per cent.[170] Thus, this results in a ranking of 'poor' for this sign.

Employability Prospects and Skills Shortages

In the UK, the employment rate for 25–64 year-olds who have completed a bachelor's or equivalent degree is 87 per cent, higher than the OECD average of

164. See ibid 31; CBI, 'Future Fit: Preparing Graduates for the World of Work' (Report, CBI, March 2009) 10, 12–13.

165. CBI, above n 164, 10, 23.

166. Ibid 10, 23.

167. Ibid 11, 21.

168. European Commission, 'Employers' Perception of Graduate Employability' (Analytical Report, Flash Eurobarometer Series #304, European Commission, November 2010) 49.

169. Santiago Budria and Ana Moro-Egido, 'Overqualification, Skill Mismatches and Wages in Private Sector Employment in Europe' (2014) 20(3) *Technological and Economic Development of Economy* 457, 463–4.

170. OECD, 'Education at a Glance 2016', above n 25, 68.

82 per cent.[171] Yet in spite of general economic recovery, significant and serious skills shortages exist.[172] Many of these shortages are in occupations where higher education qualifications are required, such as engineering, information technology and teaching.[173] Hays Global Skills Index 2016 asserts that 'skills shortages remain prevalent'.[174] England is thus ranked 'good' in relation to this criterion.

Research Quality

The UK has 37 universities listed in the top 500[175] and a population of 65.1 million.[176] The U21 Ranking for the UK is 56.0. This result is 'average'.

Global Connectivity

Connections between the UK and the international higher education community vary across the indicators considered here. Of the total tertiary enrolment in the UK in 2014, 18 per cent of students were international students.[177] In the same year, however, only 1.5 per cent of UK tertiary students were enrolled abroad.[178] Thus in relation to this criterion, the UK is ranked 'good'.

3. United States

(a) Political Context and Approach

Although US higher education policy has not traditionally been controversial, it has become more polarizing in recent times.[179] Student loan debt has escalated,

171. Ibid 103.

172. See Matthew Wall, 'Skills Shortages Holding Back the UK's Economic Recovery', *BBC News* (online), 1 December 2014 <http://www.bbc.com/news/business-30224320>; Hays, *Hays Global Skills Index 2014: United Kingdom* <http://www.hays-index.com/countries/united-kingdom/>.

173. Matthew Wall, 'Skills Shortages', above n 172. See generally *Tier 2 Shortage Occupation List—Government-Approved Version* (6 April 2014) Gov.UK <https://www.gov.uk/government/uploads/system/uploads/attachment_data/file/308513/shortageoccupationlistapril14.pdf>.

174. Hays, *Hays Global Skills Index 2016: United Kingdom* <http://www.hays-index.com/countries/united-kingdom/>.

175. Shanghai Jiao Tong University, *Academic Ranking of World Universities: Statistics,* above n 82.

176. Note that the reference measure is the United Kingdom rather than England, as this is what is used in the Shanghai Jiao Tong University rankings. Office for National Statistics, *Theme: Population* <http://ons.gov.uk/ons/taxonomy/index.html?nscl=Population>.

177. OECD, 'Education at a Glance 2016', above n 25, 339.

178. Ibid 341.

179. Susan Delacourt, *America Is Now Split on Education, Too: Delacourt* (14 July 2017) The Star <https://www.thestar.com/news/insight/2017/07/14/america-is-now-split-on-education-too-delacourt.html>.

such that it is now referred to as a '$1.3 Trillion Crisis'[180] and a 'debt bubble'.[181] Student loans are also subject to high interest rates.[182] The issue has led to student protests, calling for tuition-free college and cancellation of student debt, across the United States.[183] It also led to presidential hopeful Bernie Sanders promising to enact universal free public college tuition in the lead up to the 2016 US election.[184] Sanders' campaign was considered a long shot, yet his pursuit of the Democratic presidential nomination was far more successful than expected, and he has continued his campaign for free college education post the presidential election.[185] Polls indicate that Sanders is currently the most popular active politician in the United States, indicating that his messages are resonating with large numbers of Americans.[186]

The current approach to higher education in the United States is best characterised as a market-based model. High levels of competition exist throughout the system. Higher education institutions are generally able to charge tuition and fees on a market basis, although '[p]ublic institutions may have restrictions set by states on how much they can charge students'.[187] An example is Texas, where

180. Zack Friedman, *Student Loan Debt in 2017: A $1.3 Trillion Crisis* (21 February 2017) Forbes <https://www.forbes.com/sites/zackfriedman/2017/02/21/student-loan-debt-statistics-2017/#768317025dab>.

181. Rana Foroohar, *The US College Debt Bubble Is Becoming Dangerous* (10 April 2017) Financial Times <https://www.ft.com/content/a272ee4c-1b83-11e7-bcac-6d03d067f81f?mhq5j=e2>.

182. Joanna Walters, *Bernie Sanders: Free Public College Tuition Is the 'Right Thing to Do'* (23 October 2015) The Guardian <https://www.theguardian.com/us-news/2015/oct/22/bernie-sanders-free-public-college-tuition-higher-education>.

183. Curtis Skinner and Valerie Vande Panne, *Students across US March over Debt, Free Public College* (12 November 2015) Reuters <http://www.reuters.com/article/us-usa-college-protests-idUSKCN0T116W20151112>.

184. Bernie Sanders, *Make College Free for All* (22 October 2015) The Washington Post <https://www.washingtonpost.com/opinions/bernie-sanders-america-needs-free-college-now/2015/10/22/a3d05512-7685-11e5-bc80-9091021aeb69_story.html?utm_term=.c127e64d780e>; Walters, above n 182.

185. *It's Time to Make College Tuition Free and Debt Free*, Bernie Sanders <https://berniesanders.com/issues/its-time-to-make-college-tuition-free-and-debt-free/>.

186. Jonathan Easley, *Poll: Bernie Sanders Country's Most Popular Active Politician* (18 April 2017) The Hill <http://thehill.com/homenews/campaign/329404-poll-bernie-sanders-countrys-most-popular-active-politician>; Michael Sainato, *Poll Confirms Bernie Sanders Is the Most Popular Politician in the Country* (11 July 2017) Observer <http://observer.com/2017/07/bernie-sanders-most-popular-politician/>.

187. International Affairs Office, *Organization of U.S. Education: Tertiary Institutions* (February 2008) US Department of Education <http://www2.ed.gov/about/offices/list/ous/international/usnei/us/edlite-org-us.html>.

'[p]rior to 2003, postsecondary education ... was regulated by the state legislature.... [H]owever ... the legislature decided to deregulate university tuition and remove tuition caps'.[188] The result was a 72 per cent increase in average public university costs between 2003 and 2009.[189] As higher education institutions can charge fees on a market basis, they effectively compete with each other for students, although it should be noted that public institutions generally charge higher fees for out-of-state and international students.[190] The estimated annual average student tuition fees charged by public tertiary institutions are relatively high, amounting to $8,202 for students enrolled in bachelor's or equivalent level degrees and $10,818 for students enrolled in master's or equivalent level degrees.[191] In recent times, fees have increased 'faster than inflation'.[192] Fees are offset, however, by the availability of 'grants, tax credits, and loans'.[193]

Further aspects of competition include a lack of barriers to the higher education market and access to information. Like most other systems, the US higher education system requires higher education institutions to be accredited.[194] Lindsey Burke and Stuart M Butler argue, however, that 'accreditation has become, first and foremost, a barrier to entry' to the higher education market.[195] To this extent then, the US system is not a pure market system. Nevertheless, requirements to provide access to information are indicative of a market approach. In this respect, section 111(i) of the *Higher Education Opportunity Act* requires extensive information about higher education institutions to be published on a particular website.[196] The title of section 111—'transparency in college tuition for

188. Madeleine Green, NAFSA: Association of International Educators, Mark Darby, Charles McCullough, Andrew Previc, Brianna Roberts and Katrina Santner, 'United States Education Guidebook' (Report, Australian Education International, April 2012) 44.

189. Ibid 44–45.

190. Ibid 13.

191. Note that fees charged by independent private institutions are significantly higher, at $21,189 and $16,932 respectively. See OECD, 'Education at a Glance 2016', above n 25, 243.

192. Green, Darby, McCullough, Previc, Roberts and Santner, Association of International Educators, 'United States Education Guidebook' above n 188, 13.

193. Ibid.

194. Ibid 15.

195. Lindsey Burke and Stuart M Butler, *Accreditation: Removing the Barrier to Higher Education Reform* (21 September 2012) The Heritage Foundation <http://www.heritage.org/research/reports/2012/09/accreditation-removing-the-barrier-to-higher-education-reform>.

196. *Higher Education Opportunity Act*, Pub L No 110-315, § 111(i), stat 3078, 122, 122 (2008).

consumers'[197]—suggests the purpose of ensuring this information is available is to enable student consumers to make choices 'consistent with competition, commodity production and profit'.[198]

The US higher education system also has significant levels of privatisation countered with moderate levels of government intervention. The private sector provides the majority of funding, comprising 64 per cent of all tertiary education funding.[199] Of all higher education students in 2012, 28 per cent of tertiary education students were enrolled in independent private institutions.[200] Further, for-profit post-secondary education institutions constitute 'the fastest-growing segment of US higher education'.[201] Nevertheless, the public spend on higher education is on par with the OECD average, at $10,134 per student.[202] Further, higher education institutions are government-regulated through legislation such as the *Higher Education Opportunity Act*[203] as well as accreditation processes.[204]

Although the US higher education system cannot be described as having adopted a rights-based approach, it does share some characteristics of the approach. Human rights norms do not underpin the US approach to higher education, nor is higher education something that people are considered to be entitled to. This is particularly evident through the ability of institutions to set their own tuition and fee rates, although this is offset to some degree by the availability of financial support for students. Characteristics of a rights-based approach are, however, present. Government spending per student is approximately the same as the OECD average. Further, policies are in place to impact existing status differences.[205] Nevertheless, high levels of competition, access to information and privatisation suggest the US system is best characterised as representative of a market-based approach.

197. Ibid.

198. Simon Marginson, 'The Impossibility of Capitalist Markets in Higher Education' (2013) 28(3) *Journal of Education Policy* 353, 356. See also Roger Brown, 'Markets and Non-Markets' in Roger Brown (ed), *Higher Education and the Market* (Routledge, 2011) 6, 8–9.

199. OECD, 'Education at a Glance 2016', above n 25, 218.

200. Ibid 425.

201. Green, Darby, McCullough, Previc, Roberts, Santner, Association of International Educators, 'United States Education Guidebook' above n 188, 18.

202. Compared to the OECD average of $9,719. See OECD, 'Education at a Glance 2016', above n 25, 221.

203. *Higher Education Opportunity Act*, Pub L No 110-315, stat 3078, 122 (2008).

204. Green, Darby, McCullough, Previc, Roberts, Santner, Association of International Educators, 'United States Education Guidebook' above n 188, 15.

205. See, eg, *Higher Education Opportunity Act*, Pub L No 110-315, § 316, stat 3185, 122, 122 (2008).

(B) Evaluation

(i) Individual Transformation

Student Survey Responses

The major student survey instrument utilised in the United States is the NSSE, which has been administered to first- and senior-year undergraduate students on an annual basis since 2000.[206] All student survey measures have some limitations and the NSSE is no exception. In particular, where some student surveys are conducted across all higher education institutions, the NSSE is conducted only in those institutions that elect to participate.[207] Further, for the purposes of this analysis the NSSE is limited in that it surveys students in both the United States and Canada. Nevertheless, given the majority of participating institutions are from the United States,[208] it is contended that the NSSE results serve as a reasonable proxy for self-reported student transformation in the United States.

The NSSE survey asks students the extent to which their experience at their particular higher education institution has 'contributed to [their] ... knowledge, skills, and personal development' in relation to the following ten specified areas:[209]

- writing clearly and effectively
- speaking clearly and effectively
- thinking critically and analytically
- analysing numerical and statistical information
- acquiring job or work-related knowledge or skills
- working effectively with others
- developing or clarifying a personal code of values and ethics
- understanding people of other backgrounds (economic, racial/ethnic, political, religious, nationality, etc)
- solving complex real-world problems
- being an informed and active citizen.

206. Alexander C McCormick and Jillian Kinzie, 'Refocusing the Quality Discourse: The United States National Survey of Student Engagement' in Hamish Coates and Alexander C McCormick (eds), *Engaging University Students* (Springer, 2014) 13, 14–15.

207. Ibid 14.

208. 'Since its launch in 2000, more than 1,500 four-year colleges and universities in the US and Canada have participated in NSSE, with 640 US and 73 Canadian institutions in 2014'. National Survey of Student Engagement, 'Bringing the Institution into Focus—Annual Results 2014' (Report, National Survey of Student Engagement, 2014) 6.

209. National Survey of Student Engagement, *National Survey of Student Engagement: Summary Tables* (2016) <http://nsse.indiana.edu/html/summary_tables.cfm>.

In relation to these questions, the percentage of students that responded 'quite a bit' or 'very much' to these statements varied between 56 per cent and 81 per cent, with the average being 64.1 per cent.[210] This represents a reasonably positive picture of student self-reported individual transformation in US higher education and results in a ranking of 'average' in relation to this criterion.

Personalised Learning

Unfortunately, data relating specifically to the ratio of students to teaching staff in bachelor's, master's, doctoral or equivalent degrees in the United States is not available. The ratio of students to teaching staff in all tertiary education, however, constitutes a good proxy and is 15.[211] This is better than the OECD average of 17.[212] The United States is thus ranked 'good' in relation to this criterion.

Resources per Student

The United States has the highest level of spending on tertiary education among OECD countries. In 2013, it spent an amount equal to 2.6 per cent of GDP on higher education, compared with the OECD average of 1.5 per cent.[213] Higher education spending is also high on a per student basis. In 2013, $27,924 per tertiary education student was spent, compared with the OECD average of $15,772.[214] On the basis of this analysis, the United States is ranked 'very good' in relation to this criterion.

Institutional Autonomy

The US higher education sector is unique in its approach to institutional autonomy. Pursuant to the US *Constitution*, higher education is not a federal but a state responsibility.[215] Further, the extent to which states control higher education institutions varies.[216] In general, higher education institutions enjoy significant

210. Note that these figures represent the average responses of first-year and senior students. See ibid.

211. OECD, 'Education at a Glance 2016', above n 25, 403.

212. Ibid.

213. Ibid 206.

214. Ibid 192.

215. Molly Corbett Broad, 'Academic Freedom & Institutional Autonomy in the United States: Balancing Rights and Responsibilities' (Paper presented at Council of Europe, Strasbourg, France, 8 November 2010) 27; Peter D Eckel and Jacqueline E King, *An Overview of Higher Education in the United States: Diversity, Access, and the Role of the Marketplace* (American Council on Education, 2004) 3.

216. Corbett Broad, above n 215, 6; Eckel and King, above n 215, 3.

independence and autonomy from government.[217] This autonomy is to some extent enshrined in the *Constitution* in the form of guaranteed freedom of speech.[218] In relation to teaching, institutions generally have autonomy to determine their own curriculum, subject to peer review and professional accreditation requirements.[219] Similarly, higher education institutions are able to exercise freedom in staff recruitment.[220] In general, institutions have freedom in terms of student admission, reflected in 'institutions with a wide range of admissions selectivity',[221] although particular states may set policies regulating admissions standards.[222]

In accordance with its decentralised structure, the US higher education system has no overarching quality assurance system. Instead, it relies on peer-review processes of accreditation, 'where a team of knowledgeable academics from other institutions gathers together to assess the programs, policies and practices of the institution being evaluated'.[223] This system is thought to protect against inappropriate government intervention in higher education and has traditionally been seen as a reliable indicator of quality.[224] Nevertheless, some argue that '[h]ow effectively this system works is a subject of considerable disagreement', and its decentralised nature necessarily involves variation in the standards applied to higher education institutions.[225] On the basis of this analysis, the United States achieves a ranking of 'good'.

Commitment to Teaching and Learning

As the US higher education system is decentralised, there is no overarching national system for academic career structures. In general, teaching does have an

217. Alvaro Romo de la Rosa, 'Institutional Autonomy and Academic Freedom: A Perspective from the American Continent' (2007) 20(3) *Higher Education Policy* 275, 283.

218. Corbett Broad, above n 215, 2.

219. Charles Glenn, 'Autonomy in Education: United States' in Walter Berka, Jan De Groot and Hilde Penneman (eds), *Autonomy in Education: Yearbook of the European Association for Education Law and Policy* (Kluwer Law International, 2000) vol 3, 433, 440; Eckel and King, above n 215, 9.

220. Glenn, above n 219, 433, 436.

221. Eckel and King, above n 215, 8.

222. Ibid 3.

223. Alexander W Astin, *Accreditation and Autonomy* (18 February 2014) Inside Higher Ed <https://www.insidehighered.com/views/2014/02/18/accreditation-helps-limit-government-intrusion-us-higher-education-essay>. See also de la Rosa, above n 217, 283.

224. Corbett Broad, above n 215, 8.

225. Glenn, above n 219, 437. See also Astin, above n 223.

influence on appointment and promotion, including to tenured academic positions.[226] In this respect, higher education institutions are responsible for conducting evaluation and promotion activities.[227] Nevertheless, in the United States '[a] scholar's value on the academic market is very much based on his/her research output'. [228] This is supported by James S Fairweather, whose research found that 'despite decade-long efforts to enhance the value of teaching . . . spending more time on teaching . . . still means lower pay', and instead, research productivity remained the strongest indicator of increased pay.[229] Thus, the United States is ranked 'poor' in relation to this criterion.

(ii) Improving Society

Integration of Values

As the role of federal government in relation to the US higher education system is constitutionally limited, identifying overarching values involves making inferences from national legislation and policy documents.[230] In this respect, the *Higher Education Opportunity Act 2008* suggests that diversity, freedom of speech and association, and equal treatment should underpin the higher education system.[231] The establishment of a National Advisory Committee on Institutional Quality and Integrity suggests that importance is attached to quality.[232] Further, value is attached to the concept of college affordability.[233] Nevertheless, as the values are somewhat unclear, the United States is ranked 'poor' in relation to this criterion.

226. European University Institute, *USA, Academic Structure* (18 February 2014) <http://www.eui.eu/ProgrammesAndFellowships/AcademicCareersObservatory/AcademicCareersbyCountry/USA.aspx>.

227. Ibid.

228. Ibid.

229. James S Fairweather, 'Beyond the Rhetoric: Trends in the Relative Value of Teaching and Research in Faculty Salaries' (2005) 76(4) *The Journal of Higher Education* 401, 418. See also The Higher Education Academy, 'Reward and Recognition in Higher Education: Institutional Policies and Their Implementation' (Report, The Higher Education Academy, 2009) 2.

230. See US Department of Education, *Laws & Guidance* <http://www2.ed.gov/policy/landing.jhtml?src=go>.

231. *Higher Education Opportunity Act*, Pub L No 110-315, § 104, stat 3090, 122, 122 (2008).

232. Ibid.

233. Ibid; Green, Darby, McCullough, Previc, Roberts, Santner, Association of International Educators, 'United States Education Guidebook' above n 188, 17.

Teaching for Citizenship

To gauge the extent to which the American higher education system is focused on teaching for citizenship, a review of the following three American university websites was undertaken:

- University of California, San Diego
- East Carolina University
- The University of Kansas

In the University of California, San Diego's strategic plan five overarching university goals are identified, one of which is to deliver 'an educational and overall experience that develops students who are capable of solving problems, leading, and innovating in a diverse and interconnected world'.[234] This suggests a focus on teaching for citizenship. Website information directed towards students also indicates some focus in this direction. On the 'About UC San Diego' page it is stated that '[e]verything we do is dedicated to ensuring our students have the opportunity to become changemakers, equipped with the multidisciplinary tools needed to accelerate answers to our world's most pressing issues'.[235] This emphasis is not apparent, however, from the 'Choose UC San Diego' webpage.[236]

In comparison, East Carolina University's strategic plan suggests a strong focus on teaching for citizenship. Assisting graduates to work and serve their communities is one of the guiding principles of the University,[237] which informs its commitment to public service, including inspiring 'our students to be engaged citizens and leaders'.[238] This is somewhat echoed through its website, which states its mission as including developing 'tomorrow's leaders to serve and inspire positive change'.[239]

234. UC San Diego, *2014 Strategic Plan Executive Summary* (2014) UC San Diego <http://plan.sdsc.edu/documents/Exec-Summary-Strategic-Plan.pdf>.

235. UC San Diego, *About UC San Diego*, UC San Diego <http://ucsd.edu/about/index.html>.

236. UC San Diego, *Choose UC San Diego*, UC San Diego <https://grad.ucsd.edu/admissions/choose.html>.

237. East Carolina University, *ECU Strategic Plan 2014–2019* (17 September 2014) <http://www.ecu.edu/cs-acad/strategicplan/guiding-principles.cfm>.

238. Ibid.

239. East Carolina University, *ECU Mission Statement* (February 2014) <http://www.ecu.edu/cs-admin/chancellor/mission.cfm>.

The University of Kansas' Strategic Plan, 'Bold Aspirations', also indicates attention to teaching for citizenship through articulation of two goals:

- Preparing undergraduate students for leadership and success, and
- Preparing doctoral students as innovators and leaders.[240]

Similarly, the University's website indicates its mission is 'to educate leaders, build healthy communities, and make discoveries that change the world'.[241]

On the basis of this discussion, the United States is ranked 'very good' in relation to this criterion.

Equal Opportunity, Equal Treatment and Equity

In the United States, the percentage of 25–44 year-old non-students accessing tertiary education where their parents have below upper secondary education is 5 per cent, compared with 33 per cent where their parents have upper secondary or post-secondary non-tertiary education.[242] This is a difference of 28 per cent, significantly higher than the OECD average of 16 per cent.[243] The percentage of 25–44 year-old non-students accessing tertiary education where their parents have tertiary education is 61 per cent, a 28 per cent increase over where their parents have upper secondary or post-secondary non-tertiary education. This difference is equal to the OECD average of 28 per cent.[244] Thus, the United States is ranked 'poor' for this criterion.

Freedom for Teaching and Research

Some legal protection for freedom for teaching and research in higher education exists in the United States. The First Amendment of the United States Constitution provides that 'Congress shall make no law . . . abridging the freedom of speech'.[245] Although this provision does not appear to directly relate to academic freedom, it has been interpreted to protect freedom for teaching and

240. The University of Kansas, 'Bold Aspirations: The Strategic Plan for the University of Kansas 2012–2017' (Strategic Plan, The University of Kansas, September 2011) 9, 16.

241. The University of Kansas, *About KU* <http://www.ku.edu/about/>.

242. OECD, 'Education at a Glance 2016', above n 25, 85–86.

243. Ibid.

244. Ibid 86–87.

245. *United States Constitution* amend I.

research.[246] Nevertheless, the scope of the protection provided is unclear.[247] The 1940 Statement of Principles on Academic Freedom and Tenure is generally accepted as defining academic freedom in higher education in the United States.[248] However, although this Statement has been relied upon in some courts, it does not have the status of law.[249] Further, the United States *Higher Education Opportunity Act 2008* makes the following references to academic freedom:

- '[A]n institution of higher education should facilitate the free and open exchange of ideas';[250]
- '[N]othing in this paragraph shall be construed to modify, change, or infringe upon any constitutionally protected . . . freedom';[251]
- 'It is the intent of this section to . . . while supporting the academic freedom of faculty members to select high quality course materials for students';[252] and
- 'Nothing in this section shall be construed to supercede the institutional autonomy or academic freedom of instructors involved in the selection of college textbooks, supplemental materials, and other classroom materials.'[253]

Overall, although the Constitution and legislative provisions do provide a general statement in relation to academic freedom, elaboration on and clarity of the concept in law is lacking. Accordingly, the United States is ranked 'average' in relation to this criterion.

246. See Owen Fiss, 'The Democratic Mission of the University' (2012–2013) 76 *Albany Law Review* 735.

247. See Carol N Tran, 'Recognizing an Academic Freedom Exception to the Garcetti Limitation on the First Amendment Right to Free Speech' (2011–2012) 45 *Akron Law Review* 949; Robert Post, 'Discipline and Freedom in the Academy' (2012) 65 *Arkansas Law Review* 203; Donna R Euben, *Academic Freedom of Professors and Institutions* (May 2002) American Association of University Professors <https://www.aaup.org/issues/academic-freedom/professors-and-institutions>.

248. Euben, above n 247.

249. Ibid.

250. *Higher Education Opportunity Act 2008* 122 Stat § 104(2)(C).

251. Ibid § 104(2)(F).

252. Ibid Stat § 133(a).

253. Ibid § 133(h).

International Assistance

In 2015, the United States directed approximately 4 per cent of total official development aid towards education.[254] This compares poorly with the DAC member country average of 6.8 per cent[255] and results in a ranking for this criterion of 'poor'.

(iii) Social Efficiency

Vocational Orientation

Higher education programmes in the United States are strongly oriented towards vocational purposes. The majority of higher education students undertake internships or similar work integrated learning experiences as part of their course, with 63 per cent of students graduating in 2013 having participated in such a programme.[256] Nevertheless, despite the widespread nature of such programmes, there is concern that they 'can exacerbate socio-economic division with those from less financially well off backgrounds being less able to take advantage of opportunities'.[257] There is also a strong awareness of the importance of teaching employability skills within higher education programmes.[258] Again, however, the system does have issues in terms of translation of this awareness; colleges need to develop an improved understanding of employer needs, and assessment could be developed so as to more effectively gauge students' employability skills.[259]

Although there is a clear intention to orient higher education programmes towards graduate employability skills, employer and graduate views indicate that this has not yet been successfully achieved. Employer survey results suggest that graduates are 'woefully ill-prepared for the demands of today's (and tomorrow's) workplace'.[260] In particular, employers have indicated that two-year and

254. OECD, *Aid (ODA) by Sector and Donor [DAC5]*, above n 66.

255. Ibid.

256. Australian Workforce and Productivity Agency, above n 159, 8. See also Oakleigh Consulting Limited and Career Development Organisation, above n 158, 38–9.

257. Oakleigh Consulting Limited and Career Development Organisation, above n 158, 38–9.

258. Michael Bastedo, Batjargal Batkhuyag, Eufrasio Prates and Yaroslav Prytula, 'Educational Policies for Integrating College Competencies and Workforce Needs: Cases from Brazil, Mongolia, Ukraine, and the United States' (Issue Brief, Institute for Higher Education Policy, March 2009) 20–1.

259. Ibid 21.

260. Jill Casner-Lotto and Linda Barrington, 'Are They Really Ready to Work? Employers' Perspectives on the Basic Knowledge and Applied Skills of New Entrants to the 21st Century US Workforce' (Report, The Conference Board, Corporate Voices for Working Families, The Partnership for 21st Century Skills and The Society for Human Resource Management, 2006) 9.

four-year college graduates are 'deficient' in terms of writing in English, written communications and leadership.[261] Student survey results also indicate some dissatisfaction with the extent to which higher education assists students to develop employability skills; of first-year students, only 53 per cent felt that their higher education experience had contributed to their knowledge, skills and personal development in relation to the acquisition of job or work-related knowledge and skills.[262] For senior students the response is more positive at 68 per cent.[263] The United States is ranked 'average' in relation to this criterion.

Graduation Rates

Graduation rates in the United States are higher than the OECD average. In 2014, the first-time tertiary graduation rate (excluding international students) was 53 per cent, compared to the OECD average rate of 45 per cent.[264] Overall, this results in a 'very good' ranking for the United States in relation to this sign.

Employability Prospects and Skills Shortages

In the United States, the employment rate for 25–64 year-olds who have completed a bachelor's or equivalent degree is 81 per cent, slightly lower than the OECD average of 82 per cent.[265] Although significant skills shortages exist in trades not requiring higher education qualifications, for example 'welders, electricians, [and] machinists',[266] shortages in many professions are also apparent. Serious skills shortages in a number of sectors requiring higher education qualifications, for example 'construction, IT and technology, banking and financial, and life sciences' are present.[267] On the basis of this analysis, the United States is ranked 'poor' in relation to this criterion.

261. Ibid 11.

262. National Survey of Student Engagement, *NSSE 2014 US Grand Frequencies: First Year Students* (2014) <nsse.iub.edu/2014_institutional_report/pdf/Frequencies/Freq%20-%20FY%20by%20Major.pdf>.

263. Ibid.

264. OECD, 'Education at a Glance 2016', above n 25, 68.

265. Ibid 103.

266. Joshua Wright, *America's Skilled Trades Dilemma: Shortages Loom as Most-in-Demand Group of Workers Ages* (3 July 2013) Forbes <http://www.forbes.com/sites/emsi/2013/03/07/americas-skilled-trades-dilemma-shortages-loom-as-most-in-demand-group-of-workers-ages/>.

267. Hays, *Hays Global Skills Index 2016: United States* <http://www.hays-index.com/countries/usa/>.

Research Quality

The United States has 137 universities listed in the top 500[268] and a population of 323.15 million.[269] The U21 Ranking for the United States is 47.7. This result is 'average'.

Global Connectivity

The United States has comparatively weak connectivity with the international community. In relation to foreign student enrolment, only 4 per cent of the total tertiary enrolment in the United States in 2014 were international students.[270] In terms of domestic students enrolling in higher education overseas, only 0.3 per cent of students undertook study abroad in 2014.[271] Thus, on the basis of this data, the United States is ranked 'poor'.

C. HUMAN RIGHTS-BASED APPROACHES

1. Finland

(A) Political Context and Approach

Finland provides higher education free of charge for Finnish citizens.[272] Until recently, higher education was also provided freely to international students. Debate in relation to introducing tuition fees for international students has continued for a number of years;[273] however, in 2016, Finland announced that it would introduce tuition fees for non-EU students.[274] In this respect, the Finnish

268. Shanghai Jiao Tong University, *Academic Ranking of World Universities: Statistics*, above n 82.

269. United States Census Bureau, *US and World Population Clock* (25 February 2015) <http://www.census.gov/popclock/>.

270. OECD, 'Education at a Glance 2016', above n 25, 339.

271. Ibid.

272. Jussi Välimaa, *Why Finland and Norway Still Shun University Tuition Fees—Even for International Students* (17 February 2015) The Conversation <http://theconversation.com/why-finland-and-norway-still-shun-university-tuition-fees-even-for-international-students-36922>.

273. See Ian R Dobson, *Finland: To Fee or Not to Fee—That Is The Question* (24 January 2010) University World News <http://www.universityworldnews.com/article.php?story=2010012309222410&query=dobson>; Jan Petter Myklebust and Ian R Dobson, *Move towards Tuition Fees for Non-European Students* (2 February 2013) University World News <http://www.universityworldnews.com/article.php?story=20130127122204l8&query=dobson>.

274. Reet Sen, *Why Has Finland Introduced Tuition Fees for Non-EU Students?* (15 February 2017) Full Fabric Blog <http://blog.fullfabric.com/why-finland-introduced-tuition-fees-non-eu-students>.

Parliament passed regulations to introduce tuition fees for students coming from outside European Union and European Economic Area countries to take effect from 1 August 2017.[275]

The Finnish approach to higher education is best understood as a human rights-based approach. The right to education, including higher education, is set out in section 16 of the *Finnish Constitution*:

> Everyone has the right to basic education free of charge. Provisions on the duty to receive education are laid down by an Act.
>
> The public authorities shall, as provided in more detail by an Act, guarantee for everyone equal opportunity to receive other educational services in accordance with their ability and special needs, as well as the opportunity to develop themselves without being prevented by economic hardship.
>
> The freedom of science, the arts and higher education is guaranteed.[276]

This provision may be considered somewhat entrenched (and thus inalienable), as '[t]o amend or change the *[C]onstitution*, the majority in two consecutive Parliaments must adopt the changes'.[277] The human rights-based approach is also brought into the mainstream through legislation including the *Universities Act* and *Polytechnics Act*.[278]

In keeping with the right to higher education as set out in Article 13 of the *International Covenant on Economic, Social and Cultural Rights* (ICESCR), 'Finland's *[C]onstitution* guarantees tuition fee-free education for all students'.[279] The fee-free requirement is echoed in higher education legislation: 'Education

275. OECD, 'Education at a Glance 2016', above n 25, 238; OECD, 'Education at a Glance 2016: Finland—Country Note' (OECD 2016) 1; *Finland Introduces University Tuition Fees for Non-EU Students* (18 January 2016) <http://monitor.icef.com/2016/01/finland-introduces-university-tuition-fees-for-non-eu-students/>.

276. *Suomen perustuslaki* 11.6.1999/731, 16 [Ministry of Justice (Finland) unofficial trans, *The Constitution of Finland 11 June 1999*, s 16 <http://www.finlex.fi/fi/laki/kaannokset/1999/en19990731.pdf>].

277. Parliament of Finland, *Constitution of Finland* <http://web.eduskunta.fi/Resource.phx/parliament/relatedinformation/constitution.htx?lng=en>.

278. See *Universities Act* (Finland) 558/2009, s 41 [unofficial trans <http://www.finlex.fi/fi/laki/kaannokset/2009/en20090558.pdf>]; *Polytechnics Act* (Finland) 351/2003, s 24 [unofficial trans <http://www.finlex.fi/en/laki/kaannokset/2003/en20030351.pdf>].

279. Timo Aarrevaara, Ian R Dobson and Camilla Elander, 'Brave New World: Higher Education Reform in Finland' (2009) 21(2) *Higher Education Management and Policy* 101. See also OECD, 'Education at a Glance 2014', above n 23, 262, 265.

leading to a university degree and entrance examinations relating to student admission shall be free of charge for the student'.[280] The lack of tuition fees ensures that there is no financial discrimination in Finnish higher education. Further, following the human rights doctrine, the primary responsibility for ensuring enjoyment of the right to higher education lies with the state. This is evidently accepted by Finland, where the public provides 96 per cent of tertiary education funds,[281] amounting to a public spend of $17,168 per tertiary education student.[282] Further, Finland's education system also reflects a human rights-based approach in that it is based on principles of 'equity and equality',[283] which inform higher education policy.[284]

Finland's higher education system is representative of a human rights-based approach to higher education. Until recent legislative changes, the right to higher education has been extended not only to citizens of Finland, but to all students, regardless of nationality.[285] Human rights explicitly underpin the approach, as is evident in the constitutional and legislative provisions outlined above. Further, the system significantly differs from a market-based approach to higher education.[286] Higher education institutions do not compete in relation to fees, and are almost entirely publicly funded, and although they enjoy decision-making

280. *Universities Act* (Finland) 558/2009, s 8 [unofficial trans <http://www.finlex.fi/fi/laki/kaannokset/2009/en20090558.pdf>]. See also *Polytechnics Act* (Finland) 351/2003, s 26(1) [unofficial trans <http://www.finlex.fi/en/laki/kaannokset/2003/en20030351.pdf>].

281. OECD, 'Education at a Glance 2016', above n 25, 218.

282. Ibid 221.

283. Australian Broadcasting Corporation, 'Highly Educated Teachers the Key to Success' *Lateline*, 28 February 2012 (Pasi Sahlberg). See also Ministry of Education and Culture, *Education Policy in Finland* <http://www.minedu.fi/OPM/Koulutus/koulutuspolitiikka/?lang=en>.

284. See, eg, Ministry of Education and Culture, *Education and Research 2011–2016: A Development Plan* <http://www.minedu.fi/export/sites/default/OPM/Julkaisut/2012/liitteet/okm03.pdf>; University of Helsinki, *University of Helsinki Equality Plan 2013–2016* <http://www.helsinki.fi/henkos/tasa-arvo/equality_and_diversity_plan_2013-2016.pdf>.

285. Except where studies are provided in a foreign language, and the student is not from a European Economic Area State and does not have permanent residency in Finland. See *Universities Act* (Finland) 558/2009, ss 8, 10 [unofficial trans <http://www.finlex.fi/fi/laki/kaannokset/2009/en20090558.pdf>], *Polytechnics Act* (Finland) 351/2003, ss 26(1), 26(b) [unofficial trans <http://www.finlex.fi/en/laki/kaannokset/2003/en20030351.pdf>].

286. *Contra* Ilkka Kauppinen and Tuukka Kaidesoja, 'A Shift towards Academic Capitalism in Finland' (2014) 27 *Higher Education Policy* 23.

autonomy, universities are subject to performance agreements[287] and polytechnics are subject to government authorisation.[288]

(B) Evaluation

(i) Individual Transformation

Student Survey Responses

Finland has administered a nationwide annual student survey called *Kandipalaute* since 2013.[289] The survey is sent to students who have graduated with a bachelor's degree or have completed three years of medicine or veterinary studies during the relevant year.[290] This survey 'examines the students' satisfaction with their university and studying experience'.[291] The most recent 2016 survey includes questions relating to general competencies; however, the results were unavailable at the time of writing. The 2015 survey questions were quite different, but included questions:

- Asking business and economics students from particular institutions to rate the following skills/competence their education has given them in terms of how well it has prepared them for working life:
    - General knowledge of economics
    - Ability/skills in your major subject
    - Ability/skills in your minor subject studies
    - Communication skills in your mother tongue
    - Communication skills in the second official language
    - Communication skills in other languages
    - Entrepreneurial skills, knowledge
    - Entrepreneurial skills, attitudinal
    - Ability to work in an international environment

287. Ministry of Education and Culture, *University Education: Administration and Finance* <http://www.minedu.fi/OPM/Koulutus/yliopistokoulutus/hallinto_ohjaus_ja_rahoitus/?lang=en>.

288. Ministry of Education and Culture, *Polytechnic Education: Administration and Finance* <http://www.minedu.fi/OPM/Koulutus/ammattikorkeakoulutus/hallinto_ohjaus_ja_rahoitus/?lang=en>.

289. *Kandipalaute*, Universities Finland UNIFI <http://www.unifi.fi/kandipalaute/>.

290. *Student Feedback Survey for Bachelor Graduates 2015* (7 February 2017) Finnish Social Science Data Archive <http://urn.fi/urn:nbn:fi:fsd:T-FSD3135> 2.

291. University of Oulu, *Finnish Bachelor's Graduate Survey* (20 February 2015) <http://www.oulu.fi/english/studying/bachelors-graduate-survey>.

  - Team-working skills
  - General leadership skills
  - Skills in human resources/management
  - IT skills
  - Ability to learn new things
  - Ability to solve problems
  - Presentation skills
  - Interaction skills
  - Prerequisites for acting ethically
- Asking the extent to which education has given students good preparedness for being an artist in society
- Asking students from the Tampere University of Technology to rate the following knowledge and skills acquired during their studies:
  - Expertise/competence in your field of study
  - Critical and analytical thinking skills
  - Verbal and written communication skills
  - Language skills
  - Project management skills
  - Innovation skills
  - Interpersonal and social skills
  - Entrepreneurial skills
  - Extent to which understanding of sustainable development has broadened during studies.[292]

It is acknowledged that there are limitations attached to this data in that the questions were not asked of all students—the 2016 data will be more useful in this respect. Nevertheless, the data should provide a reasonable indicator of self-reported individual student transformation in Finnish higher education.

In relation to these questions, the percentage of students that agreed/somewhat agreed with these statements or ranked them 4 or 5 (on a 5-point scale) varied between 26.7 per cent and 96.2 per cent, with the average being 65.9 per cent.[293] This represents a reasonably positive picture of student self-reported individual transformation in Finnish higher education and results in a ranking of 'average' in relation to this criterion.

292. *Student Feedback Survey for Bachelor Graduates 2015*, above n 290.

293. Ibid.

Personalised Learning

In Finland, the student-teacher ratio in higher education for bachelor's, master's, doctoral or equivalent level degrees is 14.[294] This is better than the OECD average of 17,[295] and results in a ranking of 'very good'.

Resources per Student

In 2013, Finland's spending on higher education as a percentage of GDP was 1.8 per cent.[296] This is higher than the OECD average of 1.5 per cent.[297] In terms of spending per student, Finland compares well; in 2013 it spent $17,868 per tertiary education student, compared to the OECD average of $15,772.[298] On the basis of this analysis, Finland is ranked 'good' in relation to this criterion.

Institutional Autonomy

The Finnish higher education sector is characterised by high levels of institutional autonomy. Part of the mission of Finnish universities is to promote free academic and artistic education, and the *Universities Act 2009* explicitly grants universities freedom of teaching.[299] In this respect, Finnish universities are free to design academic content.[300] Similarly, Finnish polytechnics enjoy freedom of education within their field of operation.[301] In relation to research, both universities and polytechnics enjoy freedom to research.[302] Decisions relating to student enrolment are at the discretion of universities and polytechnics, both in terms of the number of students to be admitted and admission procedures.[303] Although

294. OECD, 'Education at a Glance 2016', above n 25, 403.

295. Ibid.

296. Ibid 206.

297. Ibid.

298. Ibid 192.

299. *Universities Act 558/2009* (Finland) ss 2(1), 6(1).

300. Estermann, Nokkala and Steinel, above n 125, 51–2.

301. *Polytechnics Act 351/2003* (Finland) ss 7(1), 16(1).

302. *Universities Act 558/2009* (Finland) ss 2(1), 6(1); *Polytechnics Act 351/2003* (Finland) s 16(1). See also Ministry of Education and Culture, *University Education in Finland* <http://www.minedu.fi/OPM/Koulutus/yliopistokoulutus/?lang=en>.

303. *Universities Act 558/2009* (Finland) ss 14(2)(10); *Polytechnics Act 351/2003* (Finland) s 21.

basic eligibility requirements are established in statute, universities and polytechnics are free to determine admission criteria.[304]

Finnish higher education autonomy extends to staff recruitment and is complemented by sector-wide accountability mechanisms. Both universities and polytechnics are free to decide on the hiring of staff.[305] Requirements relating to qualifications and recruitment procedures are established in university regulations.[306] In relation to quality assurance, universities and polytechnics are required to undertake internal and external evaluations on a regular basis.[307] In this respect, the Finnish Higher Education Evaluation Council has been established as an independent expert body to assist higher education institutions in matters relating to evaluation.[308] On the basis of this analysis, Finland is ranked 'very good' in relation to this criterion.

Commitment to Teaching and Learning

In Finland, government decrees and university regulations make provision for teachers' qualification requirements.[309] In terms of qualifications, teachers at polytechnics must have a master's degree or a postgraduate Licentiate's degree, as well as completion of pedagogical studies.[310] Teachers at universities must have a postgraduate degree.[311] The recruitment and promotions process places significant emphasis on teaching capacity. To obtain entry-level positions, applicants must prove their teaching skills via teaching experience or completion of pedagogical studies.[312] To obtain more senior positions as a lecturer or associate

304. *Universities Act 558/2009* (Finland) ss 37, 36(2); *Polytechnics Act 351/2003* (Finland) s 20(1), 22(1). See also Estermann, Nokkala and Steinel, above n 125, 46; Terhi Nokkala and Agneta Bladh, 'Institutional Autonomy and Academic Freedom in the Nordic Context—Similarities and Differences' (2014) 27 *Higher Education Policy* 1, 10.

305. *Universities Act 558/2009* (Finland) ss 17; *Polytechnics Act 351/2003* (Finland) s 29(3). See also Estermann, Nokkala and Steinel, above n 125, 38.

306. *Universities Act 558/2009* (Finland) s 31(1).

307. Ibid s 87(1); *Polytechnics Act 351/2003* (Finland) s 9(1).

308. *The Finnish Higher Education Evaluation Council (FINHEEC)*, Korkeakoulujen arviointineuvosto <http://www.finheec.fi/index.phtml?l=en&s=5>.

309. *Universities Act 558/2009* (Finland) s 31; *Polytechnics Act 351/2003* (Finland) s 30.

310. Finnish National Board of Education, *Teacher Education* <http://www.oph.fi/english/education_system/teacher_education>.

311. Ibid.

312. European University Institute, *Finland, Academic Career Structure* (28 October 2014) <http://www.eui.eu/ProgrammesAndFellowships/AcademicCareersObservatory/AcademicCareersbyCountry/Finland.aspx>.

professor, applicants must demonstrate teaching experience, including conducting a test lecture as part of the appointment process.[313] In some cases, applicants may also be required to submit a teaching portfolio to demonstrate their teaching ability.[314] According to the OECD, 'Finland has raised the social status of its teachers to a level where there are few occupations with higher status. University professors are among the most highly regarded of all professionals'.[315] Thus, Finland achieves a ranking of 'very good' in relation to this criterion.

(ii) Improving Society

Integration of Values

The values underpinning the Finnish higher education system are clearly identified in the state *Constitution* and relevant national legislation. Pursuant to the Finnish *Constitution*, equal opportunity in higher education is to be guaranteed by public authorities.[316] Further, importance is attached to freedom of higher education,[317] quality[318] and lifelong learning.[319] A strong emphasis is placed on the right of students to study,[320] but this study is directed towards 'service to country and humanity'.[321] On the basis of this analysis, Finland is ranked 'very good' in relation to this criterion.

313. Ibid.

314. Ibid.

315. OECD, 'Building a High-Quality Teaching Profession: Lessons from around the World' (Background Report for the International Summit on the Teaching Profession, OECD, 2011) 11.

316. Parliament of Finland, *Constitution of Finland* <http://web.eduskunta.fi/Resource.phx/parliament/relatedinformation/constitution.htx?lng=en>.

317. Ibid s 16; *Polytechnics Act* (Finland) 351/2003, s 24 [unofficial trans <http://www.finlex.fi/en/laki/kaannokset/2003/en20030351.pdf>] s 16(1); *Universities Act* (Finland) 558/2009, ss 2(1), 3(1), 6(1) [unofficial trans <http://www.finlex.fi/fi/laki/kaannokset/2009/en20090558.pdf>].

318. *Universities Act* (Finland) 558/2009, s 2(2) [unofficial trans <http://www.finlex.fi/fi/laki/kaannokset/2009/en20090558.pdf>].

319. *Polytechnics Act* (Finland) 351/2003, s 24 [unofficial trans <http://www.finlex.fi/en/laki/kaannokset/2003/en20030351.pdf>] s 4(1); *Universities Act* (Finland) 558/2009, ss 2(1) [unofficial trans <http://www.finlex.fi/fi/laki/kaannokset/2009/en20090558.pdf>].

320. *Universities Act* (Finland) 558/2009, s 41 [unofficial trans <http://www.finlex.fi/fi/laki/kaannokset/2009/en20090558.pdf>]; *Polytechnics Act* (Finland) 351/2003, s 24 [unofficial trans <http://www.finlex.fi/en/laki/kaannokset/2003/en20030351.pdf>] s 4(1).

321. *Universities Act* (Finland) 558/2009, ss 2(1) [unofficial trans <http://www.finlex.fi/fi/laki/kaannokset/2009/en20090558.pdf>].

Teaching for Citizenship

To gauge the extent to which the Finnish higher education system is focused on teaching for citizenship, a review of the following three Finnish university websites was undertaken:

- Aalto University
- University of Tampere
- University of Helsinki

Aalto University's strategic plan suggests a strong focus on teaching for citizenship. This is evidenced by the University's mission, which is to work 'towards a better world through . . . pioneering education . . . and by educating responsible, broad-minded experts to act as society's visionaries and change agents'.[322] This mission, together with expressed values including a 'sense of responsibility', are also communicated via the University's website information.[323]

Similarly, the University of Tampere's focus on teaching for citizenship is clear through its strategic plan 'Let's Shape the Future! Change in the University of Tampere 2010–2015'. The Plan makes clear the institution's 'social mission of educating visionaries who understand the world and change it'[324] as well as its focus in teaching to 'educate students to become responsible academic citizens and experts'.[325] This focus is echoed in the University's website information, which expresses its 'singularly clear and extensive mission to serve society'.[326]

The University of Helsinki's strategic plan is also reflective of a focus on teaching for citizenship, as evident in its expressed values.[327] In particular, the University considers that its '[g]raduates serving as experts in various fields constitute the University's most significant contribution to society'.[328]

322. Aalto University, 'Strategic Development of Aalto University' (Strategic Plan, Aalto University, January 2012) 7.

323. Aalto University, *Studying at Aalto* (3 January 2014) <http://www.aalto.fi/en/studies/about/>; Aalto University, *Brochure* <http://www.aalto.fi/en/studies/about/for_future_student/>.

324. University of Tampere, 'Let's Shape the Future! Change in the University of Tampere 2010–2015' (Strategic Plan, The University of Tampere, 15 February 2010) 5.

325. Ibid 10.

326. University of Tampere, *What Makes the University of Tampere Different?* (16 December 2010) <http://www.uta.fi/english/about/different/index.html>.

327. University of Helsinki, 'Excellence for Society: Strategic Plan for the University of Helsinki 2013–2016' (Strategic Plan, University of Helsinki, 18 January 2012) 10.

328. University of Helsinki, *University's Core Duties* (31 March 2015) <https://www.helsinki.fi/en/university/strategia-ja-johtaminen-englanti/yliopiston-tehtavat-englanti>.

On the basis of this discussion, Finland is ranked as 'very good' in relation to this criterion.

Equal Opportunity, Equal Treatment and Equity

In Finland, the percentage of 25–44 year-old non-students accessing tertiary education where their parents have below upper secondary education is 39 per cent, compared with 48 per cent where their parents have upper secondary or post-secondary non-tertiary education.[329] This is a difference of 9 per cent, significantly lower than the OECD average of 16 per cent.[330] The percentage of 25–44 year-old non-students accessing tertiary education where their parents have tertiary education is 68 per cent, a 20 per cent increase on where their parents have upper secondary or post-secondary non-tertiary education. This difference is markedly better than the OECD average of 28 per cent.[331] Although Finland's performance puts them on the borderline between 'good' and 'very good', taking all data into account they are ranked 'very good' for this criterion.

Freedom for Teaching and Research

Section 16 of the Finnish *Constitution* provides that '[t]he freedom of science, the arts and higher education is guaranteed'.[332] Further, pursuant to section 3 of the *Universities Act 2009*, '[t]he universities have autonomy, through which they safeguard scientific, artistic and higher education freedom'.[333] Section 6 provides that 'universities enjoy freedom of research, art and teaching' and 'teachers must comply with the statutes and regulations issued on education and teaching arrangements'.[334] Pursuant to section 32, academic employees cannot have their employment terminated where it would infringe on the freedom of research, art or education.[335]

329. OECD, 'Education at a Glance 2016', above n 25, 85–6.

330. Ibid.

331. Ibid 86–7.

332. Parliament of Finland, *Constitution of Finland* <http://web.eduskunta.fi/Resource.phx/parliament/relatedinformation/constitution.htx?lng=en>.

333. *Universities Act* (Finland) 558/2009, s 3 [unofficial trans <http://www.finlex.fi/fi/laki/kaannokset/2009/en20090558.pdf>].

334. Ibid s 6. Note that a similar provision is included in the *Polytechnics Act* (Finland) 351/2003, s 16 [unofficial trans <http://www.finlex.fi/en/laki/kaannokset/2003/en20030351.pdf>].

335. *Universities Act* (Finland) 558/2009, s 32 [unofficial trans <http://www.finlex.fi/fi/laki/kaannokset/2009/en20090558.pdf>].

These provisions indicate that academic freedom is a guiding principle for activity in higher education. Nevertheless, further elaboration of the meaning of academic freedom and direct attribution of freedom to academics rather than to higher education institutions would be desirable. Accordingly, Finland is ranked 'good' in relation to this sign.[336]

International Assistance

In 2015, Finland directed approximately 13 per cent of total official development aid towards education.[337] This is significantly better than the DAC member country average of 6.8 per cent[338] and results in a rating for this criterion of 'very good'.

(iii) Social Efficiency

Vocational Orientation

Finland's higher education sector has a strong vocational focus. Like Austria, the Finnish system has a dual structure, with universities focused on the delivery of scientific research and instruction and polytechnics being multidisciplinary in nature with a practical focus.[339] Although polytechnics are more practical in focus, all higher education programmes include work experience type components, which are two-thirds funded by the higher education institution and one-third funded by the host employer.[340] Further, there is a clear awareness of the importance of teaching employability skills in higher education and '[h]igher education institutions have been encouraged to cooperate with the labour market and the enterprises'.[341] Moreover, the importance placed on preparing higher education graduates for the workforce is reflected in national policy objectives and recognised in agreements between higher education institutions and the government.[342]

336. Note that this ranking accords with the ranking of 15 per cent given in Karran, Beiter and Appiagyei-Atua, above n 152, 229.

337. OECD, *Aid (ODA) by Sector and Donor [DAC5]*, above n 66.

338. Ibid.

339. Oakleigh Consulting Limited and Career Development Organisation, above n 158, 41.

340. Ibid.

341. The European Education Directory, *Finland Higher Education System* <http://www.euroeducation.net/prof/finco.htm>.

342. Ministry of Education, 'Higher Education Institutions 2009—Universities and Polytechnics as Implementers of Higher Education Policy' (Publications of the Ministry of Education, Finland 2009:51, 14 April 2010) 16–17.

Graduates and employers indicate general satisfaction with the employability outcomes of higher education in Finland. Student survey results indicate that 85 per cent of students either agreed or somewhat agreed that the skills they acquired in their education met their expectations, while 82 per cent agreed or somewhat agreed that their education met their expectations.[343] Employer survey results indicated that 95 per cent of employers either strongly agreed or agreed that the higher education graduates recruited in the last three to five years had the skills required to work in their companies.[344] Nevertheless, it should be noted that a shortage of applicants with the right skills and capabilities was identified by 49 per cent of surveyed employers as a key reason for difficulty filling vacancies,[345] and that the incidence of skill mismatch in Finland is calculated at 31.8 per cent.[346] On the basis of this discussion, Finland is ranked 'very good' in relation to this criterion.

Graduation Rates

In 2014, the Finnish first-time tertiary graduation rate (excluding international students) was 45 per cent, equivalent to the OECD average rate of 45 per cent.[347] Thus, this results in an 'average' ranking for Finland in relation to this sign.

Employability Prospects and Skills Shortages

In Finland, the employment rate for 25–64 year-olds who have completed a bachelor's or equivalent degree is 82 per cent, equivalent to the OECD average of 82 per cent.[348] Nevertheless, partly as a result of an aging population and of the changed nature of many professions, significant skills shortages do exist.[349]

343. Zan Ileski and Hannah Leichsenring, 'Kandipalaute: Results of the Second Survey Round 2013–2' (Survey Report, CHE Consult, July 2013) 19.

344. European Commission, above n 168, 24.

345. Ibid 49.

346. Budria and Moro-Egido, above n 169, 463–4.

347. OECD, 'Education at a Glance 2016', above n 25, 68.

348. Ibid 103.

349. See Salla Korpela, *How about Getting a Job in Finland? Vacancies in Healthcare, Service Sector and More* (July 2014) This is Finland <http://finland.fi/Public/default.aspx?contentid=160050>; Laura Kytölä and Aleksi Teivainen, 'Labour Shortage Hits New Sectors', *Helsinki Times* (online), 3 December 2013 <http://www.helsinkitimes.fi/finland/finland-news/domestic/8581-labour-shortage-hits-new-sectors.html>; Riikka Jakovuori, Antti Karjaluoto and Marko Rauhala, 'Finland Skills Gap Survey 2014—Finding the Skills for Finland's Future: Understanding the Gaps Can Help Prioritize Strategies' (Survey Report, Accenture, 2014).

The country's aging population has led to a shortage of healthcare professionals, which cannot be addressed via changes to the education system alone.[350] Shortages also exist in other sectors where higher education qualifications are required, including social work, information technology, engineering and electronics.[351] Thus, Finland is ranked 'poor' in relation to this criterion.

Research Quality

Finland has five universities listed in the top 500[352] and a population of 5.48 million.[353] The U21 Ranking for Finland is 67.4. This result is 'good'.

Global Connectivity

The Finnish connection with the international community is relatively strong in relation to student mobility. Of the total tertiary enrolment in Finland in 2014, 7 per cent of students were international students.[354] Similarly, in 2014, the percentage of national tertiary students enrolled abroad was 2.9 per cent.[355] This results in a ranking of 'good' for Finland in relation to this criterion.

2. Iceland

(A) Political Context and Approach

There are no tuition fees charged to domestic or international public higher education students in Iceland, although registration fees are paid.[356] Students in private higher education institutions do pay tuition fees.[357] Although tuition fees

350. Korpela, above n 349; Kytölä and Teivainen, above n 349.

351. Jakovuori, Karjaluoto and Rauhala, above n 349, 13; AGCAS Editors, *Country Profile—Finland* (March 2012) University of Kent <https://www.kent.ac.uk/careers/int/Finland.pdf>.

352. Shanghai Jiao Tong University, *Academic Ranking of World Universities: Statistics,* above n 82.

353. Statistics Finland, *Finland's Preliminary Population Figure 5 475 450 at the End of January* (24 February 2015) <http://www.stat.fi/til/vamuu/2015/01/vamuu_2015_01_2015-02-24_tie_001_en.html>.

354. OECD, 'Education at a Glance 2016', above n 25, 339.

355. Ibid 360.

356. Ministry of Education, Science and Culture, 'The Educational System in Iceland' (Monograph 6, Ministry of Education, Science and Culture, 2002) 32.

357. *Internationals Face Higher Tuition Fees* (24 October 2014) University World News <http://www.universityworldnews.com/article.php?story=20141023150110719&query=iceland>.

do not pose a political issue, students have expressed discontent with university underfunding.[358]

The Icelandic higher education system represents a human rights-based approach to higher education. The right to education is acknowledged in the Icelandic *Constitution*: Article 76 provides that '[t]he law shall guarantee for everyone suitable general education and tuition.'[359] Although this provision is unlikely to protect a right to higher education, the *Constitution* 'is largely inspired by the Danish *[C]onstitution* of the time and is seen as anachronism.'[360] Perhaps more revealing of Icelandic culture is the failed *Constitutional Bill 2011*, drafted 'with the more or less direct participation of its people.'[361] Article 24 of the Bill provided,

> Everyone shall be ensured by law the right to general education and training to his ability.
>
> Everyone who is subject to compulsory schooling shall have access to education without charge.
>
> Education shall aim at achieving comprehensive development for each individual, critical thinking and consciousness of human rights, democratic rights and obligations.[362]

The explicit mention of human rights, and the purposes of education as including 'consciousness of human rights', is indicative of an approach based on human rights. This is supported by the OECD, which asserts that 'the funding of both

358. *"Universities at Risk"—Icelandic Students Speak Out against Underfunding of Their Universities,* Global Student Voice <http://www.globalstudentvoice.org/2016/11/15/universities-risk-icelandic-students-speak-underfunding-universities/>; Ingibjörg Rósa Björnsdóttir, *Universities In Iceland Seriously Underfunded* (25 November 2013) The Reykjavík Grapevine <https://grapevine.is/news/2013/11/25/universities-in-iceland-seriously-underfunded/>; *BM72: A Call to Support LANDSSAMTÖK ÍSLENSKRA STÚDENTA Against the Underfunding of Icelandic Universities* (23 May 2017) European Students' Union <https://www.esu-online.org/?policy=call-support-landssamtok-islenskra-studenta-underfunding-icelandic-universities>.

359. *Stjórnarskrá lýðveldisins Íslands* 1944 nr. 33 17 Júní [Government Offices of Iceland (Iceland) trans, *Constitution of the Republic of Iceland* (1944) <http://www.government.is/constitution/>.

360. *Icelanders Back First 'Crowdsourced Constitution'* (22 October 2012) <http://www.euractiv.com/enlargement/icelanders-opens-way-crowdsource-news-515543>.

361. Helene Landemore, 'Inclusive Constitution-Making: The Icelandic Experiment' (2014) *The Journal of Political Philosophy* 166, 167.

362. The Constitutional Society trans, *Constitutional Bill* (29 July 2011) <http://stjornarskrarfelagid.is/?page_id=2619> art 24.

institutions and students is based on the principle that access to tertiary education is a right, rather than a privilege'.[363]

The human rights-based approach to higher education in Iceland is reflected in the importance the state attaches to non-discrimination and equality in education. The Icelandic Ministry of Education, Science and Culture, for example, states that '[a] fundamental principle of the Icelandic educational system is that everyone should have equal opportunities to acquire an education, irrespective of sex, economic status, residential local, religion, possible handicap, and cultural or social background'.[364] Although the special needs of students are not addressed in legislation, 'each university has an official policy on how to accommodate students with special needs'.[365]

Further, in relation to financial discrimination, funding is designed to ensure that financial hardship does not provide an obstacle to higher education. Tuition fees are not charged in public higher education institutions, although registration fees are charged.[366] Private higher education institutions do charge fees.[367] Student loans are available to students from the Icelandic Student Loan Fund,[368] and 63 per cent of students benefitted from student loans in 2011.[369] Like Finland, the Icelandic state accepts most of the responsibility for higher education funding, providing 91 per cent of total tertiary expenditure in 2013.[370] This amounts to $9,775 of public spending per tertiary education student per year.[371]

The Icelandic higher education system can be distinguished from market-based systems. The right to free higher education is extended not only to citizens, but to all students. This is reflective of the rights-based values that underpin the system. Further, unlike a market-based approach, as no tuition fees are charged,

363. OECD, 'Education at a Glance 2014', above n 23, 265.

364. Ministry of Education, Science and Culture, above n 356, 7.

365. Eurypedia, *European Encyclopedia on National Education Systems: Island: Support Measures for Learners in Higher Education* (14 December 2012) European Commission <https://webgate.ec.europa.eu/fpfis/mwikis/eurydice/index.php/Iceland:Support_Measures_for_Learners_in_Higher_Education>.

366. Ministry of Education, Science and Culture, 'The Educational System in Iceland', above n 356, 32.

367. Ibid.

368. Note that eligibility conditions apply. See ibid.

369. Note that data for more recent years is not available. See OECD, 'Education at a Glance 2014', above n 23, 273.

370. OECD, 'Education at a Glance 2016', above n 25, 218.

371. Ibid 221.

higher education institutions do not compete with each other for students. Although private higher education institutions do exist, the system is largely publicly funded and subject to extensive regulation. This is reflected in the reality that 'each higher education institution is directly responsible to the Ministry of Education, Science and Culture'[372] and '[t]he Icelandic Parliament is legally and politically responsible for the educational system'.[373]

(B) Evaluation

(i) Individual Transformation

Student Survey Responses

Iceland does not administer a national student survey of higher education students. Accordingly, this sign is ranked 'not applicable'.

Personalised Learning

Unfortunately, data is not available in relation to Iceland's ratio of students to teaching staff in higher education institutions after 2012. However, in that year the ratio of students to teaching staff in tertiary educational institutions was 11, compared to the OECD average of 14.[374] This result is 'very good'.

Resources per Student

Iceland's expenditure on tertiary education institutions as a percentage of GDP was 1.3 per cent in 2013, below the OECD average of 1.5 per cent.[375] In terms of spending per student, Iceland spent $11,256 per student in 2013, compared with the OECD average of $15,772 for that year.[376] Thus, Iceland is ranked 'poor' in relation to this criterion.

Institutional Autonomy

The Icelandic higher education system is characterised by strong institutional autonomy, as is made clear by the *Higher Education Institution Act 2006*, which provides that 'Higher Education Institutions are autonomous regarding their activities'.[377] Although higher education institutions are accredited only in

372. Ministry of Education, Science and Culture, 'The Educational System in Iceland', above n 356, 9.

373. Ibid 8.

374. OECD, 'Education at a Glance 2014', above n 23, 451.

375. OECD, 'Education at a Glance 2016', above n 25, 206.

376. Ibid 192.

377. *Higher Education Institution Act No 63 from 2006* (Iceland) art 2.

relation to particular areas of study,[378] they determine the programmes that they offer within those areas of study[379] as well as the conduct of teaching and assessment.[380] Similarly, Icelandic higher education institutions are able to determine the conduct of research.[381] In relation to student admission, basic requirements are set down in the *Higher Education Institution Act 2006*,[382] but institutions are able to set their own admission requirements.[383]

Institutional autonomy in Icelandic higher education extends to staff recruitment and is complemented by sector-wide quality assurance mechanisms. Higher education institutions are required to establish their own evaluation committees, and some basic qualification requirements are provided for in legislation.[384] Essentially, however, universities are free to recruit their own academic staff.[385] In relation to quality assurance mechanisms, quality is assessed via internal and external evaluations of higher education institutions.[386] The Quality Board for Icelandic Higher Education has developed a quality enhancement framework for higher education,[387] which is directed towards supporting higher education institutions in providing quality higher education.[388] On the basis of this analysis, Iceland achieves a ranking of 'very good' in relation to this criterion.

378. Ibid art 3.

379. Ibid art 7; Nokkala and Bladh, above n 304, 10.

380. *Higher Education Institution Act No 63 from 2006* (Iceland) art 7. See also Estermann, Nokkala and Steinel, above n 125, 52.

381. *Higher Education Institution Act No 63 from 2006* (Iceland) art 7.

382. Ibid art 19.

383. Ibid art 19. See also Estermann, Nokkala and Steinel, above n 125, 46; Nokkala and Bladh, above n 304, 10.

384. *Higher Education Institution Act No 63 from 2006* (Iceland) art 18.

385. Estermann, Nokkala and Steinel, above n 125, 38; Nokkala and Bladh, above n 304, 10.

386. *Higher Education Institution Act No 63 from 2006* (Iceland) art 11.

387. *National Quality Assurance and Enhancement Framework*, Iceland Academy of the Arts <http://lhi.is/english/about/quality-enhancement/quality-system-outline/>; Ministry of Education, Science and Culture, *Education* <http://eng.menntamalaraduneyti.is/education-in-iceland/Educational_system/>.

388. Rannis, 'Quality Enhancement Handbook for Icelandic Higher Education 2011' (Handbook, Rannis on behalf of the Quality Board for Icelandic Higher Education, October 2011) 5.

Commitment to Teaching and Learning
In Iceland, there is a common national career structure for academic staff.[389] The *Higher Education Institution Act 2006* and the *Act on Public Higher Education Institutions 2008* establish general qualifications for academic staff, which include completion of at least a master's degree or equivalent knowledge and experience.[390] Universities are also required to establish an evaluation committee to assess the merit of individuals that apply for academic positions.[391] Experience as a teacher is one of the criteria that influences promotion within the national academic career structure.[392] On the basis of this analysis, Iceland is ranked 'good' in relation to this criterion.

(ii) Improving Society

Integration of Values
The values underpinning the Icelandic higher education system are identified in the state *Constitution* and relevant national legislation. By guaranteeing general education for all, section 76 of the *Constitution of the Republic of Iceland* indicates that value is placed on the right of all people to education.[393] Further, legislation governing higher education institutions indicates that the creation and dissemination of knowledge and skills[394] as well as quality[395] is important. Higher education institutions are to serve society[396] and in this respect, the *Icelandic Student Loan Fund Act 1992* indicates that equality of opportunity is an important value.[397] On the basis of this analysis, Iceland is ranked 'very good' in relation to this criterion.

389. Santiago, Tremblay, Basri and Arnal, above n 50, 157.

390. *Higher Education Institution Act* No. 63 from 2006 (Iceland) art 18; *Act on Public Higher Education Institutions* No 85 from 2008 (Iceland) art 16.

391. Ibid.

392. OECD, 'OECD Reviews of Tertiary Education for the Knowledge Society' (Review vols 1 and 2, OECD, 2008) 157.

393. *Stjórnarskrá lýðveldisins Íslands* 1944 nr. 33 17 Júní [Government Offices of Iceland (Iceland) trans, *Constitution of the Republic of Iceland* (1944) <http://www.government.is/constitution/> s 76.

394. *Higher Education Institution Act* No. 63 from 2006 (Iceland) art 2.

395. Ibid ch IV.

396. *Act on Public Higher Education Institutions* No 85 from 2008 (Iceland) art 3.

397. *Icelandic Student Loan Fund Act* No 21 from 1992 (Iceland) art 1.

Teaching for Citizenship

To gauge the extent to which the Icelandic higher education system is focused on teaching for citizenship, a review of the following two Icelandic university websites was undertaken:

- University of Akureyri
- University of Iceland

There are only four public universities in Iceland and two of those institutions (Hólar University College and the Agricultural University of Iceland) do not include the relevant information on their websites. Accordingly, this review is conducted on the basis of two rather than three university websites.

The University of Akureyri's strategic plan is suggestive of some focus on teaching for citizenship. Teaching is aimed at preparing students for employment, and the institution integrates ethical and sustainability issues into all fields of study as well as upholding human rights principles in its operations.[398] This focus is also evident through the University's website information: students are prepared for future work opportunities[399] and 'acquire the ability to undertake diverse work in the future, at the same time as [they] directly participate in the development of Icelandic society'.[400]

The University of Iceland has a strong focus on teaching citizenship values, as evidenced in its 'Policy of the University of Iceland 2011–2016'.[401] The Policy expresses the University's duty to 'educate responsible young people who are capable to taking an active part in the remaking of our own society and the global community',[402] and in this respect '[s]trong emphasis is placed on strengthening ethical judgment, consciousness of sustainability and community responsibility of . . . students'.[403] This message resonates in the marketing information provided to students: the University 'places great emphasis on . . . preparing [young

398. University of Akureyri, 'Strategy of the University of Akureyri 2012–2017' (Strategic Plan, University of Akureyri, 2012) 9–10.

399. University of Akureyri, *About UNAK* <http://english.unak.is/about/about-unak/about-unak>.

400. University of Akureyri, *Rector's Address* <http://english.unak.is/about/about-unak/rectors-adress>.

401. University of Iceland, 'Policy of the University of Iceland 2011–2016' (Policy, University of Iceland, 17 December 2010).

402. Ibid 3, 21.

403. Ibid 7.

people] for taking an active part in society as well as making their mark in the global community'.[404]

On the basis of this discussion, Iceland is ranked 'very good' in relation to this criterion.

Equal Opportunity, Equal Treatment and Equity

Unfortunately, data in relation to the likelihood of participating in tertiary education, by parents' educational attainment, is not available for Iceland.[405] Accordingly, this criterion is ranked 'not applicable'.

Freedom for Teaching and Research

The Icelandic *Higher Education Act 2006* includes provisions for the protection of academic freedom. Article 2a of the Act provides that:

> Higher education institutions have an obligation to respect the academic freedom of their staff. Academic freedom entails the right of academic staff to approach the subjects they teach in a way they consider reasonable and in keeping with academic requirements. Academic freedom does not affect the responsibility of staff to follow any general code of conduct or of ethics adopted by the higher education institution concerned. The choice of research and teaching subjects in individual academic disciplines pursued at a higher education institution shall be free of the influence of the owners and financial backers of the institution.[406]

Although Article 2a constitutes a clear statement in relation to the importance of academic freedom, it defines academic freedom in relation to teaching and not in relation to research. Accordingly, Iceland is ranked 'average' in relation to this criterion.

International Assistance

In 2013, Iceland directed approximately 5 per cent of total official development aid towards education.[407] This is less than the DAC member country average of 6.8 per cent[408] and results in a rating for this criterion of 'poor'.

404. University of Iceland, 'A Dynamic Community' (Brochure, University of Iceland, May 2014) 2.

405. OECD, 'Education at a Glance 2016', above n 25, 85–7.

406. *Higher Education Institution Act* No. 63 from 2006 (Iceland) art 2a.

407. OECD, *Aid (ODA) by Sector and Donor [DAC5]*, above n 66.

408. Ibid.

(iii) Social Efficiency

Vocational Orientation

Although Iceland does not have a 'comprehensive policy that links the tertiary education system and the labour market',[409] there is a generally widespread integration of employment type experiences and skills into higher education courses. The *Higher Education Institution Act* explicitly notes the role of higher education institutions in preparing students for jobs and, in doing so, taking into account the needs of society.[410] Most students are required to gain practical experience in their particular discipline.[411] Further, government policy has been directed towards strengthening the collaboration between higher education institutions and 'industry, the business sector, [and] research institutes.'[412]

Information in relation to graduate and employer views as to the adequacy of higher education institutions in their vocational orientation also indicates a positive picture. Although surveys of Icelandic graduates are not undertaken, a number of processes are in place to ensure student involvement in quality assessments of Icelandic higher education.[413] Employer survey information is very positive: 89 per cent of surveyed employers agreed that graduates they had hired in the last three to five years had the skills to work for them,[414] and only 24 per cent of employers indicated that a shortage of applicants with the appropriate skills and capabilities was a key reason for difficulty filling vacancies.[415] In relation to this criterion, Iceland is ranked 'good'.

Graduation Rates

In 2014, Iceland had a first-time tertiary graduation rate (excluding international students) of 53 per cent, compared to the OECD average rate of 45 per cent.[416] Thus, Iceland is ranked 'very good' in relation to this sign.

409. Elvar Örn Arason, Ingunn Ólafsdóttir and Ásta Briem, 'OECD Thematic Review of Tertiary Education: National Background Report for Iceland' (Report, Educational Testing Institute of Iceland, September 2005) 32.

410. *Higher Education Institution Act* (Iceland) No 63 from 2006, art 2.

411. Arason, Ólafsdóttir and Briem, above n 409, 32.

412. Ibid, 6, 28, 89.

413. See *Higher Education Institution Act* (Iceland) No 63 from 2006, arts 12, 14; Wenche Froestad and Pål Bakken (eds), 'Student Involvement in Quality Assessments of Higher Education in the Nordic Countries' (Project Report, Nordic Quality Assurance Network in Higher Education, 2004); OECD, 'OECD Reviews of Tertiary Education for the Knowledge Society', above n 392, 282.

414. European Commission, above n 168, 24.

415. Ibid 49.

416. OECD, 'Education at a Glance 2016', above n 25, 68.

Employability Prospects and Skills Shortages

In Iceland, the employment rate for 25–64 year-olds who have completed a bachelor's or equivalent degree is 90 per cent, significantly higher than the OECD average of 82 per cent.[417] There is also little evidence of any significant skills shortages in the economy. Although there are skills shortages in the vocational sector,[418] these positions are unlikely to be filled by higher education qualified individuals. Some skills shortages in the IT, education and health sectors are noted, but do not appear to be significant.[419] Thus, Iceland achieves a ranking of 'very good' in relation to this criterion.

Research Quality

Iceland does not have any universities listed in the Shanghai Jiao Tong University top 500 rankings.[420] It is, however, difficult to compare this unfavourably with the other states considered in this analysis as the population of Iceland is only 325,671 and there are only seven universities in the country.[421] Even if Iceland's research was comparable with Sweden (the top ranking system in relation to this criterion), Iceland would only have 0.35 universities in the top 500 ranking,[422] which is in practice impossible. Thus, rather than rank Iceland poorly in this category, the ranking is 'not applicable'.

Global Connectivity

Unfortunately, data in relation to the proportion of international students studying in Iceland in 2014 is unavailable.[423] However, in 2011, the proportion of international students was 5 per cent of the total tertiary population.[424] In 2014, 13.7

417. Ibid 103.

418. Pauline Musset and Rodrigo Castañeda Valle, 'A Skills beyond School Commentary on Iceland' (Review of Vocational Education and Training, OECD, April 2013).

419. See *Work in Iceland* (December 2014) Prospects <http://www.prospects.ac.uk/work_in_iceland.htm>; Tine Andersen, Karsten Frøhlich Hougaard and Stefán Ólafsson, 'Assessment of the Labour Market in Iceland: Contract no. VC/2010/038' (Final Report, Danish Technological Institute, April 2011).

420. Shanghai Jiao Tong University, *Academic Ranking of World Universities: Statistics*, Shanghai Ranking <http://www.shanghairanking.com/ARWU-Statistics-2014.html>.

421. Statistics Iceland, *Overview* (4 March 2014) <http://www.statice.is/Statistics/Population/Overview>; QS Top Universities, *Country Guide: Study in Iceland*, Top Universities <http://www.topuniversities.com/where-to-study/europe/iceland/guide#tab=0>.

422. Population 0.33 million divided by research quality measure of 0.933 is 0.35.

423. OECD, 'Education at a Glance 2016', above n 25, 339.

424. OECD, 'Education at a Glance 2014', above n 23, 354.

per cent of Icelandic tertiary students were enrolled abroad.[425] This results in a ranking for Iceland of 'good' in relation to this criterion.

3. Sweden

(a) Political Context and Approach

There are no tuition fees for higher education in Sweden for students from EU, EEA or Nordic countries or Switzerland. Other students are required to pay application and tuition fees.[426] Although tuition fees have generated little political controversy, recent years have seen students protest against moves perceived to align with market-based policies. In 2010, the University Chancellor of Sweden, university rectors and student unions protested plans to provide extra funding to universities according to students' performance.[427] In 2013, students in Sweden protested against a government plan to shift the management of colleges and universities to private foundations.[428]

Sweden, like its Nordic neighbours Finland and Iceland, takes a human rights-based approach to its higher education system. The right to higher education clearly underpins the Swedish legislative framework relating to higher education. First, pursuant to Chapter 1, Article 2 of the first fundamental law of the *Swedish Constitution*, public institutions are obliged to 'secure the right to . . . education'.[429] Under Chapter 2, Article 18 the public institutions are responsible 'for the provision of higher education'.[430] Second, provisions of the *Riksdag Act* require the Riksdag (the national legislature)[431] to appoint a Committee on Education, which is responsible for preparing matters for Parliament concerning higher education and research, financial support for students, and appropriations relating to financial support for students and education and academic research.[432] The right to

425. OECD, 'Education at a Glance 2016', above n 25, 341.

426. *Tuition Fees and Costs*, Study in Sweden <https://studyinsweden.se/plan-your-studies/fees-and-costs/>.

427. Jan Petter Myklebust, *Sweden: Protests against Government Reward System* (2 May 2010) University World News <http://www.universityworldnews.com/article.php?story=20100429204512982>.

428. *Students to Occupy Buildings in University Protest* (14 November 2013) Sveriges Radio <http://sverigesradio.se/sida/artikel.aspx?programid=2054&artikel=5703971>.

429. *The Instrument of Government* (Sweden) ch 1 art 2.

430. Ibid ch 2 art 18.

431. See ibid ch 1 art 4.

432. *The Riksdag Act* (Sweden) 2014:801, ch 7 art 2, Appendix (11).

higher education is amongst many rights granted via the Swedish *Constitution*,[433] indicating a belief in the indivisibility, interdependence and interrelationship of human rights in Sweden.

In line with human rights principles, the Swedish approach to higher education demonstrates a commitment to equality and non-discrimination. Chapter 1, Article 2 of the first fundamental law of the Swedish *Constitution* requires public institutions to 'promote the opportunity for all to attain participation and equality in society'.[434] Further, in relation to gender equality, the *Swedish Higher Education Act* requires that '[e]quality between women and men shall always be taken into account and promoted in the operations of higher education institutions'.[435] In relation to potential financial discrimination, higher education is provided 'without charge' to citizens of European Economic Area states and Switzerland.[436] From 2011, other students have been charged fees; however scholarship programmes are established '[t]o enable students who cannot pay tuition fees to study in Sweden'.[437]

The Swedish approach to higher education has a strong emphasis on empowerment and accountability. Section 4a of the *Swedish Higher Education Act* provides that:

> Students shall be entitled to exert influence over the courses and study programmes at higher education institutions.
>
> Higher education institutions shall endeavour to enable students to play an active role in the continued development of courses and study programmes.[438]

This focus is reflected in pedagogy through an 'emphasis on independent studies'; in Sweden 'students have somewhat less teacher-led time than is usual elsewhere, mainly pursuing their studies on their own or in groups'.[439] Further, under

433. *The Instrument of Government* (Sweden) Ch 2.

434. Ibid Ch 1 art 2.

435. *The Swedish Higher Education Act* (Sweden) Swedish Code of Statutes (SFS) No. 1992:1434, ch 1 s 5 [trans, *The Swedish Higher Education Act* <http://www.uhr.se/sv/Information-in-English/Laws-and-regulations/The-Swedish-Higher-Education-Act/>].

436. Ibid.

437. The Swedish Institute, *Higher Education and Research in Sweden* (31 March 2014) <https://sweden.se/society/higher-education-and-research/>.

438. *The Swedish Higher Education Act* (Sweden) Swedish Code of Statutes (SFS) No. 1992:1434, Ch 1 s 4a [trans, *The Swedish Higher Education Act* <http://www.uhr.se/sv/Information-in-English/Laws-and-regulations/The-Swedish-Higher-Education-Act/>].

439. The Swedish Institute, above n 437.

the *Higher Education Ordinance,* higher education institutions are required to 'enable students who are participating in or have completed a course to express their experiences of and views on the course through a course evaluation to be organised by the higher education institution' the results of which must be made available to students.[440]

The Swedish approach to higher education differs from the market-based approach. The Swedish higher education system is informed by human rights norms, as evident in the Swedish *Constitution.* Moreover, although the right to free higher education is extended on the basis of citizenship, scholarship funds are in place to ensure that those without sufficient financial means are not denied their right to higher education. In contrast with the typical market-based approach to higher education, institutions do not compete with each other for students from the European Economic Area and Switzerland, as their places are tuition-free. Further, higher education is predominantly state-funded, with 90 per cent of all tertiary education spending coming from public sources.[441] Higher education is also regulated by the state, for example, under Chapter 2, section 1 of the *Swedish Higher Education Act,* '[t]he Riksdag decides which public-sector higher education institutions shall exist'.[442]

(B) Evaluation

(i) Individual Transformation

Student Survey Responses

The Swedish Higher Education Authority and its predecessor, the Swedish National Agency for Higher Education, have conducted student surveys (referred to as the Student Mirror) in 2002, 2007 and 2015.[443] The Student Mirror is

440. *The Higher Education Ordinance* (Sweden) Swedish Code of Statutes (SFS) No. 1993:100, Ch 1 s 14 [trans The Higher Education Ordinance <http://www.uhr.se/sv/Information-in-English/Laws-and-regulations/The-Higher-Education-Ordinance/>].

441. OECD, 'Education at a Glance 2016', above n 25, 218.

442. *The Swedish Higher Education Act* (Sweden) Swedish Code of Statutes (SFS) No. 1992:1434, Ch 2 s 1 [trans, *The Swedish Higher Education Act* <http://www.uhr.se/sv/Information-in-English/Laws-and-regulations/The-Swedish-Higher-Education-Act/>].

443. Högskoleverket [Swedish National Agency for Higher Education], 'Ranking of Universities and Higher Education Institutions for Student Information Purposes?' (Report 2009:27R, Högskoleverket, November 2009) 139; Blekinge Institute of Technology, *The BTH Student Mirror 2012 (Studentspegel 2012)* (2 January 2012) <http://www.bth.se/eng/news.nsf/sidor/0939edbb54f2f0a5c125798400430e6c?OpenDocument>; *Student Input Important for the Development of Swedish Higher Education* (11 September 2015) Swedish Higher Education Authority <http://english.uka.se/about-us/news--events/nyheter/2015-11-09-student-input-important-for-the-development-of-swedish-higher-education.html>.

inspired by the American NSSE and covers 'information about different dimensions of learning and personal development'.[444] In particular, it includes questions in relation to the extent to which students' education has:

- Helped them learn to analyse the basis of an idea, phenomenon or theory, to independently seek knowledge and analyse problems, and to think critically and analytically
- Taught them to organise ideas, information or experiences into new relationships and more complex questions, to evaluate information, arguments or methods to consider, for example, the reasonableness of conclusions, and to apply theories or ideas to practical problems and/or new situations
- Given them a greater understanding of people from different ethnic or cultural backgrounds
- Contributed to increased general knowledge
- Contributed to becoming involved in community issues
- Helped them to develop a greater understanding of the cultural differences between men and women
- Helped them write more clearly and understandably
- Improved their ability to argue and debate.[445]

In relation to these questions, the percentage of students that agreed with these statements varied between 44 per cent and 87 per cent, with an approximate average being 65 per cent.[446] This represents a reasonably positive picture of student self-reported individual transformation in Swedish higher education and results in a ranking of 'average' in relation to this criterion.

Personalised Learning

In Sweden, the student-teacher ratio in higher education for bachelor's, master's, doctoral or equivalent level degrees is 11, well below the OECD average of 17.[447] This results in a ranking of 'very good' for Sweden for this criterion.

444. Högskoleverket [Swedish National Agency for Higher Education], above n 443, 139.

445. Swedish Higher Education Authority, 'Student Mirror' (Draft Summary Report, Swedish Higher Education Authority, 2017).

446. Ibid. Note that the Student Mirror Summary Report does not contain specific figures for all question results. The full report is not available in English.

447. OECD, 'Education at a Glance 2014', above n 23, 451.

Resources per Student

In 2013, Sweden's expenditure on tertiary education institutions as a percentage of GDP was 1.7 per cent, above the OECD average of 1.5 per cent.[448] Expenditure per higher education student was high, at $23,219, compared to the OECD average of $15,772.[449] On the basis of this analysis, Sweden is ranked 'good' in relation to this criterion.

Institutional Autonomy

In Sweden, higher education institutions enjoy autonomy in some areas of their operations, however, they are restricted in other areas. In relation to teaching, universities are free to decide on academic content.[450] Similarly, higher education institutions enjoy freedom in relation to research. In this respect, section 6 of Chapter 1 of the *Swedish Higher Education Act 1992* provides that 'research issues may be freely selected, research methodologies may be freely developed, and research results may be freely published.'[451] In terms of student enrolment, Swedish higher education institutions are able to decide on entry requirements, but this is subject to government regulation.[452] The *Higher Education Ordinance 1993* sets out general entry requirements for higher education applicants[453] and provides that the Swedish Council for Higher Education may issue regulations concerning field-specific entry requirements.[454] In relation to staff recruitment, legislation provides for basic competency requirements for particular posts and hiring procedures.[455] Generally, however, universities are free to recruit their own academic staff.[456]

Sector-wide quality assurance mechanisms are in place in Sweden. The *Swedish Higher Education Act 1992* provides that '[q]uality assurance procedures are the shared concern of staff and students at higher education institutions.'[457] Further, the Swedish Council for Higher Education is charged with supervision

448. OECD, 'Education at a Glance 2016', above n 25, 206.

449. Ibid 192.

450. Estermann, Nokkala and Steinel, above n 125, 51–2.

451. *Swedish Higher Education Act 1992* (Sweden) ch 1 s 6.

452. Ibid ch 4 s 2; Nokkala and Bladh, above n 304, 10.

453. *Higher Education Ordinance 1993* (Sweden) ch 7 s 5.

454. *Swedish Higher Education Act 1992* (Sweden) ch 7 s 9a.

455. Ibid ch 3 s 2. See also European University Association, *Sweden* <http://www.university-autonomy.eu/countries/sweden/>.

456. *Higher Education Ordinance 1993* (Sweden) ch 3, s 6; Estermann, Nokkala and Steinel, above n 125, 38; Nokkala and Bladh, above n 304, 9.

457. *Swedish Higher Education Act 1992* (Sweden) ch 1 s 4.

of higher education institutions as well as quality evaluation of higher education in Sweden.[458] On the basis of this analysis, Sweden is ranked 'good' in relation to this criterion.

Commitment to Teaching and Learning

Legislation in Sweden indicates a strong commitment to teaching and learning in higher education. Under the *Higher Education Ordinance*, to be appointed as a professor one must demonstrate teaching expertise, and '[a]s much attention shall be given to the assessment of teaching expertise as to the assessment of research or artistic expertise'.[459] Similar requirements apply to be appointed as senior lecturer.[460] Moreover, aside from these positions and research assistant positions, to obtain other positions, applicants must demonstrate competency in teaching.[461] This requires applicants to document their teaching skills.[462] Further, junior and senior lecturers in permanent employment as well as doctoral students must have basic pedagogical training.[463] In spite of the policy emphasis on teaching, however, recent research has indicated that in the context of tenure-track positions, research is still considered to be the 'main task'.[464] On the basis of this data, Sweden achieves a ranking of 'very good' in relation to this criterion.

(ii) Improving Society

Integration of Values

The values underpinning the Swedish higher education system are clearly identified in the state *Constitution* and relevant national legislation. The *Swedish*

458. *Two New Government Authorities*, Universitets-och högskolerådet <http://www.hsv.se/nyamyndigheter>.

459. *The Higher Education Ordinance* (Sweden) Swedish Code of Statutes (SFS) No. 1993:100, Ch 4 s 3 [trans, The Higher Education Ordinance <http://www.uhr.se/sv/Information-in-English/Laws-and-regulations/The-Higher-Education-Ordinance/>].

460. Ibid.

461. Jarno Deen, 'Higher Education in Sweden' (IHEM Country Report, Centre for Higher Education Policy Studies, September 2007) 26.

462. European University Institute, *Sweden, Academic Career Structure* (30 July 2009) <http://www.eui.eu/ProgrammesAndFellowships/AcademicCareersObservatory/AcademicCareersbyCountry/Sweden.aspx>.

463. Santiago, Tremblay, Basri and Arnal, above n 50.

464. Lars Geschwind and Anders Jörnesten, 'Tenure Track Tensions: Academic Career Paths in a Deregulated Sector' (Paper presented at the SRHE Annual Research Conference, South Wales, United Kingdom, 11–13 December 2013) 3.

Constitution makes it clear that the right to education is valued in Sweden.[465] Further, quality is considered important, as indicated by the responsibility of the Swedish Higher Education Authority for quality assurance.[466] Other values that underpin the system include freedom of research,[467] student participation,[468] equality, and understanding of other countries and of international circumstances.[469] On the basis of this analysis, Sweden is ranked 'very good' in relation to this criterion.

Teaching for Citizenship

To gauge the extent to which the Swedish higher education system is focused on teaching for citizenship, a review of the following three Swedish university websites was undertaken:

- Lund University
- Stockholm University
- Linnaeus University

Lund University's Strategic Plan is suggestive of a strong focus on teaching for citizenship. Its task, to 'educate ... future knowledge producers, problem solvers and leaders'[470] aligns with the institution's vision to be 'a world-class university that works to understand, explain and improve our world and the human condition'.[471] This vision is not strongly communicated via website information

465. *The Instrument of Government* (Sweden) Ch 1 arts 2, 18.

466. *What We Do*, Swedish Higher Education Authority <http://english.uka.se/about-us/what-we-do.html>; The Swedish National Agency for Higher Education, 'The Swedish Higher Education System' (The Swedish National Agency for Higher Education, May 2012) 1. See also *The Swedish Higher Education Act* (Sweden) Swedish Code of Statutes (SFS) No. 1992:1434, ch 1 s 4 [trans, *The Swedish Higher Education Act* <http://www.uhr.se/sv/Information-in-English/Laws-and-regulations/The-Swedish-Higher-Education-Act/>].

467. *The Swedish Higher Education Act* (Sweden) Swedish Code of Statutes (SFS) No. 1992:1434, Ch 1 s 6 [trans, *The Swedish Higher Education Act* <http://www.uhr.se/sv/Information-in-English/Laws-and-regulations/The-Swedish-Higher-Education-Act/>].

468. Ibid.

469. Ibid.

470. Lund University, 'Strategic Plan 2012–2016' (Strategic Plan, Lund University, 16 February 2012) 4.

471. Ibid.

available to English-speaking students, however, aside from reference to graduate employability.[472]

Similarly, the Strategic Plan of Stockholm University evinces some attention towards teaching for citizenship. The promotion of education and knowledge is considered 'a cornerstone of the development of society' and is one of the University's main tasks.[473] In this respect, courses and programmes offered by the University are to be 'reviewed continuously in a strategic effort to . . . meet societal needs'.[474] This focus is reflected in the website information available to students: it states, '[e]ducation and research at Stockholm University make a difference. The University contributes to individual and social change through top quality education'.[475]

Linnaeus University's 'A Journey into the Future: Vision and Strategy 2015–2020' is also strongly suggestive of a focus on teaching for citizenship.[476] The University aims to provide education 'with high social relevance'[477] which assists students to 'be ready to participate in the development of society'.[478] As with all the University's activities, teaching is to be conducted 'in a way that promotes equality of opportunity, economic and social well-being, justice, and a good working environment'.[479] This focus is somewhat echoed in the website information provided to English-speaking students. The University states they 'want to enable [students] to grow' as people, and that they seek to 'add a real-life dimension' to studies.[480]

On the basis of this discussion, Sweden is ranked 'good' in relation to this criterion.

472. Lund University, *Why Study at Lund University* (14 November 2005) <http://www.lunduniversity.lu.se/international-admissions/why-study-at-lund-university>

473. Stockholm University, 'Strategies for Stockholm University 2015–2018' (Strategic Plan, Stockholm University, 2015) 10.

474. Ibid.

475. Stockholm University, *About Us* <http://www.su.se/english/about>.

476. Linnaeus University, 'A Journey into the Future: Vision and Strategy 2015–2020' (Vision and Strategy, Linnaeus University, 24 September 2014).

477. Ibid 10.

478. Ibid 6.

479. Ibid 17.

480. Linnaeus University, *This Is Linnaeus University* (25 June 2014) <http://lnu.se/education/this-is-linnaeus-university-?l=en>.

Equal Opportunity, Equal Treatment and Equity

In Sweden, the percentage of 25–44 year-old non-students accessing tertiary education where their parents have below upper secondary education is 28 per cent, compared with 31 per cent where their parents have upper secondary or post-secondary non-tertiary education.[481] This is a difference of 3 per cent, lower than the OECD average of 16 per cent.[482] The percentage of 25–44 year-old non-students accessing tertiary education where their parents have tertiary education is 52 per cent, a 21 per cent increase over where their parents have upper secondary or post-secondary non-tertiary education. This difference is markedly better than the OECD average of 28 per cent.[483] Thus, Sweden is ranked 'very good' for this criterion.

Freedom for Teaching and Research

Article 18 of the Swedish *Instrument of Government* provides that '[t]he freedom of research is protected according to rules laid down in law'.[484] Further, pursuant to section 6 of the *Swedish Higher Education Act*, '[t]he following general principles shall apply to research: research issues may be freely selected, research methodologies may be freely developed, and research results may be freely published'.[485]

Although these provisions do constitute statements in relation to academic freedom, they lack elaboration. Further, they are significantly limited in that they refer only to freedom for research and not freedom for teaching. Accordingly, Sweden is ranked 'poor' in relation to this criterion.[486]

International Assistance

In 2013, Sweden directed approximately 2 per cent of total official development aid towards education.[487] This compares very poorly with the DAC member

481. OECD, 'Education at a Glance 2016', above n 25, 85–86.

482. Ibid.

483. Ibid 86–87.

484. *The Instrument of Government* (Sweden) ch 2 art 18.

485. *The Swedish Higher Education Act* (Sweden) Swedish Code of Statutes (SFS) No. 1992:1434, ch 1 s 6 [trans, *The Swedish Higher Education Act* <http://www.uhr.se/sv/Information-in-English/Laws-and-regulations/The-Swedish-Higher-Education-Act/>].

486. Note that this ranking accords with the ranking of 5 per cent given in Karran, Beiter and Appiagyei-Atua, above n 152, 229.

487. OECD, *Aid (ODA) by Sector and Donor [DAC5]*, above n 66. See also Swedish International Development Cooperation Agency, Openaid.se <http://www.openaid.se/aid/sweden/world/all-organisations/education/2014/>; Swedish International Development Cooperation Agency, Openaid.se <http://www.openaid.se/aid/2014/>.

country average of 6.8 per cent[488] and results in a rating for this criterion of 'very poor'.

(iii) Social Efficiency

Vocational Orientation

Partly as a result of the Bologna process, there has been an increasing focus on employability in relation to Swedish higher education.[489] One manifestation of this focus is a 'growing dialogue between employers and universities and colleges about the content and organization of their courses'.[490] This dialogue has resulted in the creation of a new form of vocational post-secondary education, which has been 'designed, constructed and carried out in partnerships between employers and educational providers'.[491] Further, higher education quality assurance systems in Sweden reflect an importance attached to graduate employability.[492]

Graduate and employer survey data indicates a general satisfaction with the outcomes of Swedish higher education. Student surveys indicate that 90 per cent of students were satisfied with their courses and that approximately 84 per cent of students would enrol in the same programme again.[493] Students, however, were not satisfied with the 'lack of work-related content in their education'.[494] In terms of employer views, in a European Commission survey 98 per cent of employers indicated that the graduates that they had hired in the last three to five years had the skills required to work for them.[495] In terms of reasons for difficulty in filling vacancies, however, 42 per cent of Swedish employers identified a shortage of applicants with the right skills and capabilities as a key reason.[496] Thus, in relation to this criterion, Sweden is ranked 'good'.

488. OECD, *Aid (ODA) by Sector and Donor [DAC5]*, above n 66.

489. See generally Elinor Edvardsson Stiwne and Mariana Gaio Alves, 'Higher Education and Employability of Graduates: Will Bologna Make a Difference?' (2010) 9(1) *European Educational Research Journal* 32.

490. Egbert de Weert, 'Perspectives on Higher Education and the Labour Market: Review of International Policy Developments' (Thematic Report, Centre for Higher Education Policy Studies, December 2011) 27.

491. Ibid.

492. Ibid 51.

493. Stiwne and Alves, above n 489, 40.

494. Kristina Josefson, Jenny Pobiega and Christian Stråhlman, 'Student Participation in Developing Student Feedback' (2011) 17(2) *Quality in Higher Education* 257, 261.

495. European Commission, above n 168, 24.

496. Ibid 49.

Graduation Rates

In 2014, Sweden had a first-time tertiary graduation rate (excluding international students) of 36 per cent, compared to the OECD average rate of 45 per cent.[497] Thus, Sweden is ranked 'very poor' in relation to this sign

Employability Prospects and Skills Shortages

In Sweden, the employment rate for 25–64 year-olds who have completed a bachelor's or equivalent degree is 90 per cent, significantly higher than the OECD average of 82 per cent.[498] Although some skills shortages exist in the economy, including in sectors requiring higher education qualifications such as education, engineering, healthcare and information technology,[499] these shortages do not appear to be significant.[500] Thus, Sweden is ranked 'very good' in relation to this criterion.

Research Quality

Sweden has eleven universities listed in the top 500[501] and a population of 9.97 million.[502] The U21 Ranking for Sweden is 93.3. This result is 'very good'.

Global Connectivity

The proportion of international students studying in Sweden in 2014 was 6 per cent.[503] Similarly, 4.2 per cent of Swedish tertiary students were enrolled abroad in the same year.[504] On the basis of this data, Sweden is ranked 'good' in relation to this criterion.

497. OECD, 'Education at a Glance 2016', above n 25, 68.

498. Ibid 103.

499. See *Labour Shortage List,* Work in Sweden <http://work.sweden.se/how-to-find-a-job/labour-shortage-list/>.

500. See OECD, *Sweden's Skills Snapshot* <http://skills.oecd.org/informationbycountry/sweden.html>; Hays, *Hays Global Skills Index 2014: Sweden* <http://www.hays-index.com/countries/sweden/>.

501. Shanghai Jiao Tong University, *Academic Ranking of World Universities: Statistics,* above n 82.

502. Statistics Sweden, *Population Statistics* (31 December 2014) <http://www.scb.se/en_/Finding-statistics/Statistics-by-subject-area/Population/Population-composition/Population-statistics/>.

503. OECD, 'Education at a Glance 2016', above n 25, 339.

504. Ibid 341.

D. CONCLUSION

This chapter has presented case studies of six different state higher education policies, with a view to determining whether policies that align with a human rights-based approach as opposed to a market-based approach to higher education are more likely to assist a state to meet the purposes of higher education. The initial analysis of each system identified whether the system could be categorised as adopting a market-based or human rights-based approach. Subsequent analysis evaluated each system against the signs of a successful higher education system as indicated by measures identified in Chapter 3 (see Appendix A).[505]

The analysis undertaken in this chapter indicates that higher education policy informed by human rights, as opposed to market principles, is more likely to enable individual transformation in students. Figure 4.1 shows that the Finnish, Icelandic and Swedish higher education policies are more likely to enable individual transformation than those policies representative of a market-based approach. This outcome is unsurprising, given that human rights, by nature, focus on the individual, whereas market-based approaches are arguably more macro in focus.

In terms of the objective of improving society, this chapter indicates that higher education policy informed by human rights, as opposed to market principles, is more likely to do so. Where policies based on human rights ranked on average

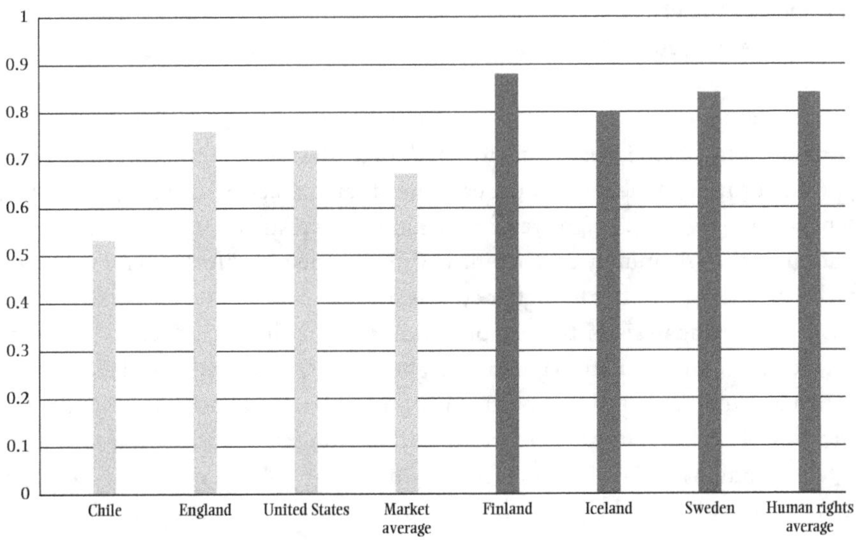

Figure 4.1 Individual Transformation.

505. See Figure 4.4 for graphical summary country comparison.

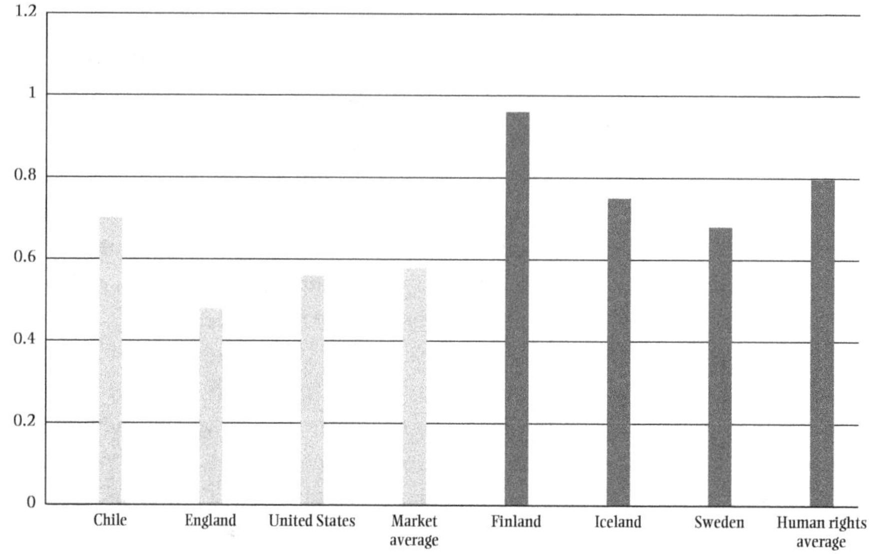

Figure 4.2 Improving Society.

80 per cent, market-based systems ranked 58 per cent (rounded to the nearest full percentage point) (Figure 4.2). These results may be explained, perhaps, by the importance that human rights-based systems place on the contribution of higher education to society.

It may be expected that market-based higher education policy, as opposed to policy informed by human rights, would be more likely to have a positive impact on the economy. The analysis in this chapter, however, suggests that this is not the case. Rather, the Finnish, Icelandic and Swedish systems (ranked 79 per cent) appear to be more beneficial for the economy than market-based systems (ranked 59 per cent) (Figure 4.3). The reasons behind these results warrant further investigation, as they seemingly undermine key justifications put forward for adopting market-based approaches to higher education.

Overall, the analysis in this chapter indicates that higher education systems that are based on international human rights norms, as opposed to those underpinned by a market-based approach, are more likely to enable achievement of the purposes of higher education teaching and learning. Each of the human rights systems profiled here—Finland, Iceland and Sweden—fared better in relation to the signs of a successful higher education system than the market-based systems that were considered (Figure 4.4).

Of course, this analysis has limitations. The identification of objectives of higher education set out in Chapter 3 is inherently normative in nature; in particular, the purported goal of social mobility has been discounted from this

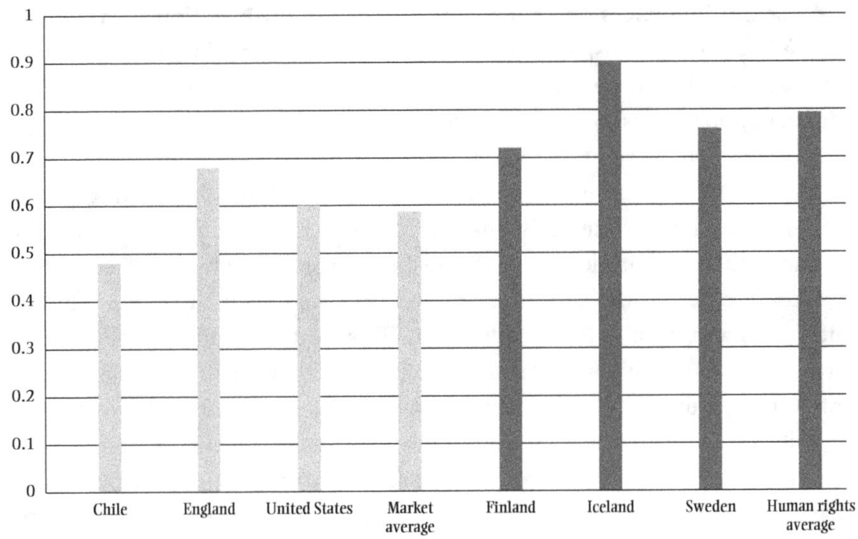

Figure 4.3 Social Efficiency.

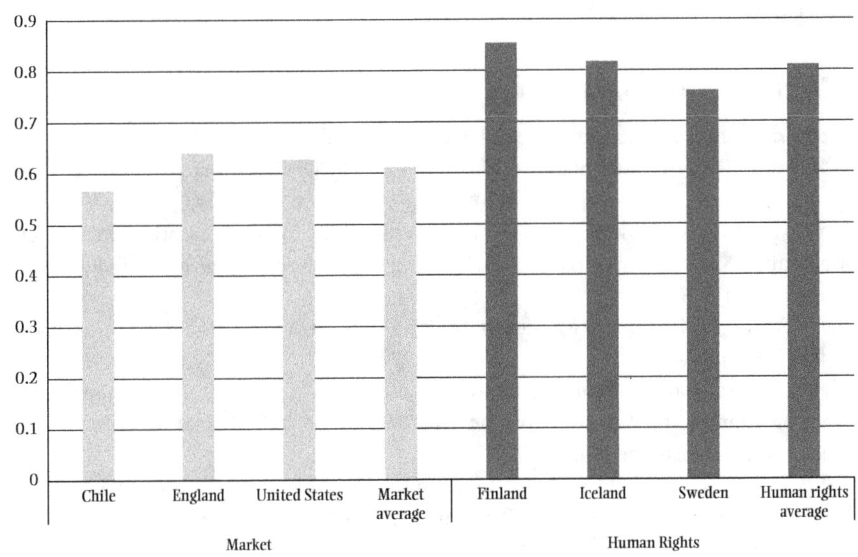

Figure 4.4 Overall Performance.

analysis. Further, in terms of measuring the achievement of these objectives, by necessity, particular measures of higher education purposes were focused upon. Broadening the scope of analysis in this respect may provide a more detailed view of the advantages and disadvantages of different approaches to higher education. Finally, the selection of particular states for analysis, and the exclusion of other states, clearly influences the conclusions drawn. Consideration of additional higher education systems, in particular those from low or middle income countries, may provide a more complete picture of the advantages and disadvantages of different approaches to higher education.

It is asserted, however, that the results of this analysis are sufficiently rigorous that they should be taken into account in higher education policymaking. Where states endeavour to enable individual transformation, improve society and prepare individuals for participation in the workforce through higher education, they should consider the adoption of policy measures that align with a human rights-based approach to higher education. This would include enacting legislation and policy to implement Article 13 of the ICESCR, mainstreaming human rights throughout the higher education sector, ensuring that higher education is equally accessible to all, establishing mechanisms to enable the participation of students and staff in higher education processes, and ensuring accountability mechanisms are in place to provide access to remedies where the right to higher education is denied.[506]

REFERENCE LIST

A. Articles/Books/Reports

Aarrevaara, Timo, Ian R Dobson and Camilla Elander, 'Brave New World: Higher Education Reform in Finland' (2009) 21(2) *Higher Education Management and Policy* 101

Adcroft, Andy, Jon Teckman and Robert Willis, 'Is Higher Education in the UK Becoming More Competitive?' (2010) 23(6) *International Journal of Public Sector Management* 578

Ainley, Patrick, 'The New "Market-State" and Education' (2004) 19(4) *Journal of Education Policy* 497

Andersen, Tine, Karsten Frøhlich Hougaard and Stefán Ólafsson, 'Assessment of the Labour Market in Iceland: Contract no. VC/2010/038' (Final Report, Danish Technological Institute, April 2011)

AUSSE, 'Respondent Characteristics Report' (Report, AUSSE, December 2012)

Australasian Survey of Student Engagement, '2012 Institution Report' (Report, AUSSE, 2012)

Australian Chamber of Commerce and Industry, 'Learning to Work: A Helping Hand for Young Australians' (Report, Australian Chamber of Commerce and Industry, April 2014)

Bauer, B and K Stieg, 'Open Access Publishing in Austria: Development and Future Perspectives' (2010) 3(52) *Bulletin of the Transilvania University of Brasov* 271

506. See Chapter 2 for a detailed explanation of a human rights-based approach to higher education.

Bexley, Emmaline, Richard James and Sophie Arkoudis, 'The Australian Academic Profession in Transition: Addressing the Challenge of Reconceptualising Academic Work and Regenerating the Academic Workforce' (Report, Department of Education, Employment and Workplace Relations, September 2011)

Brown, Roger, 'Markets and Non-Markets' in Roger Brown (ed), *Higher Education and the Market* (Routledge, 2011) 6

Brunner, José Joaquín, 'Chile's Higher Education: Between Market and State' (1993) 25(1) *Higher Education* 35

Brunner, José Joaquín, 'Chile: Challenges to Autonomy and Accountability in a Privatized Context' (2013) 3 *Leadership and Governance in Higher Education* 1

Budria, Santiago and Ana Moro-Egido, 'Overqualification, Skill Mismatches and Wages in Private Sector Employment in Europe' (2014) 20(3) *Technological and Economic Development of Economy* 457

Calderon, Angel J, Ian R Dobson and Neil Wentworth, 'Recipe for Success: Year 12 Subject Choice and the Transition from School to University' (2000) 9(1) *Journal of Institutional Research* 111

Cardak, Buly A and Chris Ryan, 'Participation in Higher Education in Australia: Equity and Access' (2009) 85(271) *The Economic Record* 433

Casner-Lotto, Jill and Linda Barrington, 'Are They Really Ready to Work? Employers' Perspectives on the Basic Knowledge and Applied Skills of New Entrants to the 21st Century US Workforce' (Report, The Conference Board, Corporate Voices for Working Families, The Partnership for 21st Century Skills and The Society for Human Resource Management, 2006)

CBI, 'Future Fit: Preparing Graduates for the World of Work' (Report, CBI, March 2009)

Chalmers, Denise and Kate Thomson, 'Snapshot of Teaching and Learning Practice in Australian Universities' (Report, Australian Learning & Teaching Council, 2008)

Cini, Lorenzo and César Guzmán-Concha, 'Student Movements in the Age of Austerity: The Cases of Chile and England' (2017) 16(5) *Social Movement Studies* 1

Clark, Tom, 'Under No Circumstances Resolve the Main Problem: Higher Education Policy Overview in Australia' (2004) 46(2) *Australian Universities Review* 12

Coomans, Fons, 'Content and Scope of the Right to Education as a Human Right and Obstacles to Its Realization' in Yvonne Donders and Vladimir Volodin (eds), *Human Rights in Education, Science and Culture: Legal Developments and Challenges* (UNESCO Publishing, 2007) 183

De Weert, Egbert, 'Perspectives on Higher Education and the Labour Market: Review of International Policy Developments' (Thematic Report, Centre for Higher Education Policy Studies, December 2011)

Deen, Jarno, 'Higher Education in Sweden' (IHEM Country Report, Centre for Higher Education Policy Studies, September 2007)

Dodds, Anneliese, 'The British Higher Education Funding Debate: The Perils of "Talking Economics"' (2011) 9(3) *London Review of Education* 317

Edvardsson Stiwne, Elinor and Mariana Gaio Alves, 'Higher Education and Employability of Graduates: Will Bologna Make a Difference?' (2010) 9(1) *European Educational Research Journal* 32

Emerson, Craig and Sharon Bird, 'Assuring Quality while Reducing the Higher Education Regulatory Burden' (Australian Government, May 2013)

Estermann, Thomas and Enora Bennetot Pruvot, 'EUA Autonomy Scorecard: Ireland 2014 Update' (Report Update, European University Association, 2014)

Estermann, Thomas and Terhi Nokkala, 'University Autonomy in Europe I' (Project Report, European University Association, November 2009)

Estermann, Thomas, Terhi Nokkala and Monika Steinel, 'University Autonomy in Europe II: The Scorecard' (Project Report, European University Association, 15 November 2011)

European Commission, 'Employers' Perception of Graduate Employability' (Analytical Report, Flash Eurobarometer Series #304, European Commission, November 2010)

Fairweather, James S, 'Beyond the Rhetoric: Trends in the Relative Value of Teaching and Research in Faculty Salaries' (2005) 76(4) *The Journal of Higher Education* 401

Fiss, Owen, 'The Democratic Mission of the University' (2012–2013) 76 *Albany Law Review* 735

Froestad, Wenche and Pål Bakken (eds), 'Student Involvement in Quality Assessments of Higher Education in the Nordic Countries' (Project Report, Nordic Quality Assurance Network in Higher Education, 2004)

Glendenning, Dympna, 'Autonomy in Education: Irish Report' in Walter Berka, Jan De Groot and Hilde Penneman (eds), *Autonomy in Education: Yearbook of the European Association for Education Law and Policy* (Kluwer Law International, 2000) vol 3, 363

Glendinning, Irene, 'Responses to Student Plagiarism in Higher Education across Europe' (2014) 10(1) *International Journal for Educational Integrity* 4

Glendinning, Irene, Krzysztof Jóźwik and Agnieszka Michałowska-Dutkiewicz, 'Impact of Policies for Plagiarism in Higher Education across Europe: Plagiarism Policies in Austria' (Report, December 2013)

Glenn, Charles, 'Autonomy in Education: United States' in Walter Berka, Jan De Groot and Hilde Penneman (eds), *Autonomy in Education: Yearbook of the European Association for Education Law and Policy* (Kluwer Law International, 2000) vol 3, 433

Green, Madeleine, NAFSA: Association of International Educators, Mark Darby, Charles McCullough, Andrew Previc, Brianna Roberts and Katrina Santner, 'United States Education Guidebook' (Report, Australian Education International, April 2012)

Guggenberger, Helmut, Maria Keplinger and Martin Unger, 'Country Report on Employability and Mobility of Bachelor Graduates in Austria' (Report presented at the International Conference 'Employability and Mobility of Bachelor Graduates in Europe', Berlin, 30 September–1 October 2010)

Gunn, Andrew, 'The Role of Political and Policy Studies in Higher Education Policy Research' 1 *Theory and Method in Higher Education Research* 27

Hantrais, Linda, *International Comparative Research: Theory, Methods and Practice* (Palgrave Macmillan, 2009)

Hauptman, Arthur M, 'Assessing Market Mechanisms for Higher Education in New Zealand and Australia' (2003) 32 *International Higher Education* 20

Hedlund, Turid and Annikki Roos, 'FinnOA 10 Years of Open Access Work and a Road Map for the Future' (2013) 2 *Sciecom Info* 3

Heyneman, Stephen P, 'The Concern with Corruption in Higher Education' in Tricia Bertram Gallant (ed), *Creating the Ethical Academy: A Systems Approach to Understanding Misconduct and Empowering Change* (Routledge and Kegan Paul, 2010) 13

Higher Education Authority, 'What Do Graduates Do?—The Class of 2013: An Analysis of the Universities and Colleges of Education First Destination of Graduates Survey 2014' (Survey Report, Higher Education Authority, December 2014)

Higher Education Strategy Group, 'National Strategy for Higher Education to 2030' (Report, Department of Education and Skills, January 2011)

Högskoleverket [Swedish National Agency for Higher Education], 'Ranking of Universities and Higher Education Institutions for Student Information Purposes?' (Report 2009:27R, Högskoleverket, November 2009)

Holmwood, John and Gurminder K Bhambra, 'The Attack on Education as a Social Right' (2012) 111(2) *The South Atlantic Quarterly* 392

Ileski, Zan and Hannah Leichsenring, 'Kandipalaute: Results of the Second Survey Round 2013–2' (Survey Report, CHE Consult, July 2013)

Implementation Oversight Group, 'Draft Implementation Progress Report for National Strategy for Higher Education' (Report, Department of Education and Skills, Quarter 4 2012)

Jakovuori, Riikka, Antti Karjaluoto and Marko Rauhala, 'Finland Skills Gap Survey 2014—Finding the Skills for Finland's Future: Understanding the Gaps Can Help Prioritize Strategies' (Survey Report, Accenture, 2014)

Johnston, Ron, 'England's New Scheme for Funding Higher Education through Student Fees: "Fair And Progressive"?' (2013) 84(2) *The Political Quarterly* 200

Josefson, Kristina, Jenny Pobiega and Christian Stråhlman, 'Student Participation in Developing Student Feedback' (2011) 17(2) *Quality in Higher Education* 257

Karran, Terence, Klaus Beiter and Kwadwo Appiagyei-Atua, 'Measuring Academic Freedom in Europe: A Criterion Referenced Approach' (2017) 1(2) *Policy Reviews in Higher Education* 209

Kauppinen, Ilkka and Tuukka Kaidesoja, 'A Shift towards Academic Capitalism in Finland' (2014) 27 *Higher Education Policy* 23

Kosmützky, Anna, 'The Precision and Rigor of International Comparative Studies in Higher Education' (2016) 2 *Theory and Method in Higher Education Research* 199

Kottmann, Andrea, 'Higher Education in Austria' (Country Report, Centre for Higher Education Policy Studies, July 2008)

Landemore, Helene, 'Inclusive Constitution-Making: The Icelandic Experiment' (2014) 23(2) *The Journal of Political Philosophy* 166

Leer, Jane, 'Higher Education in Chile: A Study of Youth Perceptions' (2011) 1(1) *Penn State Journal of International Affairs* 27

Linde, Peter, 'Beyond OA-Policy' (2010) 2 *Sciecom Info* 3

Marginson, Simon, 'The Impossibility of Capitalist Markets in Higher Education' (2013) 28(3) *Journal of Education Policy* 353

McCormick, Alexander C and Jillian Kinzie, 'Refocusing the Quality Discourse: The United States National Survey of Student Engagement' in Hamish Coates and Alexander C McCormick (eds), *Engaging University Students* (Springer, 2014)

McGann, Kara and Geraldine Anderson, 'National Survey of Employers' Views of Irish Higher Education Outcomes' (Survey Report, IBEC, 14 December 2012)

Mercieca, Paul and Peter Macauley, 'A New Era of Open Access?' (2008) 39(4) *Australian Academic & Research Libraries* 243

Mitchell, Mark, 'Graduate Salary & Graduate Recruitment Trends Survey 2012' (Survey Report, Gradireland, May 2012) 9, 12.

National Survey of Student Engagement, 'Bringing the Institution into Focus—Annual Results 2014' (Report, National Survey of Student Engagement, 2014)

Neuhäuser, Rudolf, 'Institutional Autonomy versus Government Control (The New University Act in Austria)' (2004) 16(1) *Higher Education Management and Policy* 19

Nokkala, Terhi and Agneta Bladh, 'Institutional Autonomy and Academic Freedom in the Nordic Context—Similarities and Differences' (2014) 27 *Higher Education Policy* 1

Norton, Andrew, 'Taking University Teaching Seriously' (Report No 2013-8, Grattan Institute, July 2013)

Norton, Andrew, 'Mapping Australian Higher Education 2014–15' (Report No 2014-11, Grattan Institute, October 2014)

Oakleigh Consulting Limited and Career Development Organisation, 'Increasing Opportunities for High Quality Higher Education Work Experience: Report to HEFCE by Oakleigh Consulting Ltd and CRAC' (Report, Oakleigh Consulting Limited and Career Development Organisation, July 2011)

OECD, 'Building a High-Quality Teaching Profession: Lessons from around the World' (Background Report for the International Summit on the Teaching Profession, OECD, 2011)

Örn Arason, Elvar, Ingunn Ólafsdóttir and Ásta Briem, 'OECD Thematic Review of Tertiary Education: National Background Report for Iceland' (Report, Educational Testing Institute of Iceland, September 2005)

Park, Chris, 'In Other (People's) Words: Plagiarism by University Students—Literature and Lessons' (2003) 28(5) *Assessment & Evaluation in Higher Education* 471

Pechar, Hans, 'Austrian Higher Education Meets the Knowledge Society' (2004) 34(3) *The Canadian Journal of Higher Education* 55

Penneman, Hilde, 'Autonomy in Education: Review of the Country Reports' in Walter Berka, Jan De Groot and Hilde Penneman (eds), *Autonomy in Education: Yearbook of the European Association for Education Law and Policy* (Kluwer Law International, 2000) vol 3, 29

Penneman, Hilde, 'Synoptic Review of the Country Reports' in Walter Berka, Jan De Groot and Hilde Penneman (eds), *Autonomy in Education: Yearbook of the European Association for Education Law and Policy* (Kluwer Law International, 2000) vol 3, 41

Picasso, Vicki and Liam Phelan, 'The Evolution of Open Access to Research and Data in Australian Higher Education' (2014) 11(3) *RUSC Universities and Knowledge Society Journal* 122

Post, Robert, 'Discipline and Freedom in the Academy' (2012) 65 *Arkansas Law Review* 203

Radloff, Alexandra and Hamish Coates, 'Engaging University Students in Australia' in Hamish Coates and Alexander C McCormick (eds), *Engaging University Students* (Springer, 2014) 53

Raza, Reehana, 'Examining Autonomy and Accountability in Public and Private Tertiary Institutions' (Report, Human Development Network and World Bank, November 2009)

Romo de la Rosa, Alvaro, 'Institutional Autonomy and Academic Freedom: A Perspective from the American Continent' (2007) 20(3) *Higher Education Policy* 275

Santiago, Paulo, Karine Tremblay, Ester Basri and Elena Arnal, 'Tertiary Education for the Knowledge Society' (Report vol 2, OECD, 2008)

Schibany, Andreas, 'Austrian Research and Technology Report 2013' (Report, Federal Ministry of Science and Research, Federal Ministry for Transport, Innovation, and Technology and Federal Ministry of Economy, Family, and Youth, 2013)

Schwartz, Steven, 'Big Ideas for Australian Universities' (2009) 21(2) *Higher Education Management and Policy* 38

Southwell, Deborah, 'Good Practice Report: Revitalising the Academic Workforce' (Report, Australian Learning and Teaching Council, 2012)

Student Survey.IE, 'The Irish Survey of Student Engagement (ISSE): Results from 2014' (Report, Student Survey.IE, November 2014)

Student Survey.IE, 'The Irish Survey of Student Engagement (ISSE): Results from 2016' (Report, Student Survey.IE, November 2016)

Student Survey.IE, 'The Irish Survey of Student Engagement (ISSE)—Effective Feedback and Uses of ISSE Data: An Emerging Picture' (Report, Student Survey.IE, January 2015)

Swedish Higher Education Authority, 'Student Mirror' (Draft Summary Report, Swedish Higher Education Authority, 2017)

Teichler, Ulrich and Ester Ava Höhle, *The Work Situation of the Academic Profession in Europe: Findings of a Survey in Twelve Countries* (Springer Science & Business Media, 2013)

Tertiary Education Quality and Standards Agency, 'Report on Student Academic Integrity and Allegations of Contract Cheating by University Students' (Report, Tertiary Education Quality and Standards Agency, 12 March 2015)

The Higher Education Academy, 'Reward and Recognition in Higher Education: Institutional Policies and Their Implementation' (Report, The Higher Education Academy, 2009)

Thorsteinsdóttir, Sólveig, 'OA Mandates and the Nordic Countries' (2010) 1 *Sciecom Info* 1

Tomlinson, Michael, 'The Impact of Market-Driven Higher Education on Student-University Relations: Investing, Consuming and Competing' (2016) 29 *Higher Education Policy* 149

Tran, Carol N, 'Recognizing an Academic Freedom Exception to the Garcetti Limitation on the First Amendment Right to Free Speech' (2011–2012) 45 *Akron Law Review* 949

Turner, Rebecca and David Gosling, 'Rewarding Excellent Teaching: The Translation of a Policy Initiative in the United Kingdom' (2012) 66(4) *Higher Education Quarterly* 415

Uribe, Daniel and Juan Salamanca, 'Country Background Report—Chile: OECD Thematic Review of Tertiary Education' (Country Background Report, Higher Education Division, Ministry of Education, June 2007)

Welch, Anthony, 'Evidence-Based Policy: Epistemologically Specious, Ideologically Unsound' in Helen Proctor, Patrick Brownlee and Peter Freebody (eds), *Controversies in Education: Orthodoxy and Heresy in Policy and Practice* (Springer, 2015) 63

B. Cases/Constitutions/Legislation

Act on Public Higher Education Institutions No 85 from 2008 (Iceland)

Act on Quality Assurance in Higher Education 2012 (Austria)

Constitution of the Republic of Chile 1980

Education Reform Act 1988 (UK)

Establish the General Law of Education (2 July 2010) Biblioteca del Congreso Nacional de Chile <https://www.leychile.cl/Navegar?idNorma=1006043#free0> art 3 [Google Chrome trans]

Federal Act on Private Universities (Austria), Federal Gazette 1 No 74/2011 <http://wissenschaft.bmwfw.gv.at/home/studies/legislation/>

Federal Act on the External Quality Assurance in Higher Education and the Agency for Quality Assurance and Accreditation Austria (Austria), Federal Law Gazette 1 No 74/2011 <http://wissenschaft.bmwfw.gv.at/home/studies/legislation/>

Federal Act on University of Applied Sciences Degree Programmes (Austria), Federal Law Gazette No 340/1993 <http://wissenschaft.bmwfw.gv.at/home/studies/legislation/>

Fixes the Refunded, Coordinated and Systematized Text of the Political Constitution of the Republic of Chile (4 May 2017) Biblioteca del Congreso Nacional de Chile <https://www.leychile.cl/Navegar?idNorma=242302> ch 3 art 19(11) [Google Chrome trans]

Higher Education (Higher Amount) (England) Regulations 2010 (UK) No 3020 <http://www.nationalarchives.gov.uk/doc/open-government-licence/>

Higher Education and Research Bill 2016-17 (Cth)

Higher Education Institution Act 2006 (Iceland) No 63

Higher Education Opportunity Act, Pub L No 110-315, stat 3078, 122, 122 (2008)

Higher Education Ordinance 1993 (Sweden)

Higher Education Research and Reform Amendment Bill 2014 (Cth)

Higher Education Standards Framework (Threshold Standards) 2015 (Cth)

Higher Education Support Act 2003 (Cth)

Icelandic Student Loan Fund Act No 21 from 1992 (Iceland)

Institutes of Technology Act 2006 (Ireland) No 25 of 2006

Polytechnics Act 351/2003 (Finland)

Quality Assurance and Qualifications (Education and Training) Act 2012 (Ireland)

Stjórnarskrá lýðveldisins Íslands 1944 nr. 33 17 Júní [Government Offices of Iceland (Iceland) trans, *Constitution of the Republic of Iceland* (1944) <http://www.government.is/constitution/>

Student Grant Scheme 2014 (Ireland) SI No 201 of 2014

Student Support Act 2011 (Ireland) No 4 of 2011

Suomen perustuslaki 11.6.1999/731, 16 [Ministry of Justice (Finland) unofficial trans, *The Constitution of Finland 11 June 1999*, <http://www.finlex.fi/fi/laki/kaannokset/1999/en19990731.pdf>]

Swedish Higher Education Act 1992 (Sweden)

Tertiary Education Quality and Standards Agency Act 2011 (Cth)

The Higher Education Ordinance (Sweden) Swedish Code of Statutes (SFS) No. 1993:100

The Instrument of Government (Sweden)

The Riksdag Act (Sweden) 2014:801

United States Constitution

Universities Act 1997 (Ireland) No 24 of 1997

Universities Act 2002 (Austria)

Universities Act 558/2009 (Finland)

University of Applied Sciences Studies Act—FHStG (Austria)

C. Official international documents

Third Period Reports Submitted by States Parties under Articles 16 and 17 of the Covenant: Addendum: Australia, UN Doc E/1994/104/Add.22 (23 July 1998)

D. Other

'Chile to Have Free Higher Education by 2016', *TeleSUR* (online), 4 December 2014 <http://www.telesurtv.net/english/news/Chile-to-Have-Free-Higher-Education-by-2016-20141204-0049.html>

Aalto University, 'Strategic Development of Aalto University' (Strategic Plan, Aalto University, January 2012)

Aalto University, *Brochure* <http://www.aalto.fi/en/studies/about/for_future_student/>

Aalto University, *Studying at Aalto* (3 January 2014) <http://www.aalto.fi/en/studies/about/>

About the NSS, The National Student Survey <http://www.thestudentsurvey.com/about.php>

AGCAS Editors, *Country Profile—Finland* (March 2012) University of Kent <https://www.kent.ac.uk/careers/int/Finland.pdf>

Ali, Aftab, *Graduate Debt in England Higher than Any Other English-Speaking Country* (28 April 2016) The Independent <http://www.independent.co.uk/student/student-life/finances/graduate-debt-in-england-higher-than-any-other-english-speaking-country-a7004666.html>

Astin, Alexander W, *Accreditation and Autonomy* (18 February 2014) Inside Higher Ed <https://www.insidehighered.com/views/2014/02/18/accreditation-helps-limit-government-intrusion-us-higher-education-essay>

AUSSE, 'Student Engagement Questionnaire' (Questionnaire, AUSSE, 2012)

Austin, Anthony, Maree Heffernan and Nikki David, 'Academic Authorship, Publishing Agreements and Open Access: Survey Results' (Research Project, Open Access to Knowledge (OAK) Law Project, May 2008)

Australian Broadcasting Corporation, 'Highly Educated Teachers the Key to Success' *Lateline*, 28 February 2012 (Pasi Sahlberg)

Australian Bureau of Statistics, *Population Clock* (12 January 2017) <http://www.abs.gov.au/ausstats/abs%40.nsf/94713ad445ff1425ca25682000192af2/1647509ef7e25faaca2568a90015 4b63?OpenDocument>

Australian Council for Educational Research, 'Entering Higher Education in Australia' (LSAY Briefing Paper No 6, Australian Council for Educational Research, January 2003)

Australian Government, 'Commonwealth Supported Places (CSP) & Higher Education Loan Program (HELP) Handbook 2014' (Handbook, 2014)

Australian National University, 'ANU by 2020' (Strategic Plan, Australian National University, 2011)

Australian National University, *Choose ANU* <http://www.anu.edu.au/study/choose-anu>

Australian Workforce and Productivity Agency, 'Work Integrated Learning: AWPA Scoping Paper' (Scoping Paper, Australian Workforce and Productivity Agency, undated)

Austria Higher Education System, The European Education Directory <http://www.euroeducation.net/prof/ausco.htm>

Austria Population (23 February 2015) Country Meters <http://countrymeters.info/en/Austria>

Austrian Times, 'Austria Threatened with Skills Shortage' (14 November 2006) <http://austriantimes.at/news/Business/2006-11-14/133/Austria_threatened_with_skills_shortage>

Baker, Simon, *Applications to UK Universities down 4 Per Cent, Says UCAS* (13 July 2017) Times Higher Education <https://www.timeshighereducation.com/news/applications-uk-universities-down-4-cent-says-ucas>

Barrett, David, 'The Cheating Epidemic at Britain's Universities', *The Telegraph* (online), 5 March 2011 <http://www.telegraph.co.uk/education/educationnews/8363345/The-cheating-epidemic-at-Britains-universities.html>

Baskerville, Steve, 'A Guide to UK Higher Education and Partnerships for Overseas Universities' (Research Series 11, UK Higher Education International Unit, July 2013)

Bastedo, Michael, Batjargal Batkhuyag, Eufrasio Prates and Yaroslav Prytula, 'Educational Policies for Integrating College Competencies and Workforce Needs: Cases from Brazil, Mongolia, Ukraine, and the United States' (Issue Brief, Institute for Higher Education Policy, March 2009)

Björnsdóttir, Ingibjörg Rósa, *Universities in Iceland Seriously Underfunded* (25 November 2013) The Reykjavík Grapevine <https://grapevine.is/news/2013/11/25/universities-in-iceland-seriously-underfunded/>

Blekinge Institute of Technology, *The BTH Student Mirror 2012 (Studentspegel 2012)* (2 January 2012) <http://www.bth.se/eng/news.nsf/sidor/0939edbb54f2f0a5c125798400430e6c?OpenDocument>

BM72: A Call to Support LANDSSAMTÖK ÍSLENSKRA STÚDENTA against the Underfunding of Icelandic Universities (23 May 2017) European Students' Union <https://www.esu-online.org/?policy=call-support-landssamtok-islenskra-studenta-underfunding-icelandic-universities>

Boston University, 'Choosing to Be Great: A Vision of Boston University—Past, Present, and Future—The University's Strategic Plan' (Strategic Plan, Boston University, 19 November 2007)

Boston University, *The Difference Is Our DNA* <http://www.bu.edu/info/about/dna/>

Brady, Brian and Kunal Dutta, '45,000 Caught Cheating at Britain's Universities' *The Independent* (online), 11 March 2012 <http://www.independent.co.uk/news/education/education-news/45000-caught-cheating-at-britains-universities-7555109.html>

Bretag, Tracey, 'Australian Unis Should Take Responsibility for Corrupt Practices in International Education', *The Conversation* (online), 20 April 2015 <https://theconversation.com/australian-unis-should-take-responsibility-for-corrupt-practices-in-international-education-40380>

Browne, Lord John, Michael Barber, Diane Doyle, David Eastwood, Julia King, Rajay Naik and Peter Sands, *Securing a Sustainable Future for Higher Education: An Independent Review of Higher Education Funding & Student Finance* (Review, 12 October 2010)

Burke, Lindsey and Stuart M Butler, *Accreditation: Removing the Barrier to Higher Education Reform* (21 September 2012) The Heritage Foundation <http://www.heritage.org/research/reports/2012/09/accreditation-removing-the-barrier-to-higher-education-reform>

Cashmore, Annette, Chris Cane and Robert Cane, 'Rebalancing Promotion in the HE Sector: Is Teaching Excellence Being Rewarded?' (HEA Research Series, The Higher Education Academy, 3 July 2013)

Chile Police, Students Clash amid Rally for Free Education (22 June 2017) PressTV <http://presstv.ir/Detail/2017/06/22/526138/Chile-protest-higher-education-fee>

Chile Population, Trading Economics <http://www.tradingeconomics.com/chile/population>

Chile: Students Protest to Demand Universal Education (21 June 2017) teleSUR <http://www.telesurtv.net/english/news/Chile-Students-Protest-to-Demand-Universal-Education-20170621-0010.html>

Citizens Information Board, *Third-Level Student Fees and Charges* (9 October 2014) <http://www.citizensinformation.ie/en/education/third_level_education/fees_and_supports_for_third_level_education/fees.html>

Collini, Stefan, *Voters Should Be Enraged by Higher Education Profiteering* (6 June 2017) The Guardian <https://www.theguardian.com/education/2017/jun/06/higher-education-profiteering-tuition-fees-universities>

Corbett Broad, Molly, 'Academic Freedom & Institutional Autonomy in the United States: Balancing Rights and Responsibilities' (Paper presented at Council of Europe, Strasbourg, France, 8 November 2010)

Council of Legal Education and Board of Examiners, *About Us* (23 March 2015) <http://www.lawadmissions.vic.gov.au/>

CQ University, 'Strategic Plan 2015–2020: "Strong to Great"' (Strategic Plan, CQ University, 1 January 2015)

CQ University, *Welcome: Vice-Chancellor's Welcome* <https://www.cqu.edu.au/about-us/structure/organisation/welcome>

Craven, Greg, 'Pyne's Fine Words Fell on Deaf Ears', *The Australian* (Australia), 12 March 2014

Deakin University, *Why Choose Deakin?* (25 May 2015) <http://www.deakin.edu.au/study-at-deakin/why-choose-deakin>

Deakin University, 'LIVE the Future: Agenda 2020' (Strategic Plan, Deakin University, 2014)

De Gayardon, Ariane, *England Embraces the Delusion of Free Tuition* (14 July 2017) University World News <http://www.universityworldnews.com/article.php?story=20170712153136573>

Delacourt, Susan, *America Is Now Split on Education, Too: Delacourt* (14 July 2017) The Star <https://www.thestar.com/news/insight/2017/07/14/america-is-now-split-on-education-too-delacourt.html>

Delargy, Orlaith, 'The Graduate: What's Wrong with Learning for Learning's Sake?' *The Irish Times* (online), 15 February 2014 <http://www.irishtimes.com/life-and-style/the-graduate-what-s-wrong-with-learning-for-learning-s-sake-1.1692106>

Department for Business, Innovation & Skills, *2010 to 2015 Government Policy: Higher Education Participation* (8 May 2015) <https://www.gov.uk/government/publications/2010-to-2015-government-policy-higher-education-participation/2010-to-2015-government-policy-higher-education-participation>

Department for Business, Innovation & Skills, *Higher Education: Students at the Heart of the System* (White Paper, 2011)

Department for Business, Innovation and Skills, 'National Strategy for Access and Student Success in Higher Education' (Strategy, Office for Fair Access and Higher Education Funding Council for England, April 2014)

Department of Employment, 'Skill Shortage List Australia' (Departmental Document, Department of Employment, 8 August 2014)

Dobson, Ian R, *Finland: To Fee or Not to Fee—That Is the Question* (24 January 2010) University World News <http://www.universityworldnews.com/article.php?story=20100123092224108&query=dobson>

Dobson, Ian R, 'Full Circle: The Return to User-Pays in Australian Higher Education' (Paper presented at First RESUP International Conference, Paris, 1–3 February 2007)

Dublin City University, 'Transforming Lives and Societies: Strategic Plan 2012–2017' (Strategic Plan, Dublin City University, 2012)

Dublin City University, *Discovering DCU, Dublin City University* <http://dcu.ie/discovering-dcu.shtml>

Easley, Jonathan, *Poll: Bernie Sanders Country's Most Popular Active Politician* (18 April 2017) The Hill <http://thehill.com/homenews/campaign/329404-poll-bernie-sanders-countrys-most-popular-active-politician>

East Carolina University, *ECU Mission Statement* (February 2014) <http://www.ecu.edu/cs-admin/chancellor/mission.cfm>

East Carolina University, *ECU Strategic Plan 2014–2019* (17 September 2014) <http://www.ecu.edu/cs-acad/strategicplan/guiding-principles.cfm>

Eckel, Peter D and Jacqueline E King, *An Overview of Higher Education in the United States: Diversity, Access, and the Role of the Marketplace* (American Council on Education, 2004)

Euben, Donna R, *Academic Freedom of Professors and Institutions* (May 2002) American Association of University Professors <https://www.aaup.org/issues/academic-freedom/professors-and-institutions>

European University Association, *Ireland* <http://www.university-autonomy.eu/countries/ireland/>

European University Association, *Sweden* <http://www.university-autonomy.eu/countries/sweden/>

European University Association, *United Kingdom* <http://www.university-autonomy.eu/countries/united-kingdom/>

European University Institute, *Sweden, Academic Career Structure* (30 July 2009) <http://www.eui.eu/ProgrammesAndFellowships/AcademicCareersObservatory/AcademicCareersbyCountry/Sweden.aspx>

European University Institute, *Finland, Academic Career Structure* (28 October 2014) <http://www.eui.eu/ProgrammesAndFellowships/AcademicCareersObservatory/AcademicCareersbyCountry/Finland.aspx>

European University Institute, *Ireland, Academic Career Structure* (7 November 2014) <http://www.eui.eu/ProgrammesAndFellowships/AcademicCareersObservatory/AcademicCareersbyCountry/Ireland.aspx>

European University Institute, *United Kingdom, Academic Career Structure* (24 October 2014) <http://www.eui.eu/ProgrammesAndFellowships/AcademicCareersObservatory/AcademicCareersbyCountry/UnitedKingdom.aspx>

European University Institute, *USA, Academic Career Structure* (18 February 2014) <http://www.eui.eu/ProgrammesAndFellowships/AcademicCareersObservatory/AcademicCareersbyCountry/USA.aspx>

Eurypedia, *European Encyclopedia on National Education Systems: Island: Support Measures for Learners in Higher Education* (14 December 2012) European Commission <https://webgate.ec.europa.eu/fpfis/mwikis/eurydice/index.php/Iceland:Support_Measures_for_Learners_in_Higher_Education>

Finland Introduces University Tuition Fees for Non-EU Students (18 January 2016) <http://monitor.icef.com/2016/01/finland-introduces-university-tuition-fees-for-non-eu-students/>

Finnish National Board of Education, *Teacher Education* <http://www.oph.fi/english/education_system/teacher_education>

Fitzgerald, Kyran, 'Skills Shortage Is a Job That Needs Fixing', Irish Examiner (online), 3 March 2014 <http://www.irishexaminer.com/business/skills-shortage-is-a-job-that-needs-fixing-260641.html>

Fitzgerald, Kyran, 'Skills Shortage Will Delay Recovery', *Irish Examiner* (online), 6 October 2014 <http://www.irishexaminer.com/business/skills-shortage-will-delay-recovery-290019.html>

Foroohar, Rana, *The US College Debt Bubble Is Becoming Dangerous* (10 April 2017) Financial Times <https://www.ft.com/content/a272ee4c-1b83-11e7-bcac-6d03d067f81f?mhq5j=e2>

Friedman, Zack, *Student Loan Debt in 2017: A $1.3 Trillion Crisis* (21 February 2017) Forbes <https://www.forbes.com/sites/zackfriedman/2017/02/21/student-loan-debt-statistics-2017/#768317025dab>

Geschwind, Lars and Anders Jörnesten, 'Tenure Track Tensions: Academic Career Paths in a Deregulated Sector' (Paper presented at the SRHE Annual Research Conference, South Wales, United Kingdom, 11–13 December 2013)

Graf, Lukas, *The Hybridization of Vocational Training and Higher Education in Austria, Germany, and Switzerland* (25 November 2013) Higher Education Development Association <http://uv-net.uio.no/wpmu/hedda/2013/11/25/guest-blogger-the-hybridization-of-vocational-training-and-higher-education-in-austria-germany-and-switzerland/>

Grants & Cooperations, Center of Excellence <http://www.studyinaustria.at/grants_cooperations/>

Green, David, *It's Time to Radically Rethink University Tuition Fees* (13 July 2017) The Guardian <https://www.theguardian.com/higher-education-network/2017/jul/13/its-time-to-radically-rethink-university-tuition-fees>

Group of Eight Australia, *The Australian Higher Education System* <https://go8.edu.au/page/australian-higher-education-system>

Guggenberger, Helmut, 'Aspects of Transition and Professional Success. Some Findings from Austrian Graduate Surveys' (Paper presented at the International Conference on Employability of Graduates & Higher Education Management Systems, Vienna, 22–23 September 2011)

Gunn, Andrew, *Six Things You Need to Know about the Higher Education Bill* (4 April 2017) The Conversation <http://theconversation.com/six-things-you-need-to-know-about-the-higher-education-bill-74945>

Hanson, Hayley E, *Final Rules Issued for Higher Education Compliance with the Violence Against Women Act* (21 October 2014) Higher Education Legal Insights <http://www.highereducationlegalinsights.com/2014/10/final-rules-issued-for-higher-education-compliance-with-the-violence-against-women-act/>

Hays, *Hays Global Skills Index 2014: Ireland* <http://www.hays-index.com/countries/ireland/>

Hays, *Hays Global Skills Index 2014: United Kingdom* <http://www.hays-index.com/countries/united-kingdom/>

Hays, *Hays Global Skills Index 2014: Sweden* <http://www.hays-index.com/countries/sweden/>

Hays, *Hays Global Skills Index 2016: Chile* <http://www.hays-index.com/countries/chile/>

Hays, *Hays Global Skills Index 2016: United Kingdom* <http://www.hays-index.com/countries/united-kingdom/>

Hays, *Hays Global Skills Index 2016: United States* <http://www.hays-index.com/countries/usa/>

Hays, *Hays Global Skills Index 2016: Australia* <http://www.hays-index.com/countries/australia/>

Higher Education Authority, *Open Access to Scientific Information* (11 November 2013) <http://www.hea.ie/en/policy/research/open-access-scientific-information>

Hoeckel, Kathrin, *Learning for Jobs: OECD Reviews of Vocational Education and Training—Austria* (OECD, 2010)

Humphreys, Joe, 'Staff-Student Ratios "Considerably out of Line" with International Norms', *The Irish Times* (online), 12 June 2014 <http://www.irishtimes.com/news/education/staff-student-ratios-considerably-out-of-line-with-international-norms-1.1829034>

ICEF Monitor, *Market Snapshot: Chile* (22 October 2013) <http://monitor.icef.com/2013/10/market-snapshot-chile/>

Iceland Academy of the Arts, 'Iceland Academy of the Arts: Strategic Plan 2013–2017' (Strategic Plan, Iceland Academy of the Arts, 2013)

Iceland Academy of the Arts, *About the Academy* <http://lhi.is/english/about/>

Icelanders Back First 'Crowdsourced Constitution' (22 October 2012) <http://www.euractiv.com/enlargement/icelanders-opens-way-crowdsource-news-515543>

Improving Quality at Higher Education Institutions in Chile (24 November 2016) United Nations Educational, Scientific and Cultural Organization/International Institute for

Educational Planning <http://www.iiep.unesco.org/en/improving-quality-higher-education-institutions-chile-3786>

International Affairs Office, *Organization of U.S. Education: Tertiary Institutions* (February 2008) US Department of Education <http://www2.ed.gov/about/offices/list/ous/international/usnei/us/edlite-org-us.html>

Internationals Face Higher Tuition Fees (24 October 2014) University World News <http://www.universityworldnews.com/article.php?story=20141023150110719&query=iceland>

Ireland Population, Trading Economics <http://www.tradingeconomics.com/ireland/population>

It's Time to Make College Tuition Free and Debt Free, Bernie Sanders <https://berniesanders.com/issues/its-time-to-make-college-tuition-free-and-debt-free/>

Kandipalaute (1 January 2017) Universities Finland UNIFI <http://translate.googleusercontent.com/translate_c?depth=1&hl=en&prev=search&rurl=translate.google.com.au&sl=fi&sp=nmt4&u=http://www.unifi.fi/wp-content/uploads/2017/01/Kandipalaute_kyselyn_valtakunnallinen_osa_20170101.pdf>

Kandipalaute, *Kandipalaute,* Universities Finland UNIFI <http://www.unifi.fi/kandipalaute/>

Kelpie, Colm, *Concerns over Major Skills Shortages in Key Sectors* (26 September 2014) Independent.ie <http://www.independent.ie/business/irish/concerns-over-major-skills-shortages-in-key-sectors-30616706.html>

Kiley, Penny, *Are Irish Graduates Work-Ready?* (14 June 2012) Gradireland <https://gradireland.wordpress.com/2012/06/14/are-irish-graduates-work-ready/>

Kingkade, Tyler, 'Prosecutors Rarely Bring Charges in College Rape Cases', *Huffington Post* (online), 18 June 2014 <http://www.huffingtonpost.com/2014/06/17/college-rape-prosecutors-press-charges_n_5500432.html>

Korpela, Salla, *How about Getting a Job in Finland? Vacancies in Healthcare, Service Sector and More* (July 2014) This is Finland <http://finland.fi/Public/default.aspx?contentid=160050>

Kytölä, Laura and Aleksi Teivainen, 'Labour Shortage Hits New Sectors', *Helsinki Times* (online), 3 December 2013 <http://www.helsinkitimes.fi/finland/finland-news/domestic/8581-labour-shortage-hits-new-sectors.html>

Labour Shortage List, Work in Sweden <http://work.sweden.se/how-to-find-a-job/labour-shortage-list/>

Lancaster University, 'Our Strategy for 2020' (Strategic Plan, Lancaster University)

Lancaster University, *Five Great Reasons* <http://www.lancaster.ac.uk/study/why-lancaster/>

Letter from Australian Permanent Mission to the United Nations in Geneva to the Office of the High Commissioner for Human Rights, 18 April 2012

Letter from Ruairi Quinn, Minister for Education and Skills, to Mr John Hennessy, Chair Higher Education Authority, 30 May 2013

Linnaeus University, *This Is Linnaeus University* (25 June 2014) <http://lnu.se/education/this-is-linnaeus-university-?l=en>

Linnaeus University, 'A Journey into the Future: Vision and Strategy 2015–2020' (Vision and Strategy, Linnaeus University, 24 September 2014)

Lund University, 'Strategic Plan 2012–2016' (Strategic Plan, Lund University, 16 February 2012)

Lund University, *Why Study at Lund University* (14 November 2005) <http://www.lunduniversity.lu.se/international-admissions/why-study-at-lund-university>

McKenzie, Phillip, 'The Transition from Education to Work in Australia Compared to Selected OECD Countries' (Paper presented at the Sixth International Conference on Post-Compulsory Education and Training', Gold Coast, Queensland, 2 December 1998)

McLennan, Belinda and Shay Keating, 'Work-Integrated Learning (WIL) in Australian Universities: The Challenges of Mainstreaming WIL' (Paper presented at ALTC NAGCAS National Symposium, Melbourne, June 2008)

Mercieca, Paul, 'Publication Patterns of Australian Academics and the Impact on Open Access Publishing' (Paper presented at Victorian Association for Library Automation Inc Conference, Melbourne, 5–7 February 2008)

Ministry of Education and Culture, *Education and Research 2011–2016: A Development Plan* <http://www.minedu.fi/export/sites/default/OPM/Julkaisut/2012/liitteet/okm03.pdf>

Ministry of Education and Culture, *Education Policy in Finland* <http://www.minedu.fi/OPM/Koulutus/koulutuspolitiikka/?lang=en>

Ministry of Education and Culture, *Polytechnic Education: Administration and Finance* <http://www.minedu.fi/OPM/Koulutus/ammattikorkeakoulutus/hallinto_ohjaus_ja_rahoitus/?lang=en>

Ministry of Education and Culture, *University Education in Finland* <http://www.minedu.fi/OPM/Koulutus/yliopistokoulutus/?lang=en>

Ministry of Education and Culture, *University Education: Administration and Finance* <http://www.minedu.fi/OPM/Koulutus/yliopistokoulutus/hallinto_ohjaus_ja_rahoitus/?lang=en>

Ministry of Education, 'Higher Education Institutions 2009—Universities and Polytechnics as Implementers of Higher Education Policy' (Publications of the Ministry of Education, Finland 2009:51, 14 April 2010)

Ministry of Education, Science and Culture, 'The Educational System in Iceland' (Monograph 6, Ministry of Education, Science and Culture, 2002)

Ministry of Education, Science and Culture, *Education* <http://eng.menntamalaraduneyti.is/education-in-iceland/Educational_system/>

MODUL University Vienna, *History and Values* <https://www.modul.ac.at/history-values/>

Morgan, John, *University Tuition Fee Cap of £9,250 Confirmed for 2017–18* (21 July 2016) Times Higher Education <https://www.timeshighereducation.com/news/university-tuition-fee-cap-of-nine-thousand-two-hundred-and-fifty-pounds-confirmed-for-2017-2018>

Morris, David, *Be It Enacted: The Higher Education and Research Act* (27 April 2017) Wonkhe <http://wonkhe.com/blogs/be-it-enacted-the-higher-education-and-research-act-2017/>

Musset, Pauline and Rodrigo Castañeda Valle, 'A Skills beyond School Commentary on Iceland' (Review of Vocational Education and Training, OECD, April 2013)

Myklebust, Jan Petter and Ian R Dobson, *Move towards Tuition Fees for Non-European Students* (2 February 2013) University World News <http://www.universityworldnews.com/article.php?story=20130127122204l8&query=dobson>

Myklebust, Jan Petter, *Sweden: Protests against Government Reward System* (2 May 2010) University World News <http://www.universityworldnews.com/article.php?story=20100429204512982>

National Health and Medical Research Council, *NHMRC's Policy on the Dissemination of Research Findings* (9 December 2014) <https://www.nhmrc.gov.au/grants-funding/policy/nhmrc-open-access-policy>

National Overview on the Issue of Employability of Bachelor Graduates in Austria, Austrian Federal Ministry of Science and Research <http://www.ond.vlaanderen.be/hogeronderwijs/bologna/actionlines/documents/Employability_Austria.pdf>

National Quality Assurance and Enhancement Framework, Iceland Academy of the Arts <http://lhi.is/english/about/quality-enhancement/quality-system-outline/>

National Steering Committee on Open Access Policy, 'National Principles for Open Access Policy Statement' (Statement, National Steering Committee on Open Access Policy, 23 October 2012)

National Student Survey Results 2016 (5 October 2016) Higher Education Funding Council for England <http://www.hefce.ac.uk/lt/nss/results/2016/>

National Student Survey, The National Student Survey <www.thestudentsurvey.com/content/NSS2015_Questionnaire.pdf>

National Survey of Student Engagement, *National Survey of Student Engagement: Summary Tables* (2016) <http://nsse.indiana.edu/html/summary_tables.cfm>

National Survey of Student Engagement, *NSSE 2014 US Grand Frequencies: First Year Students* (2014) <nsse.iub.edu/2014_institutional_report/pdf/Frequencies/Freq%20-%20FY%20by%20Major.pdf>

National University of Ireland Maynooth, 'Strategic Plan 2012–2017' (Strategic Plan, National University of Ireland Maynooth, 2012)

National University of Ireland Maynooth, *Why Maynooth?* Maynooth University <https://www.maynoothuniversity.ie/study-maynooth/why-maynooth>

Nikolau, Lisa, *Chile Continues Debate over Inequality in Higher Education* (3 January 2017) Humanosphere <http://www.humanosphere.org/basics/2017/01/chile-continues-debate-over-inequality-in-higher-education/>

Office for National Statistics, *Theme: Population* <http://ons.gov.uk/ons/taxonomy/index.html?nscl=Population>

Organisation for Economic Cooperation and Development and World Bank, 'Tertiary Education in Chile' (Reviews of National Policies for Education, OECD and World Bank, 2009)

Organisation for Economic Cooperation and Development and World Bank, 'The Bío Region, Chile' (Review of Higher Education in Regional and City Development, OECD-World Bank, August 2009)

Organisation for Economic Cooperation and Development, 'Higher Education in Ireland' (Reviews of National Policies for Education, OECD, 2006)

Organisation for Economic Cooperation and Development, 'OECD Reviews of Tertiary Education for the Knowledge Society' (Review vol 1 and vol 2, OECD, 2008)

Organisation for Economic Cooperation and Development, 'Quality Assurance in Higher Education in Chile' (Reviews of National Policies for Education, OECD, November 2012)

Organisation for Economic Cooperation and Development, 'Reviews of National Policies for Education: Quality Assurance in Higher Education in Chile 2013' (Review, OECD, 2013)

Organisation for Economic Cooperation and Development, *Aid (ODA) by Sector and Donor [DAC5]* (30 April 2015) <http://stats.oecd.org/Index.aspx?datasetcode=TABLE5>

Organisation for Economic Cooperation and Development, *Survey of Higher Education Systems* <www.oecd.org/edu/imhe/32503573.PDF>

Organisation for Economic Cooperation and Development, *Sweden's Skills Snapshot* <http://skills.oecd.org/informationbycountry/sweden.html>

Organisation for Economic Cooperation and Development, 'Education at a Glance 2016: Finland—Country Note' (OECD 2016)

Organisation for Economic Cooperation and Development, 'Education at a Glance 2014: OECD Indicators' (OECD, 2014)

Organisation for Economic Cooperation and Development, 'Education at a Glance 2016: OECD Indicators' (OECD, 2016)

Parliament of Finland, *Constitution of Finland* <http://web.eduskunta.fi/Resource.phx/parliament/relatedinformation/constitution.htx?lng=en>

Pells, Rachel, *Universities Given Permission to Increase Tuition Fees Every Year* (28 April 2017) The Independent <http://www.independent.co.uk/news/education/education-news/university-tuition-fees-uk-rise-increase-every-year-government-higher-education-courses-study-a7707291.html>

Polglaze, Ray, 'Chile: Students Set to Win Free Higher Education', *Green Left Weekly* (online), 1 April 2014 <https://www.greenleft.org.au/node/56187>

Pontificia Universidad Católica de Valparaíso, 'Strategic Development Plan 2011–2016' (Strategic Plan, Pontificia Universidad Católica de Valparaíso, 2011)

Pontificia Universidad Católica de Valparaíso, *Welcome* <http://www.ucv.cl/english/>

QS Top Universities, *Country Guide: Study in Iceland*, Top Universities <http://www.topuniversities.com/where-to-study/europe/iceland/guide#tab=0>

Quality and Qualifications Ireland, *About Us* <http://www.qqi.ie/Pages/About-Us.aspx>

Quality Assurance Agency, *About Us* <http://www.qaa.ac.uk/about-us>

Radloff, Ali, *Australasian Survey of Student Engagement (AUSSE)* <https://www.acer.edu.au/ausse/background>

Ramsay, Max, *Oxford University Students Are Latest to Boycott Student Survey in Protest over Tuition Fee Hikes* (12 January 2017) The Independent <http://www.independent.co.uk/student/news/oxford-university-students-protest-tuition-fees-hike-boycott-student-survey-satisfaction-tef-sorana-a7523781.html>

Rannis, 'Quality Enhancement Handbook for Icelandic Higher Education 2011' (Handbook, Rannis on behalf of the Quality Board for Icelandic Higher Education, October 2011)

Ratcliffe, Rebecca, *Students and Lecturers March against Tories' Education Bill* (20 November 2016) The Guardian <https://www.theguardian.com/world/2016/nov/19/students-lecturers-march-tories-education-bill-brexit-eu>

Rodríguez-Ponce, Emilio, 'Time for Change in Chilean Higher Education', *University World News* (online), 20 December 2013 <http://www.universityworldnews.com/article.php?story=20131219150048533>

Ronai, Kara, 'The Cost of Higher Education: Lessons from the Australian Context for Finland', *Kielikoulutuspolitiikan verkosto* (online), 13 May 2015 <http://www.kieliverkosto.fi/article/the-cost-of-higher-education-lessons-from-the-australian-context-for-finland/>

Sainato, Michael, *Poll Confirms Bernie Sanders Is the Most Popular Politician in the Country* (11 July 2017) Observer <http://observer.com/2017/07/bernie-sanders-most-popular-politician/>

Sanchez Diaz, Ignacio, *Higher Education Reform Debated in Chile* (2 January 2017) Inside Higher Ed <https://www.insidehighered.com/blogs/world-view/higher-education-reform-debated-chile>

Sanders, Bernie, *Make College Free for All* (22 October 2015) The Washington Post <https://www.washingtonpost.com/opinions/bernie-sanders-america-needs-free-college-now/2015/10/22/a3d05512-7685-11e5-bc80-9091021aeb69_story.html?utm_term=.c127e64d780e>

Sen, Reet, *Why Has Finland Introduced Tuition Fees for Non-EU Students?* (15 February 2017) Full Fabric Blog <http://blog.fullfabric.com/why-finland-introduced-tuition-fees-non-eu-students>

Shanghai Jiao Tong University, *Academic Ranking of World Universities 2016: Australia,* Shanghai Ranking <http://www.shanghairanking.com/World-University-Rankings-2016/Australia.html>

Shanghai Jiao Tong University, *Academic Ranking of World Universities 2016: Austria* <http://www.shanghairanking.com/World-University-Rankings-2016/Austria.html>

Shanghai Jiao Tong University, *Academic Ranking of World Universities 2016: Ireland* <http://www.shanghairanking.com/World-University-Rankings-2016/Ireland.html>

Shanghai Jiao Tong University, *Academic Ranking of World Universities: Statistics,* Shanghai Ranking <http://www.shanghairanking.com/ARWU-Statistics-2016.html>

Shanghai Jiao Tong University, *Academic Ranking of World Universities: Statistics,* Shanghai Ranking <http://www.shanghairanking.com/ARWU-Statistics-2014.html>

Shortage Occupations List 2015, Federal Government website on migration <http://www.migration.gv.at/en/types-of-immigration/permanent-immigration-red-white-red-card/skilled-workers-in-shortage-occupations/shortage-occupations-list-2015.html>

Skinner, Curtis and Valerie Vande Panne, *Students across US March over Debt, Free Public College* (12 November 2015) Reuters <http://www.reuters.com/article/us-usa-college-protests-idUSKCN0T116W20151112>

Statistics Austria, *Total Population* (18 November 2014) <http://www.statistik.at/web_en/statistics/population/population_censuses_register_based_census_register_based_labour_market_statistics/totaL_population/index.html>

Statistics Finland, *Finland's Preliminary Population Figure 5 475 450 at the End of January* (24 February 2015) <http://www.stat.fi/til/vamuu/2015/01/vamuu_2015_01_2015-02-24_tie_001_en.html>

Statistics Iceland, *Overview* (4 March 2014) <http://www.statice.is/Statistics/Population/Overview>

Statistics Sweden, *Population Statistics* (31 December 2014) <http://www.scb.se/en_/Finding-statistics/Statistics-by-subject-area/Population/Population-composition/Population-statistics/>

Stockholm University, 'Strategies for Stockholm University 2015–2018' (Strategic Plan, Stockholm University, 2015)

Stockholm University, *About Us* http://www.su.se/english/about

Stone, Jon, *Jeremy Corbyn: Scrap Tuition Fees and Give Students Grants Again, Says Labour Leadership Contender* (16 July 2017) The Independent <http://www.independent.co.uk/news/uk/politics/scrap-tuition-fees-and-give-students-grants-again-says-labours-jeremy-corbyn-10392769.html>

Student Feedback Survey for Bachelor Graduates 2015 (7 February 2017) Finnish Social Science Data Archive <http://urn.fi/urn:nbn:fi:fsd:T-FSD3135>

Student Input Important for the Development of Swedish Higher Education (11 September 2015) Swedish Higher Education Authority < http://english.uka.se/about-us/news--events/nyheter/2015-11-09-student-input-important-for-the-development-of-swedish-higher-education.html>

Student Survey.IE, *Survey Results*, Student Survey.IE <http://studentsurvey.ie/wordpress/survey-results/>

Students to Occupy Buildings in University Protest (14 November 2013) Sveriges Radio <http://sverigesradio.se/sida/artikel.aspx?programid=2054&artikel=5703971>

Swedish International Development Cooperation Agency, Openaid.se <http://www.openaid.se/aid/2014/>

Swedish International Development Cooperation Agency, Openaid.se <http://www.openaid.se/aid/sweden/world/all-organisations/education/2014/>

Syokos, Alexandra, 'Students Bring out Mattresses in Huge "Carry That Weight" Protest against Sexual Assault' *Huffington Post* (online), 29 October 2014 <http://www.huffingtonpost.com/2014/10/29/carry-that-weight-columbia-sexual-assault_n_6069344.html>

Teeter, Derek T, *10 Questions College and University Leaders Should Ask about Title IX Sexual Misconduct "2.0" Compliance* (12 December 2014) Higher Education Legal Insights <http://www.highereducationlegalinsights.com/2014/12/10-questions-college-and-university-leaders-should-ask-about-title-ix-sexual-misconduct-2-0-compliance/>

Tertiary Education Quality and Standards Agency, *About TEQSA* <http://www.teqsa.gov.au/about>

The Constitutional Society trans, *Constitutional Bill* (29 July 2011) <http://stjornarsk-rarfelagid.is/?page_id=2619>

The European Education Directory, *Finland Higher Education System* <http://www.euroeducation.net/prof/finco.htm>

The Finnish Higher Education Evaluation Council (FINHEEC), Korkeakoulujen arviointineuvosto <http://www.finheec.fi/index.phtml?l=en&s=5>

The Open University, 'Strategic Plan 2012–2017: Securing the Mission' (Strategic Plan, The Open University, 2015)

The Open University, *What It's Like to Study* <http://www.open.ac.uk/courses/what-study-like>

The Swedish Institute, *Higher Education and Research in Sweden* (31 March 2014) <https://sweden.se/society/higher-education-and-research/>

The Swedish National Agency for Higher Education, 'The Swedish Higher Education System' (The Swedish National Agency for Higher Education, May 2012)

The University of Kansas, 'Bold Aspirations: The Strategic Plan for the University of Kansas 2012–2017' (Strategic Plan, The University of Kansas, September 2011)

The University of Kansas, *About KU* <http://www.ku.edu/about/>

The University of Melbourne, *Our Courses* (11 June 2016) <https://futurestudents.unimelb.edu.au/courses/world-standard-education>

Thompson, Mary Anne, *Employment Outlook: Chile* (1 April 2014) Going Global <http://www.goinglobal.com/articles/1160/>

Thousands of Chilean Students Take to Streets Demanding Education Reform (11 April 2017) teleSUR <http://www.telesurtv.net/english/news/Thousands-of-Chilean-Students-Take-to-Streets-Demanding-Education-Reform-20170411-0022.html>

Tier 2 Shortage Occupation List—Government-Approved Version (6 April 2014) Gov.UK <https://www.gov.uk/government/uploads/system/uploads/attachment_data/file/308513/shortageoccupationlistapril14.pdf>

Tuition Fees, Center of Excellence <http://www.studyinaustria.at/study_in_austria/tuition_fees/>

Tuition Fees and Costs, Study in Sweden <https://studyinsweden.se/plan-your-studies/fees-and-costs/>

Two New Government Authorities, Universitets-och högskolerådet <http://www.hsv.se/nyamyndigheter>

UCAS, *Undergraduate Tuition Fees and Student Loans,* UCAS <https://www.ucas.com/ucas/undergraduate/finance-and-support/undergraduate-tuition-fees-and-student-loans>

UC San Diego, *2014 Strategic Plan Executive Summary* (2014) UC San Diego <http://plan.sdsc.edu/documents/Exec-Summary-Strategic-Plan.pdf>

UC San Diego, *About UC San Diego,* UC San Diego <http://ucsd.edu/about/index.html>

UC San Diego, *Choose UC San Diego,* UC San Diego <https://grad.ucsd.edu/admissions/choose.html>

United Nations Educational, Scientific and Cultural Organization, *Global Open Access Portal: Australia* <http://www.unesco.org/new/en/communication-and-information/portals-and-platforms/goap/access-by-region/asia-and-the-pacific/australia/#topPage>

United Nations Educational, Scientific and Cultural Organization, *Global Open Access Portal: Austria* (December 2013) <http://www.unesco.org/new/en/communication-and-information/portals-and-platforms/goap/access-by-region/europe-and-north-america/austria/>

United Nations Educational, Scientific and Cultural Organization, *Global Open Access Portal: Chile* (December 2013) <http://www.unesco.org/new/en/communication-and-information/portals-and-platforms/goap/access-by-region/latin-america-and-the-caribbean/chile/>

United Nations Educational, Scientific and Cultural Organization, *Global Open Access Portal: Finland* (December 2013) <http://www.unesco.org/new/en/communication-and-information/portals-and-platforms/goap/access-by-region/europe-and-north-america/finland/>

United Nations Educational, Scientific and Cultural Organization, *Global Open Access Portal: Iceland* (December 2013) <http://www.unesco.org/new/en/communication-and-information/portals-and-platforms/goap/access-by-region/europe-and-north-america/iceland/>

United Nations Educational, Scientific and Cultural Organization, *Global Open Access Portal: Ireland* (December 2013) <http://www.unesco.org/new/en/communication-and-information/portals-and-platforms/goap/access-by-region/europe-and-north-america/ireland/>

United Nations Educational, Scientific and Cultural Organization, *Global Open Access Portal: Sweden* (December 2013) <http://www.unesco.org/new/en/communication-and-information/portals-and-platforms/goap/access-by-region/europe-and-north-america/sweden/>

United Nations Educational, Scientific and Cultural Organization, *Global Open Access Portal: United Kingdom of Great Britain and Northern Ireland* <http://www.unesco.org/new/en/communication-and-information/portals-and-platforms/goap/access-by-region/europe-and-north-america/united-kingdom-of-great-britain-and-northern-ireland/>

United Nations Educational, Scientific and Cultural Organization, *Global Open Access Portal: United States of America* <http://www.unesco.org/new/en/communication-and-information/portals-and-platforms/goap/access-by-region/europe-and-north-america/usa/>

United States Census Bureau, *US and World Population Clock* (25 February 2015) <http://www.census.gov/popclock/>

Universidad Arturo Prat, *Strategic Definitions: Vision* (2014) Universidad Arturo Prat <http://www.unap.cl/mk/pei/files/assets/basic-html/page10.html> [Google Chrome trans]

Universidad Arturo Prat, *The University I Want,* Universidad Arturo Prat <http://www.unap.cl/admision/2017/unap.html> [Google Chrome trans]

Universidad de Antofagasta, *Plan de Desarrollo Estrategico Convenio Plurianual 2016–2020,* Universidad de Antofagasta <http://intranetua.uantof.cl/plan_desarrollo/> [Google Chrome trans]

Universidad de Los Lagos, University, Universidad de Los Lagos <http://www.ulagos.cl/contenido03.php?id=1> [Google Chrome trans]

"Universities at Risk"—Icelandic Students Speak Out against Underfunding of Their Universities, Global Student Voice <http://www.globalstudentvoice.org/2016/11/15/universities-risk-icelandic-students-speak-underfunding-universities/>

Universities Australia, 'A National Internship Scheme: Enhancing the Skills and Work-Readiness of Australian University Graduates' (Position Paper No 3/08, Universities Australia, May 2008)

Universities Australia, 'Submission to the Review of Higher Education Regulation' (Submission, Universities Australia, June 2013)

University of Akureyri, 'Strategy of the University of Akureyri 2012–2017' (Strategic Plan, University of Akureyri, 2012)

University of Akureyri, *About UNAK* <http://english.unak.is/about/about-unak/about-unak>

University of Akureyri, *Rector's Address* <http://english.unak.is/about/about-unak/rectors-adress>

University of Bath, 'University Strategy 2013–2016: A World-Class University in a World Heritage City' (Strategic Plan, University of Bath, 2013)

University of Bath, *Rankings and Reputation* <http://www.bath.ac.uk/about/rankings/index.html>

University of Helsinki, 'Excellence for Society: Strategic Plan for the University of Helsinki 2013–2016' (Strategic Plan, University of Helsinki, 18 January 2012)

University of Helsinki, *University of Helsinki Equality Plan 2013–2016* <http://www.helsinki.fi/henkos/tasa-arvo/equality_and_diversity_plan_2013-2016.pdf>

University of Helsinki, *University's Core Duties* (31 March 2015) <https://www.helsinki.fi/en/university/strategia-ja-johtaminen-englanti/yliopiston-tehtavat-englanti>

University of Iceland, 'Policy of the University of Iceland 2011–2016' (Policy, University of Iceland, 17 December 2010)

University of Iceland, 'A Dynamic Community' (Brochure, University of Iceland, May 2014)

University of Limerick, 'Strategic Plan 2011–2015: Pioneering & Connected' (Strategic Plan, University of Limerick, 2011)

University of Limerick, *Why Choose UL?* <http://www.ul.ie/>

University of Oulu, *Finnish Bachelor's Graduate Survey* (20 February 2015) <http://www.oulu.fi/english/studying/bachelors-graduate-survey>

University of Tampere, 'Let's Shape the Future! Change in the University of Tampere 2010–2015' (Strategic Plan, The University of Tampere, 15 February 2010)

University of Tampere, *What Makes the University of Tampere Different?* (16 December 2010) <http://www.uta.fi/english/about/different/index.html>

University of Vienna, 'University of Vienna 2015 Development Plan' (Development Plan, University of Vienna, 27 January 2012)

University of Vienna, *Why Study Here?* <http://www.univie.ac.at/en/study/admission/why-study-here/>

US Department of Education, *Laws & Guidance* <http://www2.ed.gov/policy/landing.jhtml?src=go>

Välimaa, Jussi, *Why Finland and Norway Still Shun University Tuition Fees—Even for International Students* (17 February 2015) The Conversation <http://theconversation.com/why-finland-and-norway-still-shun-university-tuition-fees-even-for-international-students-36922>

Van der Brugge, Eva and Daniel Edwards, 'Australia in Context: An International Perspective on Our Higher Education System' (Research Briefing vol 2, no 2, Australian Council for Educational Research, July 2012)

Van Onselen, Peter, 'Australia Orders Plagiarism Review', *The Australian* (online), 26 November 2014 <https://www.insidehighered.com/news/2014/11/26/australian-government-orders-inquiry-foreign-student-plagiarizing>

Visentin, Lisa, 'Corruption Rife in International Student Sector of Leading Australian Universities, ABC's Four Corners Reports', *The Sydney Morning Herald* (online), 20 April 2015 <http://www.smh.com.au/nsw/corruption-rife-in-international-student-sector-of-leading-australian-universities-abcs-four-corners-reports-20150420-1mp64t.html>

Von Prondzynski, Ferdinand, 'Reconfiguring the Irish System of Higher Education' (14 February 2012) A University Blog: Diary of Life and Strategy inside and outside the University <https://universitydiary.wordpress.com/tag/national-strategy-for-higher-education/>

Wall, Martin, 'End to Public Service Staff Moratorium Announced in Budget', *The Irish Times* (online), 14 October 2014 <http://www.irishtimes.com/business/end-to-public-service-staff-moratorium-announced-in-budget-1.1963225>

Wall, Matthew, 'Skills Shortages Holding Back the UK's Economic Recovery', *BBC News* (online), 1 December 2014 <http://www.bbc.com/news/business-30224320>

Walters, Joanna, *Bernie Sanders: Free Public College Tuition Is the 'Right Thing to Do'* (23 October 2015) The Guardian <https://www.theguardian.com/us-news/2015/oct/22/bernie-sanders-free-public-college-tuition-higher-education>

Webster University, 'Strategic Plan for Webster University in Vienna: 2013–2018' (Strategic Plan, Webster University, 30 August 2013)

Webster University, *Why Webster University* <http://webster.ac.at/why-webster-university>

What We Do, Swedish Higher Education Authority <http://english.uka.se/about-us/what-we-do.html>

Wilkoszewski, Harald, 'Education at a Glance 2014—Country Note: Austria' (Country Note, OECD)

Williams, James, 'What Do Students Deserve? Concerns Mount over Quality of Expanding Higher Education', *The Conversation* (online), 28 May 2014 <http://theconversation.com/what-do-students-deserve-concerns-mount-over-quality-of-expanding-higher-education-27041>

Wilson, Robin, 'Why Colleges Are on the Hook for Sexual Assault' *The Chronicle of Higher Education* (online), 6 June 2014 <http://chronicle.com/article/Why-Colleges-Are-on-the-Hook/146943/>

Wilson, Sir Tim, 'A Review of Business-University Collaboration' (Review, February 2012)

Woodley, Naomi, 'University Students to Undertake Work Experience as Part of National Strategy to Boost Their "Job Readiness"' *ABC News* (11 March 2015) <http://www.abc.net.au/news/2015-03-11/national-strategy-aims-to-improve-job-readiness-of-uni-students/6297716>

Work in Iceland (December 2014) Prospects <http://www.prospects.ac.uk/work_in_iceland.htm>

Wright, Joshua, *America's Skilled Trades Dilemma: Shortages Loom as Most-in-Demand Group of Workers Ages* (3 July 2013) Forbes <http://www.forbes.com/sites/emsi/2013/03/07/americas-skilled-trades-dilemma-shortages-loom-as-most-in-demand-group-of-workers-ages/>

Conclusion

A. PURPOSE AND FINDINGS

Over the last few decades, there has been significant change in higher education. Although higher education has historically been provided to a minority elite in traditional lecture- and tutorial-style settings, these norms are rapidly changing. Globalisation, the massification of higher education, rapidly changing technology, and changing workforce needs, among other factors, have all contributed to a need to rethink the delivery of higher education.

In light of the historical and continuing inequality in higher education, the international obligations that many states have accepted, as well as the general lack of attention given to the human right to higher education, this book has sought to identify what a human rights-based approach to higher education would look like. Further, in the context of our rapidly changing world, this book endeavoured to determine whether the adoption of a human rights-based approach to higher education policy, as opposed to a market-based approach, might be more likely to enable a state to meet the purposes of higher education teaching and learning.

Analysis of the market and human rights-based approaches to higher education led to the conclusion that, at least in theory, the human rights-based approach is more likely to enable a state to meet the purposes of higher education teaching

The Human Rights-Based Approach to Higher Education. Jane Kotzmann.
© Oxford University Press 2018. Published 2018 by Oxford University Press.

and learning. Further, analysis of state higher education policies that might be considered to represent these approaches confirmed this conclusion.

B. THE CHALLENGES OF ADVOCATING FOR A HUMAN RIGHTS-BASED APPROACH TO HIGHER EDUCATION POLICY

The broad conclusion of this book, that a human rights-based approach to higher education policy is more likely to enable the achievement of higher education purposes than a market-based approach, is not surprising. Common sense indicates that where a higher education policy focuses on ensuring that all individuals have access to quality higher education, then teaching and learning results are likely to be superior to those of policies that lack such focus or prioritise other objectives. What is (perhaps) surprising is the contentiousness of this conclusion. It may prove difficult to persuade policymakers to redirect higher education policy away from market-based approaches towards those that prioritise quality higher education for all individuals, if only because citizens may be unwilling to shoulder the associated tax burden.[1]

A number of strategic considerations should be kept in mind by advocates of a human rights-based approach to higher education policy. In particular, advocates will need to address the content of the human right to higher education, the competing nature of rights claims, the lack of familiarity with the idea of human rights being applied to higher education and the likely political resistance to the application of human rights in this area.[2]

This book has gone some way towards addressing some of these strategic considerations. Although human rights standards, including the right to higher education, can be 'vague and ambiguous',[3] Chapter 1 of this book outlined the scope and content of the right to higher education, and also sought to raise awareness of some of the complexities associated with the right. Second, by focusing specifically on the right to higher education and undertaking an analysis to determine whether a human rights-based approach might have more value than a market-based approach, this book has sought to familiarise stakeholders with the concept of human rights applying in the higher education sector. Third, this book

1. See John Tobin, 'Understanding a Human Rights Based Approach to Matters Involving Children: Conceptual Foundations and Strategic Considerations' in Antonella Invernizzi and Jane Williams (eds), *The Human Rights of Children: From Visions to Implementation* (Ashgate Publishing, 2011) 61, 75–88.

2. See ibid 76.

3. Ibid 77.

has focused on the potential instrumental reasons, rather than intrinsic reasons, for an adoption of a human rights-based approach to higher education. Part of the reason for this focus is that instrumental justifications may be more likely to appeal to higher education policymakers.[4]

The issue of resolving competing rights claims, and in particular determining the allocation of scarce resources in order to enable rights enjoyment, will also require consideration. The nature of the human right to higher education is that it requires significant government funding. Yet there are other equally pressing, and possibly more pressing, rights which also require government funding, such as the rights to health,[5] primary and secondary education[6] and social security.[7] This book has not attempted to provide guidance on the way in which these competing rights claims should be resolved. Advocates of a human rights-based approach to higher education policy will need to address this issue, and in this respect should draw upon human rights principles to guide suggested approaches.[8]

C. UTILITY OF THE DISCUSSION

Putting aside the likely success, or otherwise, of advocating for a human rights-based approach to higher education, the analysis undertaken in this book has utility. It has sought to raise consciousness of the relevant issues and to substantiate the arguments by reference to evidence. This task is useful in a number of respects. First, making evidence-based assertions as to the utility of a human rights-based approach to higher education is likely to operate as an accountability mechanism in itself. In this respect, Ross Willing explains that '[d]rawing out arguments from Government as to why they are moving away from a desired model, can be an important outcome of a rights based analysis'.[9] Second, placing the discussion in an evidence-based context exposes the inaccuracy of some claims made in relation to state recognition of human rights. Charles J Russo, for example, claims that 'few could argue that American educators fail to afford students significant

4. Ibid 82–84.

5. *International Covenant on Economic, Social and Cultural Rights*, opened for signature 19 December 1966, 993 UNTS 3 (entered into force 3 January 1976) art 12.

6. Ibid art 13.

7. Ibid art 9.

8. Tobin, above n 1, 79–80.

9. Ross Willing, 'The Right to Education in Australia: A Case Study of Higher Education Policy' (2014) 2(2) *UNSWLJ Student Series* 1, 18.

protections that meet or exceed virtually all international standards',[10] but the results of this book suggest that this statement may be disputed.

The implications of this book may also have broader ramifications. Positioning the discussion of how best to approach higher education policy in an evidence-based context may assist in influencing law and policymakers away from ideological approaches and towards embracing approaches to higher education supported by evidence. In this respect, the book builds on the work of the OECD in compiling data on education, and will assist states to identify (and hopefully adopt) policies that are more likely to enable them to achieve the purposes of higher education teaching and learning.[11] Thus, by placing the discussion of how best to deliver higher education in an evidence-based context, the intention is that some contribution to improved policymaking may be achieved.

D. TOWARDS A HIGHER EDUCATION 'UTOPIA'

This research also represents an attempt to identify a 'feasible utopia' for higher education and to contribute to debate about the public interest nature of the university.[12] Ronald Barnett explains his concept of 'feasible utopia' as options that '[i]n the best of all *possible* worlds . . . could just be realised even if it is unlikely that they will be'.[13]

A utopia for higher education is an imagined state of affairs in which everything in a higher education system is perfect. This should be understood in terms of the objectives of a higher education system. Thus, in a higher education utopia, the higher education system would enable individual students to undertake significant transformation. As a result of higher education experiences, students would be transformed in that they would gain significant skills and knowledge,

10. Charles J Russo, 'Reflections on Education as a Fundamental Human Right' (2010) 20(2) *Education Law Journal*, 87, 98.

11. Organisation for Economic Cooperation and Development, 'Education at a Glance 2014: OECD Indicators' (OECD, September 2014) 15.

12. See Kathleen Lynch, 'New Managerialism, Neoliberalism and Ranking' (2014) 13 *Ethics in Science and Environmental Politics* 141, 141; Kathleen Lynch, 'Neo-Liberalism and Marketisation: The Implications for Higher Education' (2006) 5(1) *European Educational Research Journal* 1, 1; Kathleen Lynch, 'International League Tables and Rankings in Higher Education: An Appraisal' in Imelda Elliott, Michael Murphy, Alain Payeur, Raymond Duval (eds), *Mutations de L'Enseignement Supérieur et Internationalisation* (De Boeck, 2011) 19, 41.

13. Ronald Barnett, *Being a University* (Routledge, 2011) 4. See also Ronald Barnett and Carolina Guzman, 'The Human Rights University: A Feasible Utopia' in Claudia Brunner and Josefine Scherling (eds), *Bildung, Menschenrechte, Universitat. Menschenrechts-Bildung and Hochschulen im Wandel als gesellschaftliche Herausforderung* (Drava Verlag, 2012) 269–88.

the capacity for critical reasoning and an understanding of themselves. Further, students would gain an understanding of different perspectives, come to see the world in a different way, and develop their morals and values.

A higher education utopia would also see the realisation of social betterment and social efficiency goals. The higher education system would effect important improvements to society. It would educate students in a manner that accords with the state's vision for society, members of higher education institutions would act in a manner congruent with this vision, and students would use their acquired skills and knowledge to contribute to the community. Further, it would work towards social justice ends, including the equal treatment of individuals and equal access to higher education. Finally, the utopian higher education system would educate and train individuals for subsequent employment, ensuring a productive and skilled labour force and benefiting both the individual concerned as well as the economy at large.

Although a higher education utopia can be broadly described in this way, countless variations of what such a system would look like can be imagined. In the context of this research, a utopian higher education system would look quite different from a market-based as compared to a human rights-based perspective. From a market-based viewpoint, the key role of the state is to ensure that the market for higher education operates effectively. In a market utopia, the market for higher education would be high functioning, ensure that the price for higher education is kept low and thus safeguard the broad accessibility of higher education. If wide access to higher education is facilitated, more individuals would have the opportunity to be transformed through the experience and to develop employability skills. Implementation of a market perspective would also underpin a view of society in which equality exists via application of the universal rules of the market, and in which the freedom to teach and learn is unobstructed by government intervention.

Although a market-based utopia is conceptually interesting, this research suggests that it is not *feasible* in that it cannot be readily achieved in practice. In contrast, this research suggests that a human rights-based higher education utopia *is* feasible. Within a human rights paradigm, the state plays a key role in ensuring that the higher education system is framed such that the right to higher education may be enjoyed by all. This requires positive action from the top down in terms of legislation and policy, as well as from the bottom up in terms of understanding of and commitment to human rights by individuals involved in the system. Such an approach goes beyond simply ensuring broad access to higher education. The human rights paradigm is concerned with the quality of educational offering and thus with ensuring the potential for individual transformation, in particular with facilitating the development of morals and values that accord with the concept of human rights. In turn, the human rights approach focuses not only on social justice through broad access, but also through the promotion of a vision of a socially just society.[14] Thus, it is also concerned with enabling individuals' employability.

The human rights-based higher education utopia may sound more utopian than a market-based higher education utopia. Yet this research suggests that unlike the market-based picture, it constitutes a *feasible* utopia; it can be and has been (at least somewhat) realised in a number of states. Thus, although the recommendations in this book are admittedly ambitious, they are also doable in genuinely progressive societies, as is demonstrated by the human rights-based approach case studies in Chapter 4. The challenge, therefore, for individuals and for states who are truly committed to achieving the goals of higher education teaching and learning, is to accumulate the requisite political will to drive the adoption of a human rights-based approach to higher education.

REFERENCE LIST

A. Articles/Books/Reports

Barnett, Ronald, *Being a University* (Routledge, 2011)

Barnett, Ronald and Carolina Guzman, 'The Human Rights University: A Feasible Utopia' in Claudia Brunner and Josefine Scherling (eds), *Bildung, Menschenrechte, Universitat. Menschenrechts-Bildung and Hochschulen im Wandel als gesellschaftliche Herausforderung* (Drava Verlag, 2012)

Lynch, Kathleen, 'Neo-Liberalism and Marketisation: The Implications for Higher Education' (2006) 5(1) *European Educational Research Journal* 1

Lynch, Kathleen, 'International League Tables and Rankings in Higher Education: An Appraisal' in Imelda Elliott, Michael Murphy, Alain Payeur, Raymond Duval (eds), *Mutations de L'Enseignement Supérieur et Internationalisation* (De Boeck, 2011) 19

Lynch, Kathleen, 'New Managerialism, Neoliberalism and Ranking' (2014) 13 *Ethics in Science and Environmental Politics* 141

Russo, Charles J, 'Reflections on Education as a Fundamental Human Right' (2010) 20(2) *Education Law Journal* 87

Tobin, John, 'Understanding a Human Rights Based Approach to Matters Involving Children: Conceptual Foundations and Strategic Considerations' in Antonella Invernizzi and Jane Williams (eds), *The Human Rights of Children: From Visions to Implementation* (Ashgate Publishing, 2011) 61

Willing, Ross, 'The Right to Education in Australia: A Case Study of Higher Education Policy' (2014) 2(2) *UNSWLJ Student Series* 1

14. See generally Barnett and Guzman, above n 13.

B. Official International Documents

International Covenant on Economic, Social and Cultural Rights, opened for signature 19 December 1966, 993 UNTS 3 (entered into force 3 January 1976)

C. Other

Organisation for Economic Cooperation and Development, 'Education at a Glance 2014: OECD Indicators' (OECD, September 2014)

Appendix A

Signs and Measures of a Successful Higher Education System

Table A.1. Signs and Measures of a Successful Higher Education System

Individual transformation	Improving society	Social efficiency
• Student survey responses • Personalised learning • Resources per student • Institutional autonomy • Commitment to teaching and learning	• Integration of values • Teaching for citizenship • Equal opportunity, equal treatment and equity • Freedom for teaching and research • International assistance	• Vocational orientation • Graduation rates • Employability prospects and skills shortages • Research quality • Global connectivity

The Human Rights-Based Approach to Higher Education. Jane Kotzmann.
© Oxford University Press 2018. Published 2018 by Oxford University Press.

Appendix B

Evaluation of State Higher Education Policy—by Country

Table B.1. Chile

Measures	Very Poor (1)	Poor (2)	Average (3)	Good (4)	Very Good (5)
PURPOSE: INDIVIDUAL TRANSFORMATION					
Student survey responses	Not applicable				
Personalised learning	Not applicable				
Resources per student			✓		
Institutional autonomy			✓		
Commitment to teaching and learning		✓			
PURPOSE: IMPROVING SOCIETY					
Integration of values					✓
Teaching for citizenship				✓	
Equal opportunity, equal treatment and equity	✓				
Freedom for teaching and research				✓	
International assistance	Not applicable				
PURPOSE: SOCIAL EFFICIENCY					
Vocational orientation		✓			
Graduation rates					✓
Employability prospects and skills shortages			✓		
Research quality	✓				
Global connectivity	✓				
Total	**34/60 = 57 per cent**				

Table B.2. England

Measures	Very Poor (1)	Poor (2)	Average (3)	Good (4)	Very Good (5)
PURPOSE: INDIVIDUAL TRANSFORMATION					
Student survey responses				✓	
Personalised learning			✓		
Resources per student					✓
Institutional autonomy					✓
Commitment to teaching and learning		✓			
PURPOSE: IMPROVING SOCIETY					
Integration of values		✓			
Teaching for citizenship			✓		
Equal opportunity, equal treatment and equity		✓			
Freedom for teaching and research		✓			
International assistance			✓		
PURPOSE: SOCIAL EFFICIENCY					
Vocational orientation				✓	
Graduation rates		✓			
Employability prospects and skills shortages				✓	
Research quality			✓		
Global connectivity				✓	
Total	**48/75 = 64 per cent**				

Table B.3. United States

Measures	Very Poor (1)	Poor (2)	Average (3)	Good (4)	Very Good (5)
PURPOSE: INDIVIDUAL TRANSFORMATION					
Student survey responses			✓		
Personalised learning				✓	
Resources per student					✓
Institutional autonomy				✓	
Commitment to teaching and learning		✓			
PURPOSE: IMPROVING SOCIETY					
Integration of values		✓			
Teaching for citizenship					✓
Equal opportunity, equal treatment and equity		✓			
Freedom for teaching and research			✓		
International assistance		✓			
PURPOSE: SOCIAL EFFICIENCY					
Vocational orientation			✓		
Graduation rates					✓
Employability prospects and skills shortages		✓			
Research quality			✓		
Connectivity		✓			
Total	**47/75 = 63 per cent**				

Table B.4. FINLAND

Measures	Very Poor (1)	Poor (2)	Average (3)	Good (4)	Very Good (5)
PURPOSE: INDIVIDUAL TRANSFORMATION					
Student survey responses			✓		
Personalised learning					✓
Resources per student				✓	
Institutional autonomy					✓
Commitment to teaching and learning					✓
PURPOSE: IMPROVING SOCIETY					
Integration of values					✓
Teaching for citizenship					✓
Equal opportunity, equal treatment and equity					✓
Freedom for teaching and research				✓	
International assistance					✓
PURPOSE: SOCIAL EFFICIENCY					
Vocational orientation					✓
Graduation rates			✓		
Employability prospects and skills shortages		✓			
Research quality				✓	
Global connectivity				✓	
Total	**64/75 = 85 per cent**				

Table B.5. ICELAND

Measures	Very Poor (1)	Poor (2)	Average (3)	Good (4)	Very Good (5)
PURPOSE: INDIVIDUAL TRANSFORMATION					
Student survey responses	Not applicable				
Personalised learning					✓
Resources per student		✓			
Institutional autonomy					✓
Commitment to teaching and learning				✓	
PURPOSE: IMPROVING SOCIETY					
Integration of values					✓
Teaching for citizenship					✓
Equal opportunity, equal treatment and equity	Not applicable				
Freedom for teaching and research			✓		
International assistance		✓			
PURPOSE: SOCIAL EFFICIENCY					
Vocational orientation				✓	
Graduation rates					✓
Employability prospects and skills shortages					✓
Research quality	Not applicable				
Global connectivity				✓	
Total	**49/60 = 82 per cent**				

Table B.6. Sweden

Measures	Very Poor (1)	Poor (2)	Average (3)	Good (4)	Very Good (5)
PURPOSE: INDIVIDUAL TRANSFORMATION					
Student survey responses			✓		
Personalised learning					✓
Resources per student				✓	
Institutional autonomy				✓	
Commitment to teaching and learning					✓
PURPOSE: IMPROVING SOCIETY					
Integration of values					✓
Teaching for citizenship				✓	
Equal opportunity, equal treatment and equity					✓
Freedom for teaching and research		✓			
International assistance	✓				
PURPOSE: SOCIAL EFFICIENCY					
Vocational orientation				✓	
Graduation rates	✓				
Employability prospects and skills shortages					✓
Research quality					✓
Global connectivity				✓	
Total	**58/75 = 77 per cent**				

Appendix C

Summary Country Comparison

Table C.1. Numerical Summary Country Comparison

	Country	**Total**
Market	Chile	0.566667
	England	0.64
	United States	0.626666667
	Market average	**0.611111222**
Human Rights	Finland	0.853333333
	Iceland	0.816666667
	Sweden	0.76
	Human rights average	**0.81**

Index

Page numbers followed by "*t*" indicate tables and "*f*" indicate figures

The Human Rights-Based Approach to Higher Education. Jane Kotzmann.

© Oxford University Press 2018. Published 2018 by Oxford University Press.

www.ingramcontent.com/pod-product-compliance
Lightning Source LLC
LaVergne TN
LVHW011751200926
848484LV00003B/671